LONG ROAD
TO BOSTON

– An Autobiography of No One You'd Know –

ROSS BURNS

Copyright © 2022 Ross Burns

ISBN: 978-1-922788-60-3
Published by Vivid Publishing
A division of Fontaine Publishing Group
P.O. Box 948, Fremantle
Western Australia 6959
www.vividpublishing.com.au

A catalogue record for this
book is available from the
NATIONAL National Library of Australia
LIBRARY
OF AUSTRALIA

Main cover photo: Ethiopian Abebe Bikila winning the marathon at the Tokyo Olympics, 1964
Inset cover photo: The author on the Wadandi Track between Margaret River and Witchcliffe,
WA, May 2022 (Lauren Trickett Photography, Witchcliffe, WA)

CONTENTS

PROLOGUE

I'll never forget 16 April 2013. It was, for me, a day of immense sadness. That's not how the day began, though. On that morning, I woke up looking forward to the day ahead.

That rarely happened in my time 'up north'. I was never thrilled about lining up for the ritual sign-in at Northern Link Camp, then being breathalysed before work, after having already endured the tedious hour-long bus commute from Kangaroo Hill Village, just north-east of Dampier.

Unlike most of the other grumps on the 18-seater that morning, I remained wide awake for the slow 70-kilometre trudge to Northern Link.

Most of my workmates onboard — my fellow inmates some might say — slept or dozed fitfully after the unwelcome 4am start to the day, the gulping down of breakfast in the dry mess, the frenzied, every-man-for-himself packing of the day's crib and the race to the bus before it crawled out of the village car park.

Up over the short, steep hill, left onto Parker Point Road, left again onto the Dampier Highway heading towards Karratha, past the Burrup Peninsula turn-off and, eventually, out along Warlu Road winding through the red-brown Pilbara desert to the camp.

You missed the bus at your peril. The maths was painfully simple. Miss the bus = no work and no pay that day.

I was never excited by the trip despite the spectacular beauty of the desert landscape that emerged as the sun finally made its morning appearance. There's an eeriness about travelling to work in the dark, or working up north at all for that matter, that I often found mildly disturbing.

But this day was very different. The Boston Marathon had been run while we slept and I was anxious to get to work to check the results, as I'd done for decades, regardless of where I was in the world.

I was on the verge of being physically ill when I learned the news of the explosion of two bombs on Boylston Street, near the finish line of the race in Copley Square in downtown Boston.

The Boston Marathon was dear to my heart and I was sickened to read the news over the internet that three people had been killed and more than 260 innocent spectators injured — many shockingly so. They'd lined the route on Boylston Street to cheer on family members and friends or were simply interested onlookers who'd come to Copley Square to honour a cherished Boston tradition. They were there, on that cool, crisp Boston spring day to celebrate people of diverse ages and walks of life conquering one of the most famous marathons in the world.

Instead, cruelly, they suffered a senseless act of violence and carnage.

As a symbol, I couldn't see even a vague link between the act of terror and the race itself. Apart from the feeling it gave me of absolute horror, it first struck me as being totally illogical. Why the Boston Marathon? Where was the connection? Was it merely because the race was perceived to be a soft target? If so, the bombings were an even greater act of blatant cowardice.

Boston is the birthplace of the American revolution. The Boston Marathon had been run on Patriots' Day, the third Monday in April, every year since 1897. This incredible event is the pride of Boston and the world's oldest annual marathon.

I'm not a Bostonian. I'd never even been to Boston. Nevertheless, I felt the bombings were a personal attack, a kind of violation

— as if I'd been there on that shocking day and had experienced the brutality firsthand.

In reality, I was thousands of kilometres away in one of the remotest and most inhospitable parts of Australia. It's difficult to imagine being more physically disconnected from the marathon or from Boston itself. Yet, somehow, I was still able to associate with the attack, emotionally at least, and to feel a strong sense of outrage and grief.

Over the course of the next several days, the plan I'd had to run the Boston Marathon two years later changed dramatically — as even the best laid plans sometimes do. That plan had included a long, slow and measured build-up to the qualifying race, the Gold Coast Airport Marathon in July 2014, and then an equally methodical approach to Boston 2015. I'd scheduled a steady build-up to establish a deep base of fitness: doing it thoroughly, doing it well and doing it justice. It's the way I endeavour to do all things.

The Boston bombings on 15 April changed all that.

There are individual incidents in life that profoundly affect us, that we often regard as so-called defining moments. How we respond to these events reflects who we are as human beings. But the manner in which we respond may not always be easy to rationalise or articulate. Sometimes, for reasons that appear inexplicable to others and that are perhaps only known to us at the deepest level, we respond in a certain way simply because it 'feels right'. We don't necessarily know why, we just know that, for us, it's the right thing to do. I believe in doing what my gut 'tells' me is right. Most times it works out, sometimes not. Regardless, I tend to trust my gut-feel approach to the issues that life throws up.

After the attack, I knew I had to be in Boston for the 2014 race, a year earlier than originally scheduled. It was a way for me to pay my respects to the victims of the atrocity, to pay tribute to the city and its people, and to the history and traditions of the race itself — in my own insignificant way, to do what I could to restore the dignity and reputation of the race. To somehow help repair the damage and contribute to the healing. I expect few people to understand, but for me it was something right at that moment that I felt strongly compelled to do.

Bringing forward by a year my participation in the race meant that I'd only have a short time to qualify for Boston 2014 — far too short in fact. An attempt to secure a qualifying time at a suitable race in Australia was now only months away, realistically in either July or August 2013, and I was light years away from being marathon fit.

But, the decision to run had now been made, even if it was a somewhat irrational decision triggered by the barbaric acts of the two Boston bombers. We can't always be controlled or measured in how we behave, as much as we might prefer to be. We're human beings after all, and we often act impulsively on sheer emotion, for better or worse. Besides, my own emotional state at the time and for some years before had been, for various reasons, raw and brittle. An off-centre, out-of-character reaction to the circumstances around me was always going to be distinctly possible.

There were significant logistical, and health and medical obstacles to overcome. Like, living as a fly-in, fly-out contractor for 300 days of the year in the remote Pilbara region of Western Australia and the 80-hour working weeks that were especially gruelling for someone of my age — 61 at the time.

Although I certainly acknowledged them, these obstacles weren't insurmountable or even relevant anymore. I was now too consumed by the decision to be at the Boston starting line in 2014 to care. Somehow, I'd find a way. I'd work around it with a realistic and well thought-out plan. It was possible.

So, there it was. A mini marathon build-up (never the smartest move), followed by a qualifying race in either July or August 2013 and a qualifying time for my age group of better than 3 hours and 55 minutes. All leading to a Boston start on 21 April 2014. There was a certain madness to it but, as the Boston bombings had demonstrated so tragically, we were living in crazy and unpredictable times.

Regardless, that was now the plan.

With me, most times plans are fulfilled. But, sometimes, not.

1

LIVING THE DREAM

It was so easy then
Never making any plans
It was so easy then

Carly Simon, 'It Was So Easy'

I'm convinced it began with one of those 'what's the meaning of life?' moments.

Surely, I'm not the only person to indulge myself with that act of introspection. Although I admit to pondering over the question on an increasingly regular basis, I don't have an even vaguely satisfactory answer.

Of course, finding an answer to the 'meaning of life' question doesn't seem to matter as much anymore. It's now all about embarking upon our own personal 'journey' of self-discovery. The journey's the thing. That'll do it for most of us. That's enough, supposedly.

Crap to that.

I'd prefer at least some kind of meaning-of-life *answer* before senility takes hold in a more serious way, even if it's merely a half-baked theory. But, that's just me.

* * *

Both my wife, Diana, and I lived most of our growing-up years in Sydney beachside suburbs. I lived in and around the northern beach suburb of Manly while Di grew up in Cronulla, south of the city. For both of us, living near the ocean was part of the natural order of things. It was home to us, a physical environment in which we were comfortable. It still has the same effect. For me, the 'rat race', as I'd heard grownups call it back then, was a ferry ride away, 'over there', in the city - a frantic, noisy and intimidating place to which I ventured infrequently, usually to watch the cricket at the SCG.

Living by the beach seemed to insulate us from the frenetic pace of life experienced by others. Beach living was soothing and calming. In those days, Manly was known as 'The Village' by many locals. The life I'd carved out for myself as a kid, even if carved out subconsciously and only at surface level, was postcard perfect: relaxed, easy, clean and, somehow, almost 'shiny'. All that despite a troubled home life.

Looking back now from the bruised and battered perspective of an adult, my years as a young boy growing up near the beach were spent 'living the dream'. Surely, my childhood was as good as life gets. Surely, I was among the luckiest inhabitants of the luckiest country. It might be a rose-coloured view of a previous life — can the past ever be as idyllic as we choose to remember it? But 'those were the days'. Right?

As an adult, maybe your childhood is a space into which you occasionally retreat, or even hide, to feel safe and happy. Maybe that's just a misplaced sense of nostalgia. Regardless, as a kid and a teenager, I merely thought that my life and how I spent my time were just plain normal. It was, simply and naturally, as it was always meant to be.

I skipped through those childhood and early teenage years enjoying almost every minute, except for high school where, strangely, I felt out of place at times. I reacted in a similar way later at university and, if I'm honest, it's been like that at other stages throughout my life.

* * *

I rarely bothered myself with clothes as a kid and a teenager. Fashion and style trends are matters I've never been remotely interested in and, so I'm told, it shows. I hardly ever wore shoes or boots except to school or to play football — soccer, as we knew it then. T-shirts, jeans, shorts and loose-fitting clothes that are totally unflattering to the human form are still my favoured type of gear and a critical part of my personal, and admittedly very basic, don't-really-care-too-much dress sense. It's likely a bloke thing but I tend to be dressed by others.

Don't hold your breath waiting for me to apologise for not complying with the dress code of the lumber-, metro-, sporno- or uber-sexual. The 'power of clothes' and the closely associated quest to enhance or modify one's personal appearance? Sorry, I just don't get it.

Then again, I don't get many things about this modern, but highly confusing, world and contemporary life. Like why people rarely care to walk on the left-hand side of the footpath anymore. Or why you never seem to get the haircut that you ask, and pay, for. It's just me being out of whack with the universe, a distinct feeling of not belonging to, or being of, this world. Almost an intruder.

My lack of dress sense, or my inclination to not attribute much significance to it, is even more appropriate for me now. I've arrived at an age where people tend to forgive you if they judge from your appearance and/or lack of grooming sophistication that you've 'let yourself go'.

Fine by me. By all accounts, including mine, I have.

* * *

Later, as I drifted past my late teens, I 'grew up' and life changed. Almost overnight I became an adult and life suddenly turned fair dinkum. It was a huge shock. There were no warning signs and no transition period. I wasn't eased into it. No one whispered in my ear or pulled me aside and counselled me on what to expect. It happened without me being even casually conscious of it.

One minute I was enjoying my youth, blissfully ignorant of what was to come, and painfully naïve about many life issues happening around me and despite me. Then, almost in an instant, I'd become a 'grownup', had to frantically learn 'adulting' skills and had responsibilities thrust upon me, even if they were unwanted and not of my making. Life wasn't easy or simple anymore. The shiny, and as it happened, temporary veneer had worn off.

My modest dress code was violated. I was made to wear a suit and tie — and shoes. I was still a kid, but living in a grownup's body. Being an adult somehow forced me to look at life differently, through adult eyes, and I didn't much like what I saw. I wanted to go back to living the dream — at least my boyhood version of it. But it was too late. I was forced to put the dream on hold. Indefinitely, as it turned out.

***

Much of my non-school time in the warmer months involved long days hanging out at the beach, mainly between South Steyne and 'Freshie', in nothing more than a pair of flimsy nylon swimming trunks known variously to us kids as 'togs', 'cozzies' or 'sluggos', and even briefer than Tony Abbott's budgie smugglers.

(That's one of the very few things the ex-PM and I have in common, to be honest. We both have some historical connection with the northern beaches of Sydney. Granted, we both run and we're both lawyers by trade, but I promise that's where the commonalities end.)

One of my favourite summer pastimes back in the day was to dive for money off Manly Wharf. A bunch of us kids would wait for the ferry to arrive from Circular Quay and gather in the water at the end of the wharf behind the collision barrier and directly below the 'DIVING FOR MONEY PROHIBITED' sign. As the hordes of tourists ('Southies' to us) poured off the ferry, some of the more benevolent visitors would toss coins in, which we'd dive for.

Even at that relatively young age, I had the distinct feeling that I was aerobically blessed. I was able to out-breathe and out-dive most of the other kids and always skipped home, looking rather like an over-shrivelled prune after hours spent in the water, with more than my fair share of the day's loot. Mostly pennies but, occasionally, the odd thrippence and sixpence and, later, five and ten cent pieces when decimal currency kicked in. (Two-shilling pieces sank too fast, by the way. I'd go back later and, hopefully, retrieve them on a lower tide.) I earned my own money at an early age. I was self-sufficient and, crucially for me, felt in control.

Other days were spent on the Manly Warringah golf course selling golf balls back to golfers who'd 'lost' them, even when they'd been smacked straight down the middle of the fairway — you can work that caper out for yourself — or snorkelling for coins that had fallen through the gaps in the weathered, wooden floors of the change rooms at the Manly swimming baths.

Even in those early times, as a young boy, it was vaguely apparent to me that I was a loner. For the most part, kids of my age hung out in groups. That was just part of the deal, part of being a kid, part of being a member of a tribe. I'm sure it's always been that way, perhaps even more so for adults. I didn't consciously reject or avoid these groups. Nevertheless, I was totally and naturally at ease with being on my own.

Nothing has changed in that respect. I find contentment at an elementary level — a long walk (bush or beach) or a train ride will most often be sufficient — rather than relying on others to do the entertaining for me. I prefer to seek it out for myself (whatever 'it' is) than to have it served to me on a platter. I've never outsourced my sense of well-being.

For whatever reason, unconscious or otherwise, I never felt the urge to belong to any of the groups that were popular during my adolescence. It also never dawned on me that I was missing out.

Living near the beach, I surfed a lot but was never what you'd call a 'surfie'. I was drawn to many different forms of popular music but could never be labelled a 'mod', a 'rocker' or a 'bodgie'. I had longish blond hair, hated shoes and ties (as you know), was ambivalent about authority (at best), decidedly unambitious (still am), had discovered Woodstock and Nimbin (and longed to be at either or both) and was, at my core, attracted to alternative lifestyles. But I could never be tagged as a 'hippie'.

No-one could rightly claim that I was a member of a distinctive counterculture. I was, accidentally and weirdly, my *own* counterculture — a bit out there, in a quaint and innocent kind of way, on the outside, looking in, and constantly internalising but living comfortably within my own thoughts. I was rarely a participant in things mainstream. Not 'anti-', just 'non-' — going with the flow, but my own peculiar flow. Flowing in a subtly different direction to most but flowing to where, who knew?

Who knows even now? Certainly, not me.

That emotional (and social) non-alignment was something that I've never been sad or self-conscious about. I thought nothing of spending the entire summer holidays having scant contact with my school friends. I'd pack my own lunch and head off to watch a day's play at the SCG. I'd sit directly behind the wicket, not an inch either side, in the Sheridan stand, as far away from other spectators as possible, and watch *every* ball bowled, feeling slightly miffed by the interruption of the lunch, tea and drinks breaks. I even kept my own, handwritten, score. I was happily 'doing my own shit' without ever being conscious of it.

On other days, I'd stuff my kit bag with all the cricket gear I possessed and bus it to my school to bowl hundreds of 'leggies' and the occasional 'wrong 'un', to imaginary batsmen in the school nets. I'd take hundreds of imaginary wickets, too.

If there was anything that could be done alone, like going to the movies, where I'd seat myself in the middle of the front row if there was no one else around, I'd do it. Or, simply climb a tree and perch there for long periods. Even take off for long walks just to see how far I could wander, especially out along the northern Sydney beaches. All the while being cheerily immersed in my own thoughts, but still attuned to the sounds and smells of the physical world and atmospherics around me, before, reluctantly, having to return home.

If it wasn't for a comfortable bed and decent food, I would've been absent for days, or maybe even headed off for good. That thought, occasionally, crossed my mind. (It still does.) At home, I often felt more like a boarder than a member of a household, especially after my brother, Peter, and sister, Sheila, left. It might sound uncharitable or ungracious, but my gut kept telling me that I lived on my own. My parents just happened to reside in the same house.

Maybe that's because my mum, Margaret, and my dad, Ron, seemed to constantly be in an undeclared state of war. An atmosphere of uneasiness in our house signified a normal day. If the vibe turned even slightly edgy, you knew that aggravation was brewing and a flare-up was not far away. It was usually a sign for me to grab a cricket ball, golf club or soccer ball — the choice depended on the time of year — and 'nick off' until I'd judged it was safe to return. I learned to be a good judge. I had plenty of practice.

There must've been joyful times at home. They just don't readily spring to mind. It's the angst-filled moments that my memory recalls when I stop and download it. Those moments don't come flooding back to haunt or traumatise me, as other memories do. They're more of an occasional trickle.

I think I more or less brought myself up, observing how other people behaved (mostly badly), and aiming to not do the same. Some will say that's being grossly disrespectful to my parents who, in good faith, undoubtedly did their very best, as parents do.

Regardless, I've never been conscious of needing a mentor, or even a role model for that matter. Not even a father figure to be honest. I've always seemed to do life DIY style and consequently, I'd never contemplate taking on a 'life coach'. Even if I was drawn to it, there wouldn't be much point. I have the clear impression that the boat has well and truly sailed.

I wasn't consciously reclusive as a kid. Could you be at such an early age? It just felt normal and natural to do my own thing, purposefully, but after carefully thinking it through first. Fierce self-sufficiency, even with the inevitable stumble, has been part of my personality (such as it is) ever since, and now I tend to wear it, quietly but maybe smugly at times, almost as a badge of honour.

I learned self-reliance at an early age. In my early teens, I worked as a 'lolly boy' at the Manly Metro movie theatre and was forced to wear a hideous, embarrassing burgundy-coloured coat with gold buttons. I earned 12 cents for every dollar of sweets sold, just so I could pay for my return airfare to Port Moresby to visit Peter, who worked there at the time. The cost of the return airfare, $94.00, sticks in my mind. By any measure, that's a shitload of Jaffas, Minties and Fantales.

The couple who owned the milk bar adjoining the theatre regularly engaged in their own, very public, pitched battle, which sometimes involved the hurling of real-life missiles in each other's direction. Periodically, I'd be instructed by Mrs (this wasn't part of my job description, mind you) to go forth and haul Mr out of one of the countless local watering holes where he'd ensconce himself until he'd summoned the courage to battle with Mrs. From memory, he won few battles. All he could manage was to bluster and turn red in the face, as men do. In any case, she was a much better shot, as women are.

I've mentioned that I didn't relish my high school years terribly much — apart from sport. My final year at Balgowlah Boys High School was supposed to be 1969. For several reasons, I didn't achieve the results I'd hoped for, so I decided to go back the next year and repeat sixth form. My parents had no say in it. (They weren't even consulted.) I lasted about three weeks. Aside from a couple of exceptions, my teachers treated me as a failure. It hadn't registered with them that, just maybe, they'd failed *me*. So, I figured, stuff them. There was nothing they could teach me that I couldn't learn on my own.

(I've never been inherently respectful of many forms of authority, especially when the exponents of it take themselves seriously, usually with zero justification. The more earnest they appear, the more ridiculous they look. Generally, though, I've resigned myself to go along with authority – in a conscious effort to be a 'good citizen' - but with little enthusiasm or conviction.)

I studied at home on my own for the rest of 1970, achieved the results I needed and gained entry into the University of Sydney Law Faculty. More DIY — this time DIY home schooling. I made it work for me.

I'd briefly lost control of my future, and then reclaimed it. The sense of self-worth I feel when I have control, and the greater, hollow feeling of impotence when I lose it, have remained deeply embedded in me ever since.

* * *

With a few exceptions, I avoid crowds whenever I can. I have the strong inclination to not be wherever a crowd is. I rarely mix comfortably in any kind of gathering, feeling equally ill at ease in most social or professional environments: large family events, the theatre, with groups of conference participants, restaurant diners, party goers, footie fans, drinking groups, (especially) lawyers, or even just a bunch of work colleagues. A crowd to me is two people, one of whom includes me.

I've never been what you'd call 'one of the boys'. Whenever I pluck up enough courage to speak in such groups, my words stumble, fumble and dribble out like incoherent, unconvincing gibberish. I'm crap at banter. Office banter is the worst. The clever retorts and one-liners elude me. I often think of something smart to say two days after the event.

Painfully shy, socially backward — put any tag on it that suits, and many people have or have tried to — the bottom line is: I missed my calling. The guy representing the Lighthouse Keepers Association of Australia failed to turn up on school Careers Night when I was desperate for professional guidance. He was probably a deliberate no-show because of the potential crowd.

That's one of the great attractions of long-distance running: being alone, but never feeling lonely. There's a monumental difference. More on that later.

The one exception to my tendency towards crowd aversion, and people avoidance, was playing soccer. I lived, ate and breathed it for 16 seasons. Soccer-charged blood pumped furiously through my body and attached itself to every fibre, if that's what blood does. Soccer was part of my DNA, if soccer can be. I was even proud to be a member of a team, mostly with the Seaforth Soccer Club in Sydney.

Soccer was one of the few endeavours I'll admit to being good at. And I was far better than average, too, representing New South Wales as a 16-year-old and even playing a couple of years as a professional in my late teens. I would've played for nothing but it was so cool to be paid.

In stark contrast to other aspects of my life then or since, I felt totally comfortable on the soccer field. I was fast, fit, a ferocious tackler and super aggressive. Hot-headed and quick-tempered, at times I displayed a nasty streak and was regularly in trouble with the referees, who I regarded as superfluous. Curiously, I was never afraid to speak my mind with *them*, articulately, but with the roughest of tongues.

It was a standing joke among my teammates to insert an imaginary key in my back before each game, pretend to wind me up and, when the whistle blew, let me go. And go I would — flat out for the duration of the match. The only things that pissed me off about soccer, apart from the dickhead refs, were if we'd lose — thankfully, a rare event — and when the whistle sounded to end each game. I could've and would've gladly re-played each match, next time taking great care to rectify any first-time imperfections.

Soccer brought out the Jekyll and Hyde in me. Once the ref blew the whistle to start the game and I was unleashed, a switch would flick in my brain, my eyes would glaze over, adrenaline would surge and I'd go apeshit for 90 minutes. I was everything on the soccer field that I wasn't in 'real life', either then or since: confident and assured of my skills.

The odd thing was that I played like a lunatic for the sake of the team: to fit in, to hold my head up, to contribute — to earn respect from my teammates. It's been my choice that I have few friends, but those who I played soccer with, like Dave Flaskas (my best man), will remain close to me, and part of me, forever.

If I could go back in time, my soccer-playing days are one thing I *wouldn't* change. I miss those days. I miss my teammates, good men like Dave Vance and Billy Grant who are sadly no longer with us. And I miss that soccer made me feel there was something at which I excelled. Being among the very best.

Those were the days. Right?

* * *

As a kid, I'd walk, ride a bike or catch a bus to the beach in the warmer months, but mostly walk, which was never a chore. In fact, it was an absolute joy. There was no way I'd let my parents drive me, even if the offer had been made, which it seldom was.

I'd spend most of the day surfing on my own, 'scabbing' on the beach for discarded soft drink bottles (another nice little earner) or trekking down to Manly Wharf. There, if I wasn't diving for money, I'd perch precariously on one of the enormous wooden beams under the wharf and fish for yellow tail, sweep, mackerel, leatherjackets or any other species of fish that found its way onto my hook. This was my private patch, my secluded domain and I didn't take kindly to anyone brave enough to shimmy along the underside of the wharf and take up residence close to me. Happily, very few people did.

I was a more than decent fisherman, too. At least my cat thought so — a big, mangy old tom called Herman who swaggered his way around the neighbourhood with an unfortunate attitude problem. Herman was completely disdainful of the human race, except at feeding time when he'd smooch up and instantly become my best mate.

We were very much alike, Herman and I, except that I wasn't big, mangy or old. Manginess and oldness would come later, colliding at about the same time. Nor did I have a swagger (don't know how to) or an attitude problem (do know how to, but have learned to let it go). I hadn't quite reached the point of being disdainful of humanity either. Nor am I in any way a natural smoocher. Come to think of it, the only attribute we really did have in common was our love of fishing. Except, of course, that my mate Herman couldn't fish.

The only downside to fishing under the wharf was that the incoming ferry would occasionally give the immense wooden structure a gentle nudge as it docked and send minor shock waves down to wherever I'd squatted for the day. One day, the gentle nudge was replaced with an earth-shaking thump. The ferry captain must've been cross-eyed — or pissed. The latter happened periodically, as I recollect. I was dislodged from my perch and plunged into the harbour not far from the ferry's whirling propeller blades that had, as part of the usual stopping process, been frantically thrust into reverse to prevent its progress up the Corso.

Having survived the dunking and the near miss with the propeller blades, I was yanked out tea-bag style by a well-meaning passerby. In the panic of the moment, he dragged me to safety over one of the oyster-encrusted pylons that had, by good luck, somehow held the pier together for decades. The result was a severely lacerated foot. The ensuing spectacle must've appeared almost comical. A drenched young boy with retrieved fishing creel in one hand, jogging and hobbling several kilometres to the relative comfort of his home and mother, leaving a long trail of spattered blood in his wake. (Maybe, this was my earliest taste of the pain of the long-distance runner.)

I was a highly accident-prone kid. I spent many hours over the following years in Manly hospital having various parts of my anatomy stitched, splinted, bandaged, taped or otherwise patched up. 'More stitches than a chaff bag', as my dad was heard to say more times than I care to remember.

I'm now a highly accident-prone adult. I'm the sort of person who can set out on a harmless, leisurely stroll around the neighbourhood only to return several hours later, after becoming hopelessly lost and just stopping short of dialling 000, sporting assorted cuts, bruises and abrasions to various parts of my body — the results of some minor disaster or general act of uncoordinated clumsiness.

It may come as no surprise to learn that I became intimately acquainted with the 'shit happens' principle at a very early age. We've kept in close contact ever since and have developed a grudging tolerance of each other, though never a lasting friendship. It wasn't that I was reckless or deliberately lived life on the edge as a kid. Far from it. At best (or worst), I was a closet non-conformist. Yet shit just seemed to happen and followed me, and stuck to me, wherever I ventured forth.

Never earth-moving truckloads of the stuff, just small, irritating pellets that got flicked at me when I wasn't paying attention. I would've preferred to be the shitt-*er* but was, more consistently, the shitt-*ee*. It's certainly not always been that way since, but often enough to convince me that life pretty much 'is what it is'. I've never seen the glass as being half full or half empty. For me, it's just half a glass. No more, no less.

The 'shit happens' / 'it is what it is' principle has, ever since I can remember, been the filter through which I tend to view life and the world. Playing your hand as best you can with the cards you're dealt — acceptance, but not capitulation by any means.

There's a huge difference.

* * *

But back to that 'what's the meaning of life' moment…

Much has been written and discussed about people of my generation and the irresistible urge we have to escape to the seaside getaway or country shack and 'live the dream', whatever that actually means. Isn't living the dream, at least as we grownups perceive it, more about escaping the nightmare? Anyway.

Sea change, tree change, call it what you like. There's an obsession for many of my vintage, if not people generally, to break the shackles of the past (and present) and start afresh in a far-off place where the excess baggage of their lives can be offloaded and discarded forever – and magically discover the meaning of life in the process, and experience an epiphany or two along the way.

Even if we do nothing about it — and life often dictates that most of us don't, or simply can't, for reasons beyond our control — we at least dream about it or verbalise that we'll do it, some day.

Like a rebirth or a semi-religious, cleansing experience. Like surgically removing the nasty bits or exorcising some of the demons that we're possessed by over the years, and which we're told by society (and reinforce in each other) are nothing more than character-building 'life experiences'.

Putting cynicism/reality aside, as an adult I, too, harboured a strong desire to live the simple life (read: to hide in my childhood bubble and go fishing all day), in whatever form it might take, somewhere — anywhere — on the vast coast of eastern Australia. In other words, to be as far away as possible from wherever I was at any given moment.

That need grew stronger over the 30-something years spent in Canberra establishing a career, running a business with Diana and raising a family.

And wearing a suit and tie.

And shoes.

* * *

I'd moved to Canberra in the summer of 1975 to undertake a post-graduate law degree at the Australian National University while, at the same time, struggling to come to grips with adulthood and floating around in my DIY-life bubble.

I met Diana in mid-1975 in Sydney during the six-month compulsory practical legal training course that followed the completion of our undergraduate law degrees. As clichéd and corny as it sounds, for me it really was a case of love at first sight. I can still remember with great clarity the exact moment I first saw her: what she looked like, what she was wearing — her sparkling smile, the gorgeous honey-blond hair, the flowing creamy-coloured dress. Even the red shoes, well before they became a symbol for the sisterhood. Instantly, I knew she was unique, someone special, truly one of a kind in every sense. I've never wavered from that first impression.

I had no idea from that initial heartbeat-skipping encounter that it would end in marriage, but I was certain that she was the one for me. As luck would have it, Di agreed to marry me after we'd returned in early 1977 from the obligatory, post-university European adventure. I jumped out of the bubble long enough to deliver a not-so-romantic, 'Whaddya reckon, eh?' kind of marriage proposal.

Our European odyssey was no *Women's Weekly* World Discovery Tour by any means. We did it tough, on ten Aussie dollars a day, barely surviving at times by boiling together strands of spaghetti (which we literally counted out), eggs and dried packet vegetables in a billy fuelled by paraffin tablets we'd purchased from an army disposal store before leaving Sydney.

The only time our relationship was put to the test was one fateful day in Florence when I jacked up at the thought of hiking up the steps of yet another Catholic church with its countless 'Madonna with Child' frescos. I know it's a sad reflection on my endurance levels, but nine churches to that point had taken me beyond my limit. And it was barely lunchtime.

The options put to me that day were stark, simple and conveyed as an offer I was not meant to refuse:

'Listen. You either come with me into this church or you bugger off and get yourself an ice cream as you say you want to, in which case don't bother coming back. Your choice. Take your pick … Sport.'

Who conceded is a question that's still in hot dispute to this day, though not in my mind. Suffice to say that after much high-level negotiation, we failed to make it a perfect ten churches for the day. And we both enjoyed a gelato ('Sport' more so than Diana) in the middle of a freezing Italian winter.

That was the beginning of a relationship that's lasted over 45 years, though sorely tested many years later, as marriages often are.

It also offered more than a passing insight into the character of the amazing person I was to spend most of my life with.

We returned to Sydney towards the end of February 1977. We planned to get married straight away, much to the consternation of my soon-to-be father-in-law, Col, who, in his typical control freak/micro-manager fashion, insisted he be allowed a couple of months to organise the grand event. We compromised. I learned early on that was the only, practical, way to go with Col. The wedding day was pencilled in for 26 March.

When Col became even mildly agitated, his face would gradually turn bright crimson. His jowls would shake uncontrollably and in perfect sync with his rapidly rising blood pressure. A 'discussion' with Col was more like an industrial arbitration, even when the subject matter of the discussion was something as innocuous as deciding on the best driving route between Sydney and Canberra.

If Col acknowledged your comment with a guarded, 'Yes, that sounds about right', you could continue with your life as planned. If, on the other hand, he fired back in a dismissive tone something along the lines of: 'Well, I don't think that's quite correct', you knew with greater conviction that you were in deep shit and needed to beat a very hasty retreat to anywhere else on the planet.

That super-high-level, UN-style negotiation approach to even the most mundane life issue was understandable given Col's background. He'd spent a substantial part of his working life doing battle with the likes of Bob Hawke, in his trade union days, and Charlie Fitzgibbon, the head of the stevedoring union in Australia. Col played a prominent role in the modernisation of the Australian shipping industry, and I had great respect for what he'd accomplished in his professional life. Besides, he loved Test cricket as much as I did and, over the years, we bonded like best mates in front of the TV every Boxing Day.

The wedding itself was not, by any measure, traditional. At least in part, that was determined by the fact that we were stony broke by the time we arrived back in Australia after our European vacation. From memory, we had not much more than ten dollars between us. No bursting urgency for a pre-nup.

I thought I was being particularly smart by paying in advance for a night's accommodation at the Wentworth Hotel in Sydney. In hindsight, that really was clever, especially for a 24-year-old male who, at that stage in life, and in most respects for many years after, couldn't really distinguish his backside from his elbow. As young men can't.

Diana made her own wedding dress. I borrowed a suit for the occasion from a mate, a hideous green little number (the suit, not the mate, though there wasn't much in it) with velvet lapels and flared pants. It was very seventies, very tacky and, therefore, very me. That remains an apt description.

We had the hair to match, too. Very long, very blond, very ABBA, very Age of Aquarius. We were two happy, shiny people. I compromised and wore shoes for the event, and even a bow tie, which I ripped off as soon as the timing seemed right.

The marriage celebrations were simple, relaxed and mellow (don't forget that this was the era of the magic mushroom). The ceremony took place in the front yard of Diana's parents' home in East Lindfield and the reception was held in the backyard. There was no need for a fleet of limos to ferry us about and no hostilities were waged over the pruning of the guest list. We were flat out thinking of people to invite, especially on my side, for obvious reasons. There was no printed, gold-embossed order of service, no 20-person wedding party resembling a TV commentary team on election night, and no need to arrange valet parking.

The reception was just a laid-back celebration with assorted relatives and friends. Di's mum Mary, or Mollie as she was always known, made the wedding cake. Mollie was a kind-hearted soul who deserved sainthood or to be bronzed, at least, for enduring Col. Apart from that, she made the best apple pies and scones in the history of the universe. Age may have dulled my memory (and there have been many times when I've hoped that it would) but I swear I can smell and taste them even now. The CV wasn't all about cooking skills, though. 'The Moll', a gutsy and feisty woman in her own subdued way, had also been a volunteer driver during World War II.

My father awkwardly greeted guests as they arrived and, after nervously witnessing the formalities, scurried into the kitchen to help with the catering. He flew back to Canberra on the first available flight, which most likely had something to do with the wedding 'crowd'. Must run in the family.

The wedding was very low key by today's ludicrously extravagant benchmark. There was no fancy church, no lavish $200-a-head reception 'do' in a tasteless Taj Mahal-like venue, no rehearsals or 'practice makeovers' and not a beach or a forest in sight. And, thankfully, it was well before 'You Are the Wind Beneath My Wings' or the Adele/Taylor Swift/Beyoncé equivalent had become a compulsory part of the marriage service. We were even married DIY-style by my uncle Bruce who was then a practising Baptist minister and, in his mid-90s today, is still one of life's great characters.

But the wedding wasn't exactly Dimboola-like either. There were no blues, punch-ups or hissy fits. No tears were shed in anger and the police weren't called to break up warring factions.

Nor did it cost 'The Col' the equivalent of the gross domestic product of a developing country, or the contents of Malcolm Turnbull's spare change jar. It didn't delay Col's retirement by ten years either.

It was just a very simple celebration which we both thoroughly enjoyed and have had fond memories of ever since. Come to think of it, we actually enjoyed the occasion. (We were amongst the last to leave.) It was the wedding we both wanted. I'm not convinced that every married couple can honestly make that claim these days.

* * *

Back, again, to that 'what's the meaning of life' moment.

Truth be told, it wasn't so much a 'moment' as a gradual build-up of over 30 years of bloody hard slog doing the things that most people do: building a career, raising a family, establishing a home and just coping with everything that life throws at you. And, of course, swatting back regular offerings of the 'shit happens' principle.

Fast forward: by the time 2005 rolled around, Diana and I were thinking seriously about a very substantial lifestyle switch. By then, we'd lived and worked in Canberra for 30 years and were hanging out for a radical change: to break free, to regain control and, if not to 'live the dream', then at least to live life more on our terms, even if we weren't entirely sure what that meant.

That was the plan, anyway. But, as we all know too well, life has a habit of changing our plans. Sometimes it's for the better, sometimes it's for the worse, and sometimes you don't even see the change coming.

2

THE CANBERRA YEARS

Life is what happens to you
while you're busy making
other plans

John Lennon, 'Beautiful Boy'

My Canberra experience was intended and planned. The move there in late 1975 was meant to be short term while I completed a postgraduate law degree. I accidentally stayed for 33 years.

Before we were married, and for a short time after, Diana and I lived there in various types of accommodation. At first, we lived in Graduate House, close to the city centre. I was already living there by early 1976. Di joined me later, after we'd officially hooked up. As the name suggests, Graduate House was student accommodation, mainly for singles. As we were a double, it was incredibly cramped. The single bed, which greatly enhanced our relationship you might say, and the kitchenette, bathroom, student desk and balcony were all shoe-horned into an area of no more than about 20 square metres. (I was unaware that over 35 years later I'd be spending a sizeable portion of my time living in similarly sized digs — 'dongas' to be precise — but in vastly different circumstances. We'll come to that.)

We loved the Graduate House days. We were incredibly happy with married life and with each other, as most young and newly married couples are.

* * *

While grinding my way through a Master of Laws degree, I worked part-time in a seafood restaurant set up by my brother Peter and my father. A seafood restaurant was a novelty for Canberra in those days, but Peter and dad had seafood restaurant form that traced back to earlier times.

In the late 1960s, Peter had been the manager of a seafood restaurant, Laddie's Place, at The Spit in Sydney. I worked there in my last couple of years at high school washing dishes. I'm not proud of it but Peter has the dubious honour of being the only person who's ever sacked me from a job.

I'd scored work for two schoolmates, Gary and Ken, who had the grossly unhygienic habit of nicking broken or spoiled cheesecakes and apple pies and parking them outside the kitchen under a bush. We'd collect them after work — what was left of them, anyway, after the local fauna had dined out. I went along with the arrangement, as you do, but was never convinced it was such a brilliant idea. Inevitably, one night Peter caught us red-handed and sticky-fingered and had no choice but to give us all the boot.

Later, and throughout my undergraduate law degree, I worked at the Manly Pier Restaurant — again, a seafood restaurant and, again, washing dishes. Dad was one of the cooks there and Peter was the manager and a wine waiter at one time.

I refused to score jobs for Gary and Ken.

The setting up of the restaurant in Canberra — 'The Fishing Village' — in the mid-1970s was less difficult for Peter and dad because of their history in the industry. It was a huge success, based largely on simple, common sense restaurant principles, and laid the groundwork for our next family venture into the catering world over 30 years later. But, this time, it wasn't to have such happy memories or outcomes.

* * *

As close as Diana and I were (forced upon us by that single bed configuration), we needed a touch more space than we had at Graduate House, and in about mid-1977 we moved into a granny flat in the backyard of a house at 5 Talbot Street, Forrest.

It was a particularly freezing Canberra winter that year, as I recall. Temperatures regularly dropped to about minus six and barely reached plus 10 during the day. Although the flat was bigger than the Graduate House unit, it was still microscopic in size and had no effective heating or cooling. But as I said, we were deliriously happy with life and needed very little apart from each other.

I was finishing off the thesis for my degree and still working part-time at The Fishing Village earning the vast sum of $40 per week. Di had enrolled at the ANU in the forestry department, just for something to do, it seemed, as a way of quenching her insatiable thirst for all forms of activity and knowledge which, to date (due to ongoing hyperactivity), has never been, and never will be, entirely satisfied.

My Masters thesis was completed in 1978 and, for all I know, could still be gathering dust somewhere in the bowels of the ANU Law Library. Or perhaps it's being used as a convenient doorstop or to prop up some wonky-legged table somewhere.

Early in 1978, we took the plunge and bought our first house. It was located out in the burbs in the only area we could afford. My sister Sheila found it for us, at 15 Yarra Street, Kaleen. The house, a cute salt-and-pepper-coloured brick butter box, was purchased for

$34,950.00. That was the full sale price, not just the five per cent deposit.

We paid the deposit by credit card and took out two low interest rate mortgages. We weren't consciously part of any 'we want it all and we want it now' movement; that would come later with a heightened level of maturity and sophistication. We were just desperate to set up house together, as most newly married couples are. We lived for months with a double bed and nothing much else. Our first 'fridge' was a leaky, second-hand esky and we had no washing machine, let alone a dishwasher or microwave.

The house was certainly no McMansion and had no games room, lap pool, gym, study, ensuite, media room or reading nook — or their 1970s equivalents. Nor did we have an outdoor entertainment area, a spa, or, tragically, even a true-blue Balinese gazebo in the backyard. Our idea of alfresco living was a few bricks left over from the building of the house, which I not-too-professionally stacked on top of each other, and didn't even 'glue' together in any way (my version of DIY again), to form a very primitive barbecue. But, it cooked snags and chops. It did the job.

We made do, as you did back in the day, with what we had, which wasn't much at all.

But we did have a dog — an Australian sheepdog/kelpie cross called Jack. He was our best mate, a great running buddy for me, and we loved him to bits for the 16 years we had him. Apart from his incredible fitness, Jack was a gifted climber. More than once, we'd arrive home to find him cowering nervously on the carport roof, having peed himself senseless from sheer anxiety, after using the horizontal wooden carport gates as his personal ladder. As I get older, I know that feeling all too well, but don't extend the experience to include scaling a carport roof. As well as being ridiculously accident-prone, my climbing skills are rubbish.

Diana and I mothered/fathered two kids in rapid succession: Hamish in 1979 and Jessica in 1980. It was as if all I had to do was to look sideways at Di and she'd become pregnant. I suspect there must've been something more to do with it than just that, but knowing me, possibly not much more.

I was present at each birth and, as it happened, was more than just an interested spectator. Both labours were 24-hour affairs from go to whoa. I wasn't exactly a 'live-in dad' at the hospital, as I know some men are now, but I was the next best thing. On top of all the other medico-related assistance I administered, I had to heave Mrs Burns onto a bedpan several times during each shift, with the aid of a rudimentary block-and-tackle set-up – thus, qualifying me for an honorary degree in nursing, if not engineering.

As you'll discover, the pragmatic Mrs Burns is never backwards in coming forwards. Her instructions were very loud and very clear — and sometimes just plain loud — during each 24-hour ordeal: 'Gimme druuuugs ... I just want druuuugs!!!' The obliging hospital staff were more than happy to accommodate. Smart move. Mrs Burns isn't the most amenable patient on the planet, as you'll also learn.

I was asked at times whether I'd like a cup of tea or coffee to calm *my* nerves. 'No, gimme druuuugs! I just want druuuugs!!!' I occasionally did the tea lady thing for the nursing staff. To calm *their* nerves.

Having to 'top and tail' my dearly beloved multiple times with a damp sponge and towel was *not* covered by a chapter in the marriage manual. At the same time, I was compelled by The Col to provide a personal, blow-by-blow description of every aspect of the delivery being expertly executed by his one and only darling daughter. Obviously according to Col, such a miracle had never been performed by any other female in the history of the human race.

* * *

The Masters degree was meant to lead me to working in the constitutional law field at some stage. At one point, I had a strong hankering to be a university academic, a very bubble-conducive lifestyle, I envisaged. Although that was the plan, it didn't pan out that way.

Instead, I joined the federal Attorney-General's Department in 1978 in the parliamentary drafting area, which had nothing at all to do with constitutional law. Still, I enjoyed the challenge and count myself fortunate to have worked with some of the best and most competent lawyers I've known, including long-time friends Brendan McCarthy and Denis O'Brien.

Over a period of some 15 years, I worked my way around several divisions within the department, including business law, where I spent about six years initially in trade practices, insurance and banking law. Later, I worked in the international trade law area, specifically dealing with both domestic and international aspects of intellectual property, particularly copyright. During that period, I managed to squeeze in another law degree — such insanity. This time, a Graduate Diploma in International Law, again at the ANU.

Although it doesn't appear in the least bit sexy (positively sex*less*), copyright *was* a fascinating area and I was lucky enough to later represent the Australian Government at a number of United Nations international trade law meetings in New York and Vienna. I also represented the government at meetings of the World Intellectual Property Organization in Geneva. I loved my trips to attend the New York and Geneva meetings, which were, having regard to the often 10–12 hour working days, by no means mere international junkets or talkfests. In New York, I always stayed in uptown Manhattan not far from Central Park. By then, the late 1980s, I was well and truly into running and the before-work morning run invariably included a lap or two of the reservoir in the middle of the park, famously depicted in the opening scenes of the movie *Marathon Man* starring Dustin Hoffman and Sir Laurence Olivier.

On Sundays, I'd run a couple of laps around the outer edge of the park which was closed off to traffic on that day and turned over to a licorice-allsorts array of runners, cyclists, walkers, roller skaters and miscellaneous New York crazies. Each lap would take me past the finish line of the New York City Marathon just opposite Tavern on the Green.

* * *

Fast-forwarding again: by the early 1990s I was badly in need of a career change, despite enjoying the work. I'd been with Attorney-Generals for over 15 years and knew that I was unlikely to progress much further up the greasy pole. Even with only an ounce of smarts (I'd just groped my way out of the bubble by then), you develop a sense of where you place in the pecking order in any large organisation. It was abundantly obvious that I'd been seriously out-pecked. It was time to move on and turf the bubble once and for all.

A friend of Diana's had suggested that she start her own legal practice in Canberra as there seemed to be a niche for it, particularly in the property field. She'd worked previously as an advocate in the Veterans' Affairs Department and with the Australian Government Solicitor's Office. Diana was a dedicated and ferociously hard worker but, like me, was looking for a change, in part to be at home more for the kids, who were approaching their scary early teenage years.

So, in early 1992, Diana set up her own legal practice, working initially from an upstairs office at our home at 62 Investigator Street, Red Hill. The business was an instant success. Di was brilliant with people and very quickly established a strong client base. Of course, I did what any brave, red-blooded husband would do in the circumstances. I waited about 18 months for my highly competent wife to make a complete success of the business and then joined her.

I was more than pleased to leave the bureaucracy behind me.

Working in Attorney-Generals had been challenging and stimulating but it was time to tackle something different. If I'm honest, though, that's a convenient rationalisation for knowing that my time was up. I was treading water, possibly even sinking, though at the very least, just marking time. As you do, sometimes, during a career.

I joined the practice in November 1993. As the principal of the firm, Diana had been granted an 'unrestricted practising certificate'. Because only one UPC was necessary to operate the practice, I was happy enough with a restricted practising certificate. We'd always considered ourselves to be joint business partners even though my title was, informally, that of 'consultant'. This arrangement, as much as it suited us and reflected reality, would return to haunt us many years later in gut-wrenching fashion, particularly for Diana.

The years between the end of 1993 and 2005, as significant as they were, are not the subject of this book. Consequently, I need to hit the fast-forward button yet again and time-machine to 2005.

Hang in there, folks. We'll get to the point of the book soon, I promise. Trust me, I'm a lawyer.

* * *

By the middle of 2005, the practice had grown to the point where we were operating two separate offices: one in the inner southern Canberra suburb of Kingston and the other in the fast-growing outer northern suburb of Gungahlin. We'd long since outgrown our home office in Red Hill.

The business was booming. The volume of property and other work had increased dramatically. But, as with any business, the practice had taken its toll on both of us. It was, literally, a 24/7 proposition. Clients knew where we lived and were never too shy to land on our doorstep — even on a Sunday. As we were by then approaching our mid-fifties, we began to think in terms of making the break to a less manic lifestyle. We'd devoted mind, body and soul to the business and it had paid us back with many of the so-called trappings of success. But it was time for a change of direction.

Nothing as profound or exotic as a mid-life crisis, though. Certainly not part of life's 'journey'. You didn't consciously embark on life journeys back then. They weren't trendy, or an essential part of life, as they appear to be today. We were, pure and simple, just plain stuffed. Time for some freedom. Time, so we thought, to live the good life. It'd been put on hold long enough.

In true burnt-out Baby Boomer fashion, we began to look around for the quintessential beach shack. Both Hamish and Jess had long since moved to Melbourne so, chasing our kids around the country as parents sometimes do (what madness), we naturally gravitated towards the Victorian coast.

We spent the 2005 Christmas holidays on the Gippsland coast in south-east Victoria, feverishly exploring the surrounding seaside towns in search of the (elusive) Great Australian Sandcastle. We based ourselves in Port Albert and, from there, made several day trips and excursions to check out the local beachside towns.

Many of the places we visited were appealing but nothing really grabbed us. What we were looking for — of course, by then, we wanted it all and we wanted it now — offered direct or at least close access to the beach: part of a wish list fast becoming unattainable almost anywhere on the east coast of Australia, unless you were willing to cop an impossibly hefty price tag. (As well as wanting it all and now, we also wanted it for nothing, or bugger all, as you do.)

At the end of the first week in January 2006, as the holiday drew to a close, we'd become increasingly frustrated at not finding what we'd been searching for. We were due to leave on a Sunday for the long trip back to Canberra and took one last drive the day before, as there were still a few places we hadn't checked out. (Exhausted and at rope's end in the pursuit of ultimate peace and serenity. Go figure.)

Down to the last few possibilities, we drove through Foster and

Fish Creek, over the Tarwin River bridge and into Venus Bay. Until then, Venus Bay was nothing more to us than a name on a map. The Tarwin River flowed into Anderson Inlet and then onto the ocean, bisecting Venus Bay on one side and Inverloch on the other. It's a raw, rugged and pristine part of the world, a hidden gem, as we were soon to discover.

Venus Bay is a small coastal town with a decidedly village, almost sleepy, atmosphere. Surprisingly, we found three real estate agents in the main street, and we visited all of them, giving each, not very hopefully we thought, our beach paradise wish list. Again, nothing they showed to us seemed to fit the bill.

We'd all but given up hope and resigned ourselves to a fruitless search. While consoling each other over a cup of coffee, one of the agents we'd visited earlier spotted us from across the street, sauntered over, and told us about the forthcoming sale of a block of land for which he'd just taken instructions, but that was not yet formally on the market.

We drove to the block at 65 Jupiter Boulevard, only a short distance from the Venus Bay shops. The block, just under 1000 square metres, was nestled quietly on the edge of a cluster of towering bush-covered sand dunes. The instant attraction was the track that ran from the back of the property, through the dunes and straight onto over 20 kilometres of wild Bass Strait, ocean beach.

One walk over the block and the trek to 'Beach 1' taking less than ten minutes was all the confirmation we needed. It was just what we were looking for, another love-at-first-sight moment. An ultra-quiet location with direct beach access and several quaint country towns nearby, and only a two-hour drive to Melbourne. Backing onto a beach, and close to a river and estuary, it was also somewhere I hoped I could revive, if not relive, my boyhood love of fishing.

Two more cups of coffee later, and super buzzed as a result, our offer was accepted. We paid the deposit to the agent and signed the preliminary contract documents. Of course, we had to pay one more visit to the block for a last-minute inspection, not that we needed further convincing.

We (almost) had it all and we (almost) had it now. At least enough to satisfy that modern-day, all-pervasive, unquenchable thirst for instant nowness.

This was where we'd build our dream beach shack for holiday visits from Melbourne, where we were certain we'd end up some day, after finally leaving Canberra.

Again, that was the plan.

We returned to Canberra in early January 2006 and immediately set about determining what type of house we'd build on the block. After months of agonising and Col-style negotiation with the ever-conciliatory Mrs B, we (she) settled on a 'two-pod' design — one pod for the kitchen and living area and a separate pod for the bedrooms and bathrooms. The final concept was, naturally, conceived by the architecturally gifted Mrs Burns who, even though to this day reckons she didn't completely get what she wanted, still managed to organise a fantastic build.

Towards the end of 2007, the two pods, constructed by Prebuilt in a Melbourne warehouse, were finally transported to the site on the back of two semi-trailers and installed by crane, much to the consternation of many Venus Bay residents, who obviously hadn't experienced such wild excitement in years.

In the meantime, we were well and truly thinking of selling the business and relocating to Melbourne. Selling a legal practice is not as straightforward as might be imagined, however in the event, we were able to negotiate the sale to a local lawyer in the second half of the year.

The lawyer did not, at that stage, have an unrestricted practising certificate, which as I've already mentioned, is essential for running a legal practice. After some negotiation, we agreed that one of the conditions of the sale would be that Diana, as principal of the firm, would remain the lawyer with ultimate legal responsibility for the conduct of the practice until such time as he'd obtained his UPC. We'd been led to believe that this would be no later than November 2008. (If, upon reading the words 'legal responsibility', you immediately thought 'oh shit', you are, regrettably, spot on. Don't despair just yet, though. Save that for later. For now, read on.)

The sale proceeded on that basis, initially only applying to the business in Kingston, but later also expanding to include the Gungahlin side of the practice. In February 2008, after the sale had been 'settled', we left Canberra after some 33 years.

Canberra had been good to us. We'd raised a family there, developed our careers and operated a very successful business. We had no regrets. None. Canberra had given us the opportunity to enjoy a great lifestyle and we counted ourselves fortunate to have lived there. We still do.

At the same time, we had no regrets in leaving. None. We were long overdue for a change of lifestyle. The practice had soaked up every drop of physical and emotional energy over many years and we were more than ready for a decidedly slower pace in a completely different environment.

We just weren't ready for what was to come next, and the chain of events that would send us in a direction we could never have foreseen — and, arguably, from which we would never completely recover.

3

MARATHON MAN

Once you cross that finish line, no matter how slow or how fast, it will change your life forever.

Dick Beardsley, US Olympic Marathon runner,
The Spirit of the Marathon

I'm conscious that I appear to many people to be a rather strange human being. To people back in the day, I was a weird kid. To those same people now, and to more added along the way, I'm a weird adult. Okay, let's not mince words. Let's face reality. I admit to being a genuine misfit.

Seriously, and quite apart from other oddities that should by now be readily apparent, how many people do you know in their late sixties who run and, over many decades, have held a very strong desire to run the Boston Marathon? And who manically refuse to let it go, even if that desire has been shelved many times and for long periods?

As mentioned, I tend to shy away from people as much as possible. I don't feel compelled to engage with the community. Nevertheless, if a person needs help, I'll be there until it's 'all good'. I just won't turn up again tomorrow with a bowl of chicken soup or a David Jones food hamper. I'm unlikely to make a meal of it.

I don't crave social connection or interaction. A 'people person' I am not and I make no apologies for it. We're all seriously over-hugged and over-kissed as it is without me adding to it - aren't we? I never hang around afterwards, anywhere, for a chat (and especially not for a yarn), assuming I've been dragged there in the first place. I don't talk to people in lifts. That's why I automatically choose the stairs option. I've even been known to vacate a lift several floors before my destination on the faintest suspicion that 'good morning' might develop into 'how are you?' or, heaven forbid, a full-blown conversation.

I've never bothered to learn the 'art' of small talk. I am, however, a great exponent of the 'ask questions and listen' principle, mainly because it's an easy way to avoid saying much myself. Just steer people onto their favourite topic (usually themselves, their 'team', their kids/grandkids or, especially, their partner) and switch off. It works most times, a win–win. Good for me. Good for them. And it prevents me from having to cut the conversation short and rudely bolt for the nearest exit. A social cop-out, you might say? Plainly disrespectful? Maybe, but for me this 'life skill' is a vital shifting spanner in the personal survival toolbox.

Unsurprisingly, I don't have a 'social circle', or even a social semi-circle. I have no great desire to be included. A measure of grudging tolerance is acceptable, provided some kind soul is obliging enough to pass the salt or the tomato sauce — without me having to ask for it.

I'm reminded of a famous quote by Groucho Marx: 'I sent the club a wire stating, PLEASE ACCEPT MY RESIGNATION. I DON'T WANT TO BELONG TO ANY CLUB THAT WILL ACCEPT ME AS A MEMBER.'

I appreciate that most people during their lives create a network of family, friends, work colleagues, business associates, social club acquaintances and many others. They derive great comfort, security, friendship and inclusiveness from being part of these groups. They feel a sense of belonging to a wider association of human beings. I'm certainly no psychologist but, to me, that's a very tribal concept. It's heartening that most people build a network around them to help them survive and thrive. Most would agree that's just normal, natural and healthy. The way it should be. The order of things. I totally get it.

But there are exceptions. I'm equally convinced that there are people in the world (though maybe a small proportion) who genuinely need solitude and aloneness to survive and thrive, who find people, and the world in general, alien, threatening and hostile, and a claustrophobic and debilitating shock to the senses.

I have little doubt that I'm one of those people. We're not 'social animals'. If there's such a concept, maybe we're simply allergic to the world. Let's be clear, though. We can, and do, still function quietly and silently as worthwhile human beings. We just don't get invited to many parties. (It probably doesn't help much if you're a natural born grump, like me.)

* * *

Having said that, it's no real surprise that long-distance running has held a strong appeal to me over many years. The idea of marathon running intrigued me right from the moment I became aware of it. The aloneness of it has always been a great attraction. The simplicity. The honesty. The physical challenge. The mental strength it takes. The sense of peace and quiet contemplation it evokes. It somehow fits the personality.

I enjoy the challenge of pushing my body to its physical limits whatever they may be (and however much those physical limits may be shrinking year by year) and testing myself mentally. It's one of the few daily activities where I can be totally alone with my own thoughts. It's a time and a place where I can shut things out, where the outside world can't intrude.

I'm sure most of us devise various means to escape at times, to go to our happy place or even find somewhere to hide (if I'm any guide). Some, negatively, choose drugs, alcohol, or a similar diversion. Others, positively, paint, listen to music, garden or meditate. Running does the same for me.

More on that later.

Recollections of Tom Courtenay's character in the classic 1960s British film *The Loneliness of the Long Distance Runner* are vivid even now. It wasn't just the image of distance running itself. It was the context in which running was portrayed in the film. Having the freedom to run was the borstal boy's means of physical and emotional escape. Running was also a neat fit with his 'up yours' act of defiance at the end of the film, his disdain for conformity and authority and the brutality, repression and hypocrisy of the British youth detention system.

It appealed to me. I identified with it. After all, I was a closet radical myself, wasn't I? And I had little time for many forms of authority.

It mystifies me how I ever became a lawyer, one of the most conservative professions. I've rarely felt comfortable or at ease. A classic square peg, a member of an established order, but never feeling part of it. My internal compass reminds me regularly that the fit just isn't right, but I've chosen not to listen. Still, it's been my career for over 45 years. I've had the freedom to choose and it's been my choice, my decision. On that basis, I won't allow myself to regret making it.

If the truth be known, law was one of the few professions open to me at the time. At school I preferred the 'humanities' like history and English, so professions such as architecture, medicine, engineering, accountancy and pharmacy simply weren't available. The choices in those days were there, but nevertheless limited.

My mum was pleased I became a lawyer (mainly, I believe, for the status associated with it). For some bizarre reason, that mattered to me at the time. Keeping the oldies happy was important back then. Less call for it now, I expect. As it should be.

My mother, Margaret, left school at an early age and took up nursing. She was later obliged to give up her career to care for her sick father. Academically, she always felt she hadn't achieved what her potential promised. Later, in her fifties and sixties, she went back to complete her Higher School Certificate and then completed a Bachelor of Arts and a Master of Arts at ANU. She was a late achiever. It must run in the family.

So far as my own athletic endeavours went, my earliest memory of distance running (aside from the post-fishing-incident-at-Manly-Wharf jog home with a sliced-open foot) was winning the Balgowlah Boys High School under-12 cross-country race in 1964, then winning the North Shore Zone title, and finally, running second at the NSW State Cross Country Championships held in Centennial Park — all barefooted. This gave me my very first inkling that, maybe, I might have some distance-running talent.

My first awareness of what it might be like to be a marathon runner came from John Farrington who, at one time, lived next door to my brother Peter in Sydney's Queenscliff, and competed for Australia in the 1968 Olympic Marathon in Mexico. Farrington was known to run from home for many miles out along the northern beaches and back. That feat was difficult for me to contemplate, but intrigued me at the same time. It stuck with me over the years.

My other recollection of distance running back in those days came from around 1971 when the US filmmaker Bud Greenspan directed a documentary called *The Ethiopians*, which featured the legendary marathon runner Abebe Bikila. It was so inspiring to me that, with no planning or preparation, I took off for a run from where I lived in Manly, to Belrose, where my then brother-in-law was building a ferro-cement boat in the bush — about 15 kilometres away. I'd never done anything like it. I wanted to feel what it was like. I needed to see if I could do it. I did do it, though I could barely walk for several days afterwards.

I was fascinated by the story of Abebe Bikila. I still am today. It simply must be one of the most dramatic and traumatic sporting and life stories. Courage, simplicity, extreme willpower and great triumph freakishly mix with unimaginable tragedy.

The drama of Bikila's sporting career and personal life captured my attention instantly. His story hit me like a thunderbolt, jolting my senses and shaking me awake, much like the music and the politics of the late 1960s. His life story was a perfect example of the truth being infinitely stranger and vastly more unbelievable than fiction. Bikila may not have been a hero to me (hero worship is a notion I find hard to accept), but his accomplishments were heroic nevertheless.

His running style was effortless and flowing. His feet seemed to barely touch the ground. He hardly appeared to breathe. His expression never changed. His concentration never faltered. He conveyed the impression of being in total control of his body and mind.

I wanted to run like him. I wanted to be like him, mentally as tough as granite, disciplined and committed. He was, in his chosen endeavour, the real deal — as not all people are, though many pretend to be.

Bikila won the marathon at the Rome Olympics in 1960, running barefoot no less, only weeks after undergoing an operation for appendicitis. He won the marathon again at the Tokyo Olympics in 1964, this time wearing shoes, and then 'paced' his fellow Ethiopian, Mamo Wolde, to win the gold medal at the Mexico Olympics four years later, when Bikila could barely walk because of a broken bone in his leg, suffered only days before the race. Bikila won all but three of the marathons in which he competed.

Then came the tragedy of a car crash a few years later, which left Bikila wheelchair-bound. The image of a marathon runner being cruelly struck down in his prime and confined to a wheelchair was, to me, incomprehensible. A two-time Olympic Marathon winner unable to walk, let alone run. I couldn't imagine anything more sorrowful. And, finally, tragically, Bikila died from a cerebral haemorrhage at the age of 41.

Some claim that he died of a 'broken heart'. Though obviously not the clinical explanation, I can well appreciate the sentiment. It hit a very deep and raw nerve in me. Bikila's death didn't exactly break *my* heart but it came perilously close. As a young man grappling with his own emotional wellbeing and deep insecurities, it was one of the first times I can recall experiencing a sense of overwhelming sadness at the profoundly tragic 'fall' of another human being. It was a completely new emotion for me, and it had an acute and long-lasting effect which cannot be overstated. Even now, I tear up when I think or write about Bikila's story. I'm at a loss to explain why I'm so moved by his inspirational life and tragic death. I guess life is like that, sometimes.

The grainy footage of Bikila winning the 1964 Olympic Marathon in Tokyo was later used as a backdrop to the opening scenes of *Marathon Man*. Those scenes were shot around the reservoir in Central Park, New York — a place where, as I recalled earlier, I'd do a fair bit of running myself.

It wasn't until I started work at the Attorney-General's Department in Canberra in late 1978 that I took up running again, years after my early, fleeting, success at high school.

Lunchtime running around Lake Burley Griffin was a favourite pastime for public servants in Canberra, and still is. At the invitation of two friends, Brendan McCarthy and Denis O'Brien, I ventured out one lunchtime in late 1978, not wearing even close to the right gear of course. I kept pace with them for no more than a kilometre, around halfway across the Kings Avenue bridge, at which point my lungs almost burst and I had to perform an embarrassing U-turn and walk, dejectedly, back.

Brendan and Denis, along with their respective wives Julie and

Jacinta, have been our great friends for well over 40 years but I was less than impressed with them for giving me an unintentional hammering that day. They were going easy on me, hardly jogging, but it felt to me like a flat-out sprint. I persevered, though, and gradually improved my fitness over the summer of 1978–79.

* * *

I officially lost my marathon virginity on April Fool's Day 1979.

No joke.

After only a few months of very tentative running, I inexplicably decided to launch my marathon-running 'career'. In hindsight, that decision was a straight-out brain fade. By any measure, I was an embarrassingly inexperienced runner. As an aspiring marathon runner, I had absolutely no clue about what I was to throw myself head-long into. My only real knowledge of the race was that it was run, oddly, over a distance of 42.195 kilometres.

As I'd learn the hard way in the years to come, solid marathon preparation takes place over three to four months, but this is on the back of a long, solid build-up beforehand. My specific training for the marathon in April was a pitiful four weeks. It comprised my usual running, which wasn't much at all at that time, and two 20-mile runs in the fortnight or so before. I'd heard anecdotally that the '20-miler' (just over 32 kilometres) was an essential marathon prerequisite. I tackled it, naïvely, without a second thought. You couldn't google it back then.

That first 20-miler, which I remember with not a skerrick of fondness, was run on a dirt road from the northern suburbs of Canberra towards the New South Wales town of Gundaroo. On the return leg, I stopped several times to walk. At one point, severely dehydrated and almost hallucinating, I struggled over a barbed-wire fence to sit in and slurp from a puddle-size dam on a nearby farm, much like a toddler splashing about aimlessly in a half-filled backyard plastic wading pool.

I crawled the last few kilometres home and collapsed into bed. I was disorientated, had badly chafed inner thighs (not having discovered the wonders of Vaseline back then), blistered toes and bleeding nipples. To put it bluntly and crudely, I was way beyond just plain ratshit, having never experienced that level of physical exhaustion before.

I have since, many times. It's not fun but, bizarrely, total physical exhaustion can be incredibly satisfying at the same time. There *is* a fine line between pleasure and pain. We'll get to that.

I recovered enough to repeat the dose the following week. Such lunacy. This time, strangely, I felt more like a human being afterwards, bearing in mind the very low level from the week before that I was comparing it to.

Whatever possessed me to run the Nike International Marathon a week later (topless, mind you) in the freezing rain and in a ridiculously flimsy pair of running shoes? They weren't exactly 'Dunlop Volleys', but no more up-market than them, either. At least I finished, and in the more than respectable time of 2 hours and 51 minutes - a genuinely decent effort for my first competitive race of any kind, apart from my earlier schoolboy efforts.

I've heard that running a marathon is comparable to childbirth: painful while you're doing it, making you swear you'll never do it again, but after a few weeks or months, you forget the discomfort and start planning the next one. I can't vouch for what it's like to give birth, though, as I said earlier, I did make more than a guest appearance at the birth of each of our children. After licking my wounds for several weeks, the ones I could reach, I looked forward to the next race, as perverse as that must sound.

I'd been bitten by the marathon bug. There was something indefinable about the race that got into my head, took hold, and

41

wouldn't let go, as the quote from Dick Beardsley suggests. The rich history, the triumph and the tragedy as well as the quirkiness of the race distance itself. Although it's been pushed into the background (or half-forgotten) many times and for long periods, the marathon has never completely released its vice-like grip on me. Marathon madness has always been there, or thereabouts, lingering in the background, primed to grab me by the throat and squeeze hard when the time seems right.

Finishing that first marathon *did* change my life. It wasn't exactly a 'lightbulb moment', a notion that I have some problems with, I have to say. It wasn't cathartic either. I never seriously entertained the thought that I'd be the next Abebe Bikila. But it did instil in me an awareness that, if I could run a marathon, I could deal with most issues that life threw at me. It reinforced a sense of control — maybe merely control of a defined running distance, but control nevertheless. It was an accomplishment I'd achieved on my own — DIY-style, again — and, crucial to me, it was something that could never be taken from me. Ever.

At times, I've paid a price for that single-mindedness (or, some might say, a misplaced sense of commitment) but, most times, it's been without regret.

I joined the ACT Cross Country Club and the North Canberra Athletics Club and ran several of the weekly cross-country and road races they conducted. My level of fitness improved quickly and I began to pop out some reasonable results in the local Canberra races: no wins — the standard of distance running in the ACT was incredibly strong back then (boosted by the presence of the Australian Institute of Sport) — but a handful of more-than-respectable top ten placings.

I took a more serious and well-planned approach to the 1980 Canberra Marathon. I still have, and proudly wear, the singlet from the race. That year, I improved my time to 2 hours 40 minutes. Later, in August, I ran the Adelaide Marathon in 2 hours 35 minutes, again in the pouring rain, starting in Gawler and finishing on the Adelaide Oval.

By the time of the 1981 Canberra Marathon, I was churning through some very solid training mileage — about 120 kilometres per week. The extra work and better preparation paid off as I again lowered my personal best to 2 hours 30 minutes, falling short of the coveted sub-2:30 marathon by just 39 seconds.

I've always regarded the 1981 race as my best, mainly because it was run at a very even pace: 75 minutes and 10 seconds for the first half and 75:29 for the second. (I have no idea how I remember that stat — some things stay buried in your memory forever). I've always seen that as my key to running a successful marathon — no heroics or bravado at the start, a steady build-up, and an even pace for the rest of the race.

Conventional wisdom says that you live and learn. Some people don't, as you'll discover if you read on.

Building on a solid base of fitness from previous years, I pushed my training further and clocked up two to three months of 150-kilometre training weeks prior to the Canberra Marathon in 1982, including a regular 35-kilometre run (with Jack trotting faithfully beside me) each Sunday out along the Gundaroo dirt road. There were no issues with barbed-wire fences and wading pool-style dams this time around.

I set myself an interesting target for the 1982 race. I was to turn 30 only a few days after the event. So, naturally to me, my aim was to run *under* 2 hours 30 before *turning* 30.

The mind can play some disturbing tricks at times when you run long distances. I remember arriving at the 35-kilometre point in the race and frantically performing a mathematical calculation on what my time might be at the finish. Even in my extremely fuzzy mental state, my rough calculation indicated it'd be touch and go whether I'd sneak under the 2 hours 30 barrier.

I finally gave up fruitlessly calculating my likely finishing time, mainly because each calculation was wildly different to the one before. I simply ran the last 5 kilometres or so in a blind panic. I finished in 2 hours 29 minutes and 42 seconds: my lifetime personal best.

The result was incredibly pleasing, and the memory of the day has stayed with me ever since. The sense of achievement was a tremendous ego boost, much like my soccer-playing days as a kid. Best of all, I knew in my gut that it had been an eyeballs-out-leave-it-all-on-the-road effort. I had nothing left at the end, absolutely zero - the level of commitment from which I derive the most satisfaction, in whatever I do. Achieving potential at any given moment and in any given circumstance.

My time was good enough for me to be selected in the ACT team for the Australian Marathon Championships in Brisbane in the middle of 1982. Sadly, I ran an absolute shocker. The marathon monster crept up from behind, grabbed me by the scruff of the neck and gave me a severe belting. In its nastiest mood, it's uncaring, unforgiving and indiscriminate, and commonly inflicts all these forms of punishment at once.

I literally staggered my way to the finish line in the relatively slow time of 2 hours 38 minutes, way past the PB I'd run in the Canberra marathon that April (and maybe partly attributable to the bout of glandular fever I was diagnosed with a short time later). Worse still, I copped a dose of Canberra bashing along the way. The ACT singlet was a dead giveaway. With about 7 kilometres to go, I lurched past a group of spectators, one of whom stuck the boot in with the comment, delivered with palpable hostility: 'Here comes Malcolm bloody Fraser. Boo!!!'

As I'd long been a 'true believer' and had witnessed the sacking of the Whitlam government in 1975 while a student at ANU, the below-the-belt comment was especially galling. Even if I'd wanted to, I was too stuffed to respond and just limply shuffled past without so much as a two-fingered salute. I would've gladly settled for giving them the bird, but couldn't raise the energy to lift my arm, or even the middle finger that it required.

* * *

Throughout the first several years of my running 'career', I devoured anything and everything I could get my hands on about the sport. I had a voracious appetite for books, magazines and videos, so long as they concerned distance running.

History has always been my favourite subject and the marathon has always been my favourite sport. It was both natural and logical then that the Boston Marathon and its long and rich traditions would intrigue me from day one.

I could hardly have foreseen that the 1982 race in Brisbane would be the last marathon I'd attempt for 34 years. As usual, life and all its complexities and imperfections annoyingly plonked its giant hairy bum in the way.

And sometimes squarely on my face.

4

THE LAND THAT TIME FORGOT

Basil: Manuel … my wife informs me that you're … depressed. Let me tell you something. Depression is a very bad thing. It's like a virus. If you don't stamp on it, it spreads throughout the mind, and then one day you wake up in the morning and you … you can't face life anymore!

Sybil: And then you open a hotel.

Fawlty Towers, Episode 12: 'Basil the Rat'

In February 2008, following the settlement of the sale of our legal practice in Canberra, Diana and I escaped to pursue the good life in our newly constructed beach house in Venus Bay.

We didn't consider ourselves to have retired as such. We merely needed to break free for an extended period, kick the can down the road for a time and re-evaluate our position after that. This was no long-term cardigan and slippers plan, just an intense desire to revitalise flagging spirits and rehab frazzled bodies.

For the first several months, we genuinely felt we were living the dream, or at least near enough to the grownups' version of it. We were confident of having a secure position of relative freedom — financial and otherwise. Having slugged it out over many years, we'd finally earned the right, so we thought, to rest, recover and detox in a spectacular and peaceful part of the country.

Those first few months were taken up with the tasks of getting the house in order and establishing a garden. The physical environment is raw, rugged and challenging in that corner of the world, with Bass Strait literally a ten-minute walk away through the dunes. (There is some dispute even to this day, but we continue to maintain that the block is the closest to 'Beach 1' in all of Venus Bay — about 480 metres from back gate to beach.)

That physical environment is, at the same time, simply stunning.

Typical of the local bush, the block was heavily covered with ti-tree, banksia and other coastal native plants and shrubs. We retained as much of the existing vegetation as we could. Diana added a collection of her favourite native plants as well as a weeping cherry tree that we'd uprooted and transplanted from our previous home in Red Hill. The tree adapted incredibly well and is still there, and flourishing, today.

One of the few natural speed bumps encountered in those early months was local resident 'Wally', a large, dark brown, exceptionally combative wombat, which, for Diana, instantly assumed the mantle of public enemy number one. Wally was a single-minded and determined creature. So is my dear wife.

On most days, typically but not tranquilly, I'd be frightened awake by a piercing shriek coming from somewhere in the garden after Di had discovered which of her highly cherished plants Wally had destroyed overnight. Wally's favourite by a country mile was the passionfruit vine that Di was lovingly attempting to grow. Sad to say, Wally won that battle and rendered the passionfruit virtually cactus. I did my best to pee the poor wee plant back to life, as instructed, but my efforts were marginally worse than a giant fail, bordering on piss weak.

Despite the 'Wally wars', or 'war of the wallies' — take your pick — life in those early weeks, even months, was just as we'd envisaged. Long, care-free days pottering about in the garden. Walks on the vast expanse of beach at our back door. Stumps were drawn at 4pm sharp each day, allowing sufficient time to enjoy drinks on the deck while admiring the fruits of our day's efforts.

Life couldn't have been more peaceful or satisfying. We'd finally achieved the measure of contentment we'd hoped and planned for. We may have even edged closer to finding a few answers as to the meaning of life.

Then we made the unforgivable mistake of pinching ourselves.

Events unfolded on several fronts that would steer us in a very different direction — and not for the better, despite our very best intentions. We didn't see it coming. It crept up on us from behind when we weren't paying attention. We didn't have life sorted, as we'd imagined. We weren't bulletproof. We weren't invincible.

We'd pay a high price for letting our guard down, in more ways than one. We led with our chins. And got thumped.

* * *

It was the June long weekend in 2008 when Peter and his wife Wei came to visit.

In the spirit of 'it seemed like a good idea at the time' (which invariably, translates to: 'Seriously, I'd think twice about that one if I were you'), we all decided to make an offer on the café/bar/takeaway business in the Venus Bay shops that had been up for sale for several months. (A couple of bottles of very decent red may've influenced our thought processes too, mind you.)

Our offer was accepted and the purchase settled in late July.

We devised a clear strategy to re-establish the three businesses that operated simultaneously from the premises: the takeaway, the bar and the cafe. Our plan was calculated, simple and straightforward. We'd rebuild the businesses over a period of about 12 months to two years, value add, then sell the overall business and/or building as a going concern. Nothing long term. In and out quick. That was the intention. (We'd successfully adopted a similar approach in previous investment ventures as a group.)

The building was made up of two premises that had been joined by an archway knocked through a common wall, with the takeaway on the right-hand side and the bar and café on the left. A long, narrow kitchen straddled the width of the two shops with an enormous cool room adjoining the back of the kitchen. Beyond the takeaway and kitchen was a makeshift storeroom and two toilets. A small timber landing at the rear of the building led to a concrete slab and a sizeable, grassy backyard that held two water tanks and another small, but dilapidated, outdoor storeroom.

Structurally, the building was reasonably sound. Inside, however, the place was a shambles. The previous operator had done a runner just after the Christmas / New Year holiday period, leaving several disgruntled staff members and a long trail of furious creditors. The two shops were in the same condition they'd been in when the operator skipped town months before. He'd simply closed up at the end of the Australia Day long weekend and walked out, never to return — after pocketing the weekend's takings.

The kitchen had the appearance of being crash-tackled by a cyclone. Food-encrusted crockery, pots and pans and assorted cooking utensils had been left stacked, untouched, on metal trolleys. Smatterings of black mouse droppings lay embedded in congealed cooking oil in the deep fryers. Trays of unwashed glasses stood in the cool room. Fridges and freezers were in a disgusting state, some still spattered with chunks of rotting food. The small storeroom and the cupboards in the kitchen were stuffed with unwanted junk of all descriptions; empty beer kegs were left abandoned in passageways. Both premises were in dire need of a thorough clean, pest control and a new paint job.

As Peter and Wei lived in Canberra, and Diana had begun to commute back to Canberra to help out in our former legal practice (more on that later), the 'project management' was, largely by default, taken on by me. The number of jobs needing to be undertaken and completed before we could even think of reopening seemed endless.

- Walls and floors had to be scrubbed to remove an accumulated oily film.
- Both shops required repainting (bright red at the insistence of Mrs B) and dejunking.
- The cool room, fridges and freezers demanded a thorough clean-out and then a thorough clean.
- Rotting floor tiles that couldn't be saved had to be lifted and tossed.
- Beer and other drink lines had to be reinstalled.
- The existing deep fryers, and other equipment, were in desperate need of servicing and recommissioning — after removal of the unwanted mouse droppings.
- The leaking roof needed repair.

It was crucial to re-establish credibility, not only with the many pissed-off trade creditors but also with the local community itself. To say that the previous operator had left a sour taste would be a major understatement. I found myself in a constant state of apology and denial.

Fortunately, many of the local tradies, after some initial reassurance (like promising that they'd be paid upfront in cash) were supportive of what we were trying to achieve and genuinely keen to see VB's favourite watering hole back in business. No surprises there.

Dave the electrician serviced, or repaired if necessary, all the electrical installations. Andy the plumber and gas fitter installed a new deep fryer in the kitchen and attended to countless plumbing repair jobs. John and Paul, two semi-retired local builders, sliced a hole in the wall at the back of the takeaway to create a servery between the shop front and the kitchen. They also installed new bench space in the takeaway and outdoor eating area, an additional servery in the passageway next to the kitchen, and other shelving and cupboards.

We called the business The Fishing Village Bar & Cafe, taken from the name of Peter's former Canberra restaurant. The name had historical significance and was a good fit with the decidedly laid-back, coastal atmosphere of the town. In true Australian tradition, it was soon bestowed a nickname. The locals rebadged it The Fishy.

* * *

Venus Bay, though undeniably quaint and tranquil, is by no means a thriving hotbed of activity, at least, not for the greater part of the year. To me, that's its main attraction. If you can't find peace and quiet in Venus Bay, you won't find it anywhere on the planet. The town has a distinct 'feel the serenity' vibe which people are attracted to or not. Spying a kangaroo grazing casually on the side of the road, a horse clip-clopping calmly down the main drag or a wombat out for a morning stroll around the back roads, is kinda cute and folksy for some people or too wild west for others. There's negligible room for a middle course.

The Venus Bay shopping 'strip' is situated on the only road into town, just over a kilometre from the main ocean beach — Beach 1. Back in 2008, on one side of the street was the general store, then owned and operated by Dave and Darlene. Next door was a real estate agent, then a second real estate agent and then The Fishy.

Across the road was another cafe which opened infrequently. Next door was the town's third real estate agent, then a hairdresser, with the classic Venus Bay-sounding name Who Gives a Haircut, and, lastly, a fishing shop called Rod Bending's World of Fishing and

Beach Stuff. A pizza shop, with the far less exotic name: 'Venus Bay Pizza Shop', was located a couple of vacant blocks along from The Fishy — obviously, the Paris end of VB.

The Fishy opened for business in mid-September 2008.

We'd been trading for about three weeks, and cautiously feeling our way, when we received a phone call one morning at about 4am from the local Country Fire Authority captain reporting the shocking news that there'd been a fire at the two shops. We arrived to find that the back part of the building had been almost totally lost and a substantial part of the rest of the premises badly smoke damaged.

It's curious how, in hindsight, many real-life setbacks take on a funny or quirky side, though they never appear to be particularly funny or remotely quirky at the time. Maybe we cling onto the funny or the quirky as a defence mechanism against the underlying trauma, to help dissipate or mask the pain. Drama can somehow transform into comedy with the passing of time.

As there was a strong suggestion, including from some of the Venus Bay locals, that the fire had been deliberately lit (Diana and I were even in the frame for a time), a police forensic team attended the scene the day after the blaze. In due course, the chief forensic investigator appeared, kitted out with all the gear you'd normally associate with an episode of *CSI*. With his thick protective clothing and ultra-heavy work boots tightly gripping his legs to his knees, the 'chief' closely resembled the law enforcement version of the Michelin Man. He appeared in grave danger of toppling over just from the sheer weight of the gear he was carting around on his body. It would've taken only the slightest puff of wind at precisely the wrong moment.

Anyway, there he was sifting meticulously through all the charred rubble and debris, searching for the vital clue that would reveal the source of the fire. After hours of painstaking examination, he found it. Or claimed he had: 'I've never seen anything like this before, but I think this just may be the accelerant we've been looking for.'

The cast of assembled flunkies obviously shared the same opinion, as they all nodded in chorus-line fashion, like background political hangers-on at a TV press conference. Just as they were about to bag the mysterious blackened object, I had no choice but to deliver the heart-breaking news: 'Guys, I'm sorry to have to tell you but, for fuck's sake, it's just an extremely overcooked dim sim.'

Dejected, and even in a state of disbelief and denial, the deflated bunch of forensic experts all trouped off to file, sadly for them, a 'no suspicious circumstances' report.

But, the funny/quirky side of the drama concealed a personal mini-meltdown on my part. The devastating effects of the fire hit me hard, especially as it was, doubtless, caused by me. And certainly not by a well-and-truly-overdone dim sim.

At the end of the night before, I'd emptied cooking dregs (scraped from the bottom of the deep fryers) into a garbage bin, which I then placed on the small timber landing at the back of the shops. The still scorching-hot remains had smouldered all night, finally igniting paper that was also placed in the bin. That was the true source of the blaze, and it spread with devastating speed, as fires do.

I was shattered. Not just because of the result, but also by my absolute stupidity. No chance of the 'shit-happens' principle intervening this time to provide a convenient excuse.

At one point, I found myself on my hands and knees forlornly attempting to mop up the flooded floor with a tiny, useless kitchen sponge. Of course, my efforts made not a scrap of difference. The water was ankle deep and needed to be pumped out. It was a truly pathetic scene, so I'm told, but showed the extent of my shock and anguish.

It doesn't take much for me to beat myself up and pile on guilt up to my armpits. I promptly gave myself a proper pounding over the incident, quietly marinating, then stewing, in my own juice.

* * *

While the kitchen was long, spanning the width of both the cafe and the takeaway, the cooking area itself was tight. Almost all the cooking for both takeaway and dine-in meals was carried out in a space no more than three metres in length and one metre wide. The confined space was convenient at times but ridiculously restricting at others. It required either a shuffle of one or two steps to the right or left or a pivot on the balls of the feet. Neither movement provided a solid aerobic workout.

On the right-hand side of the cooking area were two deep fryers, one of which had been newly installed. To the left was an ancient, four-burner cooktop with an even more ancient oven underneath. Further to the left was a tiny plating-up bench, above which was another relic of a bygone era — a decrepit 600-millimetre-long griller. That was the extent of the available cooking space in the kitchen and, during the busy summer holiday months in particular, that area had to pump out hundreds of takeaway meals, day and night, as well as dine-in lunches and dinner meals. It was monu-mentally hectic and nothing short of a miracle that so much food could be cooked and dispatched from such a tight space.

So now we're up to Christmas 2008, the extensive repairs to the two shops having been completed several weeks before. The locals had warned us that we'd never cope with the Christmas holiday hordes that swelled the Venus Bay population by many thousands each year. They were almost right.

With such grave predictions, Peter and Wei and several of Wei's relatives kindly volunteered to work over the busy eight-week summer holiday period. We survived, though at times complete bedlam reigned in the two shops. Wei's brother Jun, who spoke only a little English, did much of the takeaway cooking, in the early weeks, in the front part of the takeaway. He worked his backside off and, indeed by the end of his first day, he had no problem understanding what 'flake 'n' chips' meant.

As well as Jun, an amazing bunch of dedicated family members and friends made a huge, wholehearted contribution to steering us through the Christmas / New Year mayhem. The team effort was extraordinary. Jess helped us out for a week over Christmas during her holidays. Hamish came for Christmas and ended up staying; he worked with us on and off for the next two years. Wei, her daughter Georgia, Wei's sister Jenny, niece Melissa and various other nieces and nephews clocked up many gruelling hours. Peter also toiled long and hard and put his considerable restaurant experience, energy and business skills to great use.

We'd opened in September 2008 with Dave and Darlene's young son Rohan as an apprentice chef, and his girlfriend Nicki as front-of-house and on the bar. Rohan lasted about six weeks before he landed another, and for him, better, job in a Japanese restaurant in the nearby beach town of Inverloch. It was also part of the script (could've been plucked straight from *Home and Away*) that he and Nicki broke up. Nicki promptly disappeared back to her home town of Summer Bay — whoops, Shepparton. No surprise there either.

As we were fast approaching the manic holiday period, someone had to take on the 'senior' cooking role on a permanent basis.

It could well have been a scene from a TV comedy sketch where a bedraggled bunch of poor souls line up on a military parade ground. A senior army type calls for a volunteer to step forwards and take on a dangerous mission from which there would likely be no return. I was the sorry sod who wasn't quick-witted enough to take a step backwards when the call was made. Consequently, and simply because there was no one else, I became 'head chef' — a misnomer of epic proportions.

Apart from Jun's stint of several weeks, from about December 2008 onwards, and over the next two years or so, I undertook the takeaway cooking as well as lunches and dinners for the dine-in cafe. When we were flat chat, our ponytailed and good-hearted kitchen hand, Ian, also helped with some of the takeaway cooking.

I'd had plenty of experience working in restaurant kitchens, mostly washing dishes while at high school and uni, but had exceptionally limited cooking skills. I certainly knew bugger all about how to cook a paella (for me this is a tarted-up seafood risotto but let's not quibble), a seafood pie, a seafood marinara or many of the other dishes on our dine-in menu. Being able to master such commonplace dishes may sound a trifle routine, even bland and boring, to all you professional foodies out there, but it was a black art to me.

I battled through a fast and furious learning period, based largely on trial and error, with a few (and only a few) practice runs thrown in before letting myself loose on the public. The learning curve was effectively vertical, as Rohan finished up one day and I took over the next. My training wheels were discarded overnight. I was left hoping like hell that no unsuspecting diner would order anything on the menu that I couldn't cook (which was pretty much every dish) and shitting bricks and hiding in the cool room each time an order was posted up in the kitchen.

Having to learn almost instantly how to cook restaurant-standard food isn't something you can google. And I wouldn't have known an app if it'd bitten me on the bum. Still don't.

I'd anticipated that in my later years any personal reinvention would involve taking up something sedate and calming like sculpture, pottery, or maybe bird watching. That plan died a very sudden and painful death.

Sorry Ross, you're it mate. Deal with it.

Crap to that.

Diana, appropriately, ran the bar — she likes a drink does my good wife — and generally the front-of-house side of the business. Not surprisingly, the locals mostly terrorised the bar. Food was of secondary importance, if that. Friday night was their big night. We introduced a happy hour and they were deliriously happy with that.

At the prompting of our chief entertainment officer and resident party girl, Mrs Burns, Friday and Saturday nights quickly devolved into, and quite often disintegrated into, live music (and sometimes open mic) nights. Local guys Matt Dalrymple and Geoff & Muzza were regulars at the café and popular with the Venus Bay set and Melbourne blow-ins. As were the Psycho Wombats (though arguably psycho, Mrs B's dear friend Wally was *not* a band member) and Leroy, an incredibly talented guy who played multiple instruments (including a didgeridoo) and who no one had *ever* seen wear shoes, even in the depths of a bleak South Gippsland winter. I related to him straight away. We even at one time engaged the Calcutta Cowboys, but they were a bit loud for our boutique café and, in any case, their name gave the impression of an Indian 20/20 cricket team rather than a band.

Our very favourite group was Beggs to Differ: Phil Beggs, Terry Lay, and Diana and John Rees, John being the former bass guitarist with Men at Work. Among other great tracks, the band banged out a terrific version of the old pub favourite 'Am I Ever Gonna See Your Face Again'. As anyone who frequented pubs back in the day will testify, those words traditionally prompt the bawdy crowd response, 'No way, get fucked, fuck off'. It's not a terribly polished, nuanced or sophisticated comeback, but you can't deny it's effective and, let's face it, it's easy to remember when you're half cut just before closing time and feeling in a 'no way, get fucked, fuck off' kind of mood.

The leader of the chorus at The Fishy was none other than Mrs Burns, who took to the role with unbridled enthusiasm. At that time of her life, she'd only just discovered the pleasures of the F-bomb and was determined to make up for lost time. She belted out the line with dazzling sincerity, probably because, by that time of night, she meant every word.

(It was my habit to cook the band supper when they'd finished their gig. I took extra care in preparing their meal, usually two platters of assorted seafood. They appreciated my efforts as much as I appreciated their undeniable talent and good grace. Although it'd be the end of a long and gruelling day, and I'd be dog-tired, I considered it a privilege to cook for them. It's a memory I'll always cherish.)

* * *

I'm convinced there are events in life that on their face appear inconsequential but which, inexplicably, have an impact on us at a significant personal level. One such incident for me was discovering the incredible true story of the life and death of Margaret Clement, the so-called Lady of the Swamp.

In 1907, Margaret and Jeanie Clement, two of the five Clement children, bought the property Tullaree located on the Tarwin River flats. The property is situated about 15 kilometres or so from Venus Bay, as the crow flies. The two sisters had inherited great wealth from their father and lived a grand Edwardian lifestyle at Tullaree, regularly entertaining the high society set from Melbourne. They lavishly decorated the homestead with Japanese art from their trips abroad. But World War I and the Great Depression badly affected their finances and the property gradually fell into disrepair. The drains and levee banks, constructed decades before to keep the waters of the flood-prone Tarwin River flats at bay, collapsed through neglect. In peak flood times, Tullaree became surrounded by swamp, effectively cutting off the sisters from the outside world.

Margaret and Jeanie continued to live in the property, increasingly reclusive as their physical isolation became more entrenched. With no means of regular transport, Margaret was known to traipse up to three times a week to the small township of Buffalo, 11 kilometres away, to buy provisions. In times of serious flood, she'd wade in waist-deep water for over two kilometres.

Jeanie passed away in 1950, leaving Margaret and her beloved dog Dingo alone and vulnerable on the property. In May 1952, Margaret mysteriously disappeared, never to be seen again. Speculation was rampant in the district. The most widely accepted theory was that she'd been murdered, possibly by a local with whom she'd had an ongoing dispute over the property.

In November 1978, while walking in Venus Bay, a couple stumbled upon what proved to be human remains in a shallow grave. Although never conclusively proved, and despite an extensive forensic investigation and a coronial inquiry, many believed that the bones found were the remains of Margaret Clement. Those remains were unearthed on what is now the corner of Saturn Parade and Milky Way, some 250 metres from our beach house at 65 Jupiter Boulevard. The police file remains 'open but inactive'.

At one time, Margaret was reported to have said in a newspaper interview: 'We were happy in our loneliness. We bothered nobody and nobody bothered us.'

For reasons that I'm unable to explain, the story of Margaret Clement — her life and, particularly, her death — touched a sensitive nerve. Somehow, I have a recurring and very real image of what may have been her last moments, alone, cold and traumatised. That image stayed with me and even strengthened, with a deeper personal resonance, as the years passed, particularly as I spent more time at the beach house, only a couple of streets away from where Margaret Clement may have lived her last agonising moments.

* * *

For several years before leaving Canberra, my running regime had been patchy — only three or four times a week, at best. I can't pinpoint what got in the way. Most likely a combination of heavy business commitments, creeping years and simply falling out of the daily habit. In other words, life's big, fat, hairy bum again.

Likewise, during the first couple of years that we lived in Venus

Bay, I'd only run sporadically. The bar and café swallowed up most of our time and energy, as businesses are prone to do. We'd had firsthand experience of that during our time in Canberra.

I'd reached a very low point in early 2010. Like previous years, the summer had taken its toll physically. For various reasons, some of which I'll touch on later, I was emotionally even worse off.

Cooking almost non-stop each day and working 80-hour weeks for the best part of three months in the heat of the summer, was probably the hardest physical work I'd ever taken on, at least up to that stage in my life. That kind of work was never meant for someone of my vintage. It was a huge relief when the school holidays finally spluttered to an end shortly after the Australia Day long weekend.

The cuts, bruises and hot-oil burns on my hands, face and arms (and, being accident prone, the occasional stitched finger) would heal in time. But other injuries would take longer to mend and have a more lasting impact. I'd strained my Achilles tendons in both legs, partly from the heavy work boots I wore and partly because of the sheer number of hours I spent on my feet.

In about February 2010, I decided that the best way to drag myself out of the hole I'd found myself in (and partly dug for myself), was to return to running at least in a modest way. A means to regenerate some sense of purpose and achievement. Psychologically, I felt atrocious that I'd become so unhealthy and unfit.

I began tentatively with a run/walk of about two kilometres around the dirt roads near home. It was an ideal running environment. The firm gravel roads were a near-perfect running surface and there were very few cars around after the summer holidays had passed. I worked out a circuit, which meant I could run multiple laps as my fitness progressed. If I wanted to do more, I could add an extra loop which took me past the corner of Saturn Parade and Milky Way, the possible gravesite of Margaret Clement.

Those first several weeks were painful and depressing —painful because my Achilles tendons hardly appreciated the additional stress and depressing because I was staggered at the extent to which my fitness had deteriorated, if not crashed completely.

After a couple of months, I was able to run six to eight kilometres at a time, so the progress was tracking reasonably well. But I needed a goal for motivation. Just running for the sake of fitness alone had rarely been enough for me. And if I was to work towards a goal, it had to be a big one.

In April, I tuned in to a live TV coverage of the Boston Marathon on Fox Sports. It was the first time I'd been able to watch the race live. Di sat and watched it with me and asked a few questions about the race. I'd read a few books about the Boston Marathon in my earlier running days and every year followed it avidly whether I was running much or not. When running seriously in Canberra, it'd been a long-time aim of mine to one day 'run Boston', if ever the opportunity arose. That goal stayed with me for many years, even if it'd been buried somewhat as other pressing matters (life again) piled on top.

The Boston Marathon is always run on Patriots' Day, the third Monday in April, from the small Massachusetts town of Hopkinton to Boston. Di casually mentioned that the race, coincidentally, fell around my birthday — 13 April. It hit me like a lightning bolt. I could almost hear the Hallelujah Chorus playing in a thought bubble above my head. I'd turn 60 on 13 April 2012. Why not run the Boston Marathon as a 60th birthday 'celebration'?

Now, to most people a 60th birthday is usually celebrated by something a touch more sedate like a world trip, retirement (increasingly unlikely for me by that stage), a shmicko sports car, a new set of golf clubs or maybe even an all-too-late nip and tuck. But no, I'd celebrate my 60th by running the Boston Marathon. Complete lunacy to most, it was sheer inspiration to me. Absolutely brilliant, so I thought. Now I had a purpose. Two years to train for it. I reckoned I could do it.

Why Boston? Why would anyone contemplate travelling

thousands of miles halfway around the world to run 26.2? The Boston Marathon is steeped in over 120 years of history — amazing stories of heroics, heartache and controversy, not to mention tales of marathon legends like Johnny Kelly, 'Tarzan' Brown, Clarence de Mar, Joan Benoit, Katherine Switzer and 'Boston Bill' Rodgers. Australia's Robert de Castella had won the race in 1986 in a then world best time.

Boston is not a 'manufactured' marathon course like some of the other modern-day world marathons. It hasn't been specifically, and artificially, designed to produce fast or world record times. It is what it is (a concept that appeals to me) and the course has for the most part remained the same since the inaugural race in 1897. It's a special event on the world sporting calendar and the people of Boston have embraced it as an integral part of their city's history, culture and tradition.

So, that was it. I'd turn 60 on 13 April 2012 and run the Boston Marathon on 16 April. Simple.

Not quite.

Boston is unique. You can't just rock up on the day and expect to officially compete. Boston has strict and demanding qualifying times that must be met before an aspiring runner can even be considered for entry. And even after registering as a competitor, a start is not guaranteed.

As I'd be 60 by the time of the race (just), I'd need to run a 60–64 years qualifying time from another marathon within about 12 months leading up to Boston. Counting back, I figured my best shot would be to qualify at the Gold Coast Airport Marathon to be run in July 2011. It required me to run a time of under four hours to qualify.

After that epiphany of sorts, the puzzle pieces began to fall into place. The distance, duration and intensity of my running began to crank up and I found myself reclaiming a small measure of confidence. The painful runs became less frequent and less painful. Small but noticeable increments of improvement were being tucked away within successive weeks.

* * *

In the middle of 2010, Diana and I took some much-needed time off and did the grey nomad thing for about five weeks. Not that we thought we'd quite fallen into that category, despite many geriatric-feeling moments during the crazy summer months at The Fishy. We flew to Western Australia, hired a van and travelled through the south-west. We trekked as far as Cheynes Beach on the southern coast, just past Albany. Along the way, we stopped in at Margaret River, a small coastal town just over three hours drive south of Perth. Di's niece, Yvette, had lived there for several years with her husband and children and we'd paid a flying visit to the town a few years before to attend Yvette and Tim's wedding.

From the first time we saw it, we were instantly attracted to the town. Love at first sight again? It had a relaxed and casual vibe but was big enough to enjoy all the usual services - an ideal combination of coastal village and rural country town.

I don't normally pass comments about important topics without first giving them a fair amount of thought. But I remember thinking rather impulsively at the time, 'This is my kind of place. I could easily live here.'

* * *

During my time at The Fishy I was certainly no celebrity chef, who these days is almost anyone who looks reasonably attractive on TV and can boil an egg. I fail miserably at the former and can barely navigate the latter without a minor catastrophe. I was no Heston Blumenthal. More like a cross between Rick Stein and Greasy Joe (I had infinitely more Joe in me than Rick). I never seriously considered cultivating an unlikely Neil Perry-like ponytail. And, at times, my very ordinary kitchen language would've made even Gordon Ramsay cringe — an unwelcome addition to Fishy ambience.

Our very modest cafe was never going to be awarded a Chef's Hat or make it into the Michelin restaurant guide. No matter how much you dress it up, and dress it up we did, fish and chips is never going to cut it as techno-emotional cuisine. We were never going to be awarded a global dining Oscar either. The food on our simple menu was not a fusion of Australian and Asian flavours or a fusion of anything, particularly science and art. And it was by no means eclectic. There was no French, Italian, Greek or nouveau Scando–Japanese element to it. We didn't serve snail porridge or edible tinsel that, apparently, you could dine on at Heston's joint at one time. Deconstructed coffee? Syringe-infused pastries? Eating food as an event? None of that nonsense.

As a cook, I was neither innovative nor particularly inventive. With absolutely no cooking qualifications, and limited practical experience, I just hung on by the skin of my teeth and hoped like hell I'd get through each day. Aside from the very occasional stuff-up, I think I did just that.

Out of pure necessity, our rather naïve approach was to serve good, tasty food at a reasonable price and I think we got it right. Such heresy. How dare we trivialise the culinary experience? It may be a terrible admission, but really folks, as I see it, it's only food. Like life, food (especially seafood), doesn't deserve over-analysis or over-complication. It is what it is — or should be.

Rick might agree, Joe definitely would, but I suspect few other professional 'foodies' would. It appears easier to perpetuate foodie myths and make cooking look more difficult than it needs to be. The result is that we tend to give up and retreat to our time-honoured favourites like spag bol or mince on toast — nothing wrong with either, mind you.

Although cooking for me was no art form, there was, nevertheless, a form of art to it. The art of 'flake flinging'. Sounds easy? On the face of it, yes. In practice, though, it could be a little tricky.

After lightly dusting the fillet with flour, I'd dunk it in a bowl of super-thin, tempura-like batter then un-dunk it, leaving the excess batter to drip back into the bowl. Next came the crucial, but tricky, 'fling'. Balancing the batter bowl precariously on the edge of the deep fryer (an art in itself that I catastrophically stuffed up occasionally), I'd carefully fling (in truth, skim) the fillet across the surface of the oil allowing it to slowly sink beneath the oil's surface. Once flung and having done its fling thing, the now golden fillet would magically rise to the surface waiting patiently for me to give it a gentle love tap to remove any unwanted batter bits. Once drained, the fillet would be plated up and presented with fresh salad and delicious, crispy deep-fried chips.

Like even the humblest or most menial of tasks, there was an easy way and a hard way, a correct way and a wrong way, a careful way and a reckless way, a caring way and a don't-give-a-stuff way. We chose easy, correct, careful and caring. And it worked.

* * *

The café experience isn't something I regretted but it's also not something I'd ever care to repeat. Don't let anybody attempt to tell you different: the hospitality industry is anything but glamorous, despite how the reality TV shows like *MKR* or *Master Chef* attempt to paint it. And it certainly isn't, in my view at least, for people of my vintage. It's just bloody hard work, quite often with little reward. Substitute the word 'restaurant' for 'hotel' in the Sybil Fawlty quote at the start of this chapter and you've got the picture.

Along the way, I'd learned a few more 'life skills', such as how to:

- cook paella (okay, seafood risotto — regardless, it's now my regular Christmas holiday food job)
- change beer kegs on the run

- mend faulty bore pumps
- remove unruly drunks from the bar, as gently as possible having regard to my modest physical size and considerable whimpiness (and despite having the combative Mrs B arc them up in the meantime)
- repair leaking water pipes
- deal with redbacks in the septic system
- deal with snakes under the waste oil container at the back of the café
- fend off competing trade creditors (and invent new ways to let them know, as subtly as possible, that it wasn't their turn to be paid this month — and that they should be overjoyed with the news)
- juggle stock (sometimes literally)
- make stock last (and last — I didn't quite get to the 'deep-fried nothing' stage but occasionally I got very close)
- remove more unruly drunks from the bar (after pacifying them sufficiently post arc-up phase).

Despite the many difficulties, we're proud of what we achieved. And, by 'we', I don't just mean myself and Diana. Along with Peter and Wei, we worked with a great bunch of committed staff members, in particular Hamish, without whom we surely wouldn't have been able to survive for as long as we did.

We rescued a rundown building and an abandoned business and transformed them into a venue where people could enjoy a great night out. We offered good, value-for-money food and quality entertainment in a friendly and relaxed beachside atmosphere. It wasn't five-star dining set in lavish surroundings. It was never meant to be, nor did it pretend to be.

In a short time, we attracted a loyal clientele who appreciated the café for what it was. Some of our regulars would travel from Melbourne and elsewhere to Venus Bay for the weekend just to enjoy a Saturday night out at The Fishy, sometimes even in the middle of winter on the foulest of nights when the wind would howl and the rain would blow in horizontally from Bass Strait.

Yet in the end, simple economics worked against us. We were on the wrong side of the 'revenue in, expenses out' curve. We built it and they *did* come but not in sufficient numbers, or often enough, to sustain the business over the long term, particularly in a town like Venus Bay, where the permanent population numbers only in the several hundred and the winters are particularly cold and bleak.

It was a well-thought-out plan, professionally and caringly executed but, in the end, we achieved a less than wonderful result. We threw all our available energy and talents into making it a success, but we simply couldn't make it financially viable.

We'd poured mind, body and soul into another business, this time without reaping the financial benefits we'd anticipated. It was a tough slog and it drained us physically and emotionally, just as our legal practice had in Canberra.

* * *

Throughout the same three-year period, trouble had been brewing, and finally boiled over, on another front that would have an even greater emotional and financial impact on us - something else we didn't foresee.

The gods turned their backs on us because we turned our backs on them. And we got smashed.

5

CANBERRA FALLOUT

Look what they've done to my brain, Ma
Look what they've done to my brain
Well, they picked it like a chicken bone
And I think I'm half insane, Ma
Look what they've done to my song

Melanie Safka, 'Look What They've Done to My Song, Ma'

At the time of the initial negotiations to sell our Canberra legal practice through a 'legal practice broker', we were unaware that the lawyer purchasing the practice had no unrestricted practising certificate, the essential prerequisite to the running of any legal practice. (This was disclosed to us later, as the negotiations progressed.)

As a result, and as previously mentioned, the sale proceeded on the basis that settlement of the sale would be 'conditional' on the lawyer being granted a UPC by the ACT Law Society. We fully expected, and were re-assured many times, that the certificate would be issued no later than November 2008, as a 'formality'.

Diana made frequent, almost weekly, trips back to Canberra in the months following April 2008 to work in the practice and to fulfil her obligations as the holder of the firm's UPC. I also returned to Canberra, but only periodically. The lawyer who took over the business continued with the criminal law practice he'd previously conducted in another firm, and otherwise ran our former practice on a day-to-day basis as the new 'owner'. Throughout that time, we kept the arrangement on foot in the expectation that the other lawyer would, ultimately, be granted his UPC.

During these events, we learned that his professional conduct was being scrutinised by the ACT Law Society concerning matters not connected with our practice. Largely because of this, it became clear by the end of 2008 that his acquisition of a UPC was seriously in question. His being under scrutiny was an issue we weren't aware of, or advised of by our broker, when we first negotiated the sale of the practice.

The matter drifted into 2009 with little indication of a resolution in sight. Diana made trips back to Canberra well into 2009 and even into 2010 after the busy Venus Bay holiday period had passed. Throughout this time, we continued to give assurances to the Law Society that the practice was being managed competently until the sale could be finalised.

As time went on, the more we obfuscated in the false hope that 'it would work itself out in the end', the more it didn't. By early 2010, our relations with the Law Society had deteriorated dramatically. So had our ongoing operation of the practice. It demanded and deserved full-time attention, not the part-time supervision it was receiving from us, or the inadequate supervision of our business partner. We'd painted a misleading picture of control and orderly conduct. In effect, we'd papered over the cracks.

Clearly, we had no intention of returning to Canberra to run the practice on a full-time basis. How could we? It was equally clear that the prospects of the other lawyer being granted his UPC were increasingly remote.

Slowly and agonisingly, the whole sorry affair degenerated

into an almighty mess. There needed to be a circuit-breaker. The matter had to be concluded for better or worse, and we increasingly suspected it would be the latter. Finally, we saw no alternative but to close the practice down. It'd be a drastic move and would no doubt impact badly on us in every possible way, but we felt it had to be done. We couldn't stand by and allow the conduct of the practice and our relations with the Law Society to deteriorate further. We chose the option of forcing the hand and taking the consequences.

As a first step, we decided not to renew our practising certificates at the end of June 2010. The Law Society acted almost immediately and appointed an administrator to carry on the practice in our absence until it could be wound down. The Gungahlin side of the business was, effectively, transferred to another Canberra law firm.

We engaged a legal firm to act on our behalf and explore the (remote) possibility of taking legal action against our former business partner. At the same time, we knew that the Law Society would come gunning for us over the conduct of the practice, and its inadequate supervision, and we needed legal representation.

The process was painful for both of us, but much more so for Diana. She was legally, and as far as the Law Society was concerned, the principal of the firm, although we knew between us that we ran the practice together as a partnership. Over a period of many months, Diana made numerous trips to Canberra to brief our lawyers. The experience had a draining and long-lasting emotional effect. The practice had always been her baby. She'd established it on her own in 1992 and had nurtured it ever since, developing a reputation as a successful property lawyer. At one time, she'd been named ACT Solicitor of the Year. The business had grown rapidly, largely through her own efforts and stewardship. She was hugely popular with her large client base who remained loyal to her, as she had been to them.

Now, it was all about to come crashing down and there was little we could do to prevent it. Damage control was the best we could hope for and the damage, especially financial, would doubtless be significant.

Diana has never completely admitted it, but the emotional distress she suffered and the toll it took on her were enormous. The briefing process required Diana to fess up and admit the series of mistakes and errors of judgment that the two of us had made together. Overwhelmingly, Diana took the brunt of the retribution as it unfolded in an extremely open and public way. It was her personal and professional reputation that took the most savage hit.

Although it was clearly acknowledged within the ACT legal profession that we'd been induced to cooperate in a temporary, and improper, arrangement, a considerable portion of blame for the position we found ourselves in should nevertheless be sheeted home to the decisions we made and the course of action we took together. It was also acknowledged that we'd misplaced our trust in our business partner and that the whole affair had been a tragic story. Put simply, though, we'd mismanaged the matter and would end up paying a substantial personal and financial price.

These events would have destroyed many people. But Diana has the strongest character of any person I've known. If anyone could survive the hurt and anguish, it would be her. She did just that and emerged from it, eventually, stronger and with her dignity and self-respect intact. That's more than can be said for many of the other participants in this very sorry saga.

The punishment was swift, uncompromising and brutal. Firstly, we were required to repay to the Law Society the cost of its administration of the practice. That wasn't surprising and certainly no more than was fair and reasonable. Secondly, and independently of that penalty, we had to repay the outstanding GST owed by the practice (incurred, in effect, by our business partner who had failed to set it aside during the conduct of the business) as we were, legally at least, the responsible taxpayers. Then, of course, there were our own legal costs. In early 2012, we negotiated the settlement of all outstanding liabilities. Although I've never attempted to add up every dollar that we outlaid to settle all aspects of the Canberra practice drama, and never will, each of the debts incurred, along with our own legal bill, was a substantial six figure sum.

Although it didn't wipe out the nest egg totally, the financial loss took a massive chunk out of the security we'd built up over many years, and which we intended to rely on in the future. This financial and emotional heartbreak wasn't a mere 'pulled thread in the rich tapestry of life' that we'd recover from quickly. It was a major life setback. And there was no funny or quirky side to it to relieve the tension.

It wasn't quite catastrophic, or life-threatening, but close enough.

* * *

Sadly, we live in a society that's all too willing to cast judgment and then dispense what it believes to be appropriate justice on those it deems have done wrong. Retribution is administered with almost gladiatorial fervour. The wrongdoer is stripped of their dignity, unceremoniously hauled over the coals and often branded with the 'disgraced' tag for evermore. How many different forms of punishment need to be meted out? Isn't one enough for most 'crimes'?

Diana and I felt like the unintentional victims of a high-school science laboratory experiment, like a pinned specimen insect having its limbs systematically and callously yanked from each bodily socket. And then being clinically dissected by a scalpel until its innards have been spilt out onto a petri dish for all the world to gawk at and deride.

We didn't expect, nor did we deserve, sympathy and received none. We expected punishment and took it on the chin. However, the manner in which that treatment was administered and the aspersions cast on us were cruel, demeaning and demoralising. We felt, because we were made to feel, like criminals.

* * *

On top of all the stress over the Canberra practice settlement, and partly because of it, our marriage took a severe hit. It was as if our relationship had been hijacked, dragged off to some wretched place, stripped naked and then beaten to a pulp with a steel bar.

For two people who'd rarely been out of each other's company for over 35 years, it was devastating. We'd been virtually joined at the hip and now our marriage was under serious threat. We weren't communicating, preferring for some bizarre reason to suffer in silence and ride out the pain separately, as best we could.

Instead of retreating into care and nurture mode, we beat each other up psychologically and emotionally. Some couples may have withdrawn into the foetal position together and protected each other from the outside world. Instead, we just butted heads. This was new territory for us and we were powerless to handle it. We'd always been each other's best friend but now were pulling in different directions. It was distressing and heart-wrenching.

For the most part, the atmosphere at home and in the café was excruciating. We were battling each other on a number of fronts, arguing over the way the café was being run, our flatlining financial position made far worse by the global financial crisis — and the total collapse of other investments as a result — how we were dealing with our children (both of whom were dealing with their own personal crises at the time) and how we were going to deal with the ever-worsening situation with the practice in Canberra.

At certain times, relations between us were openly hostile. At other times, the atmosphere was one of brooding silence. It reminded me of how my parents treated each other. That reminder was sickening and, at times, almost impossible to bear.

But, somehow, miraculously, and over a torturous period of many months, we *did* pull through it. And we did so by more than just sheer luck. Many things between us went unsaid because maybe they didn't need to be said. That's a state of being that evolves over time if a relationship has substance, held together not by gooey sentimentality but, notwithstanding rough times, by a mutual, deep-felt sense of admiration and respect.

No matter the trauma, we still had each other. Although it's never been acknowledged, that must have counted. Silently, almost subconsciously, we clung on to each other when it mattered most. We may've floundered, flip-flopped and downright failed for a time, but when it came to the crunch, we summoned just enough commitment and resolve to survive the shipwreck, weather the storm and wash up on the beach still holding hands.

* * *

By a long stretch, this was the hardest chapter of this book to write. It was also the last. I put off writing it as long as possible. Although I knew I had to face up to the events surrounding the fallout from winding up the practice, the trauma of having to relive it was difficult to cope with. I agonised for many months — years, even — before I could muster enough courage to delve into my subconscious, expose old and still festering wounds and face the dreadful truth.

By no means does this chapter adequately paint the entire picture of the fallout from the saga, either factually or as to the level of detail or distress. There's a separate book there to be written, but it certainly won't be written by me. This chapter is a mere snapshot of an almost unbearably tough time.

I've disliked having to do it. I haven't, in the process, purged myself of the ghosts of the past. I had hoped the process would be more cathartic. It wasn't. The ghosts still haunt me and it's a chapter in my life I'm desperate to close. I know that's unrealistic. Life rarely works that way. Still, I'll do whatever it takes not to relive it.

I'll draw a line under it now in the hope that it remains forever buried.

6

WHY RUN?

The beauty of motion, the ecstasy of freedom from a hurried, over-sophisticated world, requiring little financial cost and limited innate skills: this is the privilege of the running experience.

Robin Harvie, *Why We Run: A Story of Obsession*

Okay, the quote *is* over the top, but I expect you get the general message.

On the one hand, my running motion is anything but beautiful. Sometimes, more like a wombat on Valium. And I rarely experience the 'ecstasy of freedom'. There's no overwhelming feeling of ecstasy at the end of a 30-kilometre training run, especially if it's been hosing down sleet and rain for over three hours.

However, I certainly do have 'limited innate skills'. That part's bang on.

* * *

Over a period of well over 40 years, by any standard, I've done heaps of running. As a rough estimate, I reckon I've clocked up close to

100,000 kilometres in that time. That's about two and a half times around the circumference of planet Earth.

On that basis, you'd assume that running for me has life-or-death significance — an 'obsession', as the quote from Robin Harvie's book suggests. Sorry to disappoint. It's right up there, but consistent with my 'let's keep it real' approach to life, it's not the be all and end all. And it's certainly not an obsession.

It's true that I've had a longstanding love affair with running. For various reasons, though, I've not been entirely faithful to it in that time. There've been periods when I've neglected it badly and times when I've abandoned it completely through the pressure of everyday life stresses. And, simply, because I've judged at various times that other life issues have been more pressing.

Some years, I've run more than 6,000 kilometres. At other times, I've gone for months without running a step. Some years, I've fastidiously kept a detailed training diary. Other years, I've run so infrequently that it's been easier to keep training mileage in my head.

Running has been incredibly forgiving of my numerous infidelities. For me, that's one of its beauties. It's always been there for me whenever I've wanted or needed it. When I return, it only ever questions my current fitness level, never why I left in the first place and never whether I'm fair dinkum this time. It doesn't even enquire how long I'll stick around.

If I was forced to tag or label it, I'd confidently assert to having been an above-average runner. No chance a superstar, not even a common garden variety star. Never the next Abebe Bikila, but not a completely untalented, novice plodder either.

So why do I run? I'll come to that in due course. Let's first deal with some housekeeping trivia.

I won't waste time defending running against the usual charges, like the argument that running can't be good for your body long term (knees, joints, lower back) blah, blah, blah. I've heard it all before and I'll continue to run regardless. For me, the positives, physical and otherwise, far outweigh the negatives, whether actual (dodgy Achilles tendons etc.), imagined or just plain absurd.

Let's dispel a few other running myths, at least as they apply to me, and as bizarre as some of them might appear to you.

I don't 'commune with nature' in Kate Bush / 'Wuthering Heights' fashion when I run, although the physical environment can be relaxing and soothing, especially on a deserted beach or remote bush track.

Running is not a 'religious experience' for me as I've heard that it is for others. To me, such a concept is completely nuts. Despite my father's background and influence as a one-time Baptist minister during my early childhood, I have no religious affiliations and I've never 'found God' on the run. I have, at times, however, carried on a one-way conversation with him/her when I'm not overly impressed with the weather that he/she has dished out on the day, which is never in thankful or complimentary terms.

I don't subscribe to the mad notion that running is some kind of 'art form', although these days my pace is so snail-like that I could well be classified as a living sculpture. I could easily pass as a permanent, one-person display at MONA.

I don't use electronic devices or listen to music when I run. I'm not a gadget person, mainly because I'm inherently incompetent at making them work. I must exude a weird magnetic force that makes gizmos pack it in if I'm within a 100-metre radius. (I have the same effect on most people, mind you.) But I do confess to singing to myself occasionally, especially on a long run. Never loudly and certainly not in the form of some spiritual chant. More 'mmm' than 'om'.

For someone who has trouble remembering what he had for breakfast that morning, one tune that haunts me is 'Animal Crackers in My Soup', a song on a tape we played to the kids in the car over 40 years ago to keep the little buggers quiet. It rarely worked. The song pops into my head regularly. I've no idea why, but it haunts me. It had a substantial impact on me, clearly, but none on the kids.

Being 'haunted' by a children's song? Really? In my defence, some of the lines are a bit spooky, though more so for kids I suspect — lines like: 'Gosh, oh gee but I have fun swallowing animals one by one'.

'Eye of the Tiger' or the theme from *Chariots of Fire*? Sorry, but no. 'Animal Crackers' it is. It's all about cadence, folks.

I don't kid myself that I run in an eyes-glazed-over trance-like state like a Hopi Indian (as it's been claimed, historically at least, that they drift into), although the endorphins and other assorted natural chemicals do kick in periodically to give me a buzz.

Running doesn't 'complete' me. I don't run to keep in touch with my sensitive inner self. My inner self and I stopped being best mates long ago. We barely communicate these days. We rarely cross paths. It sticks to its business, I stick to mine: we have a perfect relationship.

I'd like to think that I don't run in response to some OCD problem, though I'm open to challenge there. Being slightly manic comes in handy at times when commitment and discipline are crucial.

I haven't taken up barefoot running like the Tarahumara Indians of northern Mexico, yet the simplicity of it appeals to me. I've disliked shoes since I was a kid, as you know.

It should be self-evident that I don't feel the least bit evangelical about running. I'm not a zealot or a devotee — of anything, quite honestly. (It's too dangerous a concept for me. I could never be a member of a cult. I simply couldn't take it seriously. I'd giggle too much, or blow raspberries, at the back of the room when no one was looking.)

I'm not an 'I run, therefore, I am' kind of person. I don't run for the 'zen' moments and I'm not on some spiritual, soul-cleansing 'journey'. I'm just a person who runs and enjoys it, although I've run very seriously at times.

I don't run to 'make a statement' appearance-wise. I don't preen, primp, prance, ponce, pose or pretend. There's no escaping the sad fact that I've now achieved crusty, broken-down old fart status. Less 'ripped' than completely in tatters.

I don't run to satisfy some perverse gear fetish either. I run in the same gear until it literally falls apart, which it has, embarrassingly, on a few occasions — like pants slipping half-mast at the midway point of a marathon, but more on that one later. For about 20 years, I ran in the same crappy blue cap that's only recently been retired because it begged me to let it go. I still have it though. I don't have the heart to bury or cremate it.

Incidentally, I don't fast. I don't purge. I don't, heaven forbid, belong to a gym. I don't, at the end of run, bellow out a primal scream. (I save that for other, more appropriate moments. Like when politicians try to sound sincere … or honest.) Neither am I into diets: gluten free, Paleo, 5:2, Keto, South Beach or otherwise.

And, finally, please don't for one microsecond assume that running is my 'passion'. It puzzles me that virtually every form of human endeavour these days must be performed with passion. Isn't it acceptable to just do things with a reasonable amount of interest? Can't we still feel good about ourselves if we operate fractionally below passion level?

Phew! I feel almost cleansed to have gotten that off my chest. I think I might've just lived through a zen moment.

Okay, now comes the hard part. It's not easy to articulate why running appeals to me the way it does. There's no one, or no one simple, answer.

Nevertheless, I'll have a crack at throwing some light on it, without wishing to sound sanctimonious (or like I'm a 'child of the universe'), mostly for the benefit of the non-runners out there, perhaps the saner members of society.

It would be simplistic to say I run just to stay fit and healthy. While that's an important part of the attraction, there's more to it. Something slightly deeper. Let me put it like this and restate what

I've touched on before. I regularly find the world to be hostile and alienating, an oppressive and exhausting place in which I get the distinct impression, like many others no doubt, that I'm consistently being beaten up.

Running gives me an escape from that. It's a place where I can feel at home, even for a short time: alone in my own space, with my own thoughts, where I do some of my best thinking. Where 'they', whoever 'they' might be at any given time, can't reach me.

Alone, but never lonely. There's a world of difference.

I've always preferred to run on my own. To be honest, I can't remember the last time I ran with another person. I'm sure this 'runs' counter to the principle that jogging along in groups, and thus engaging with fellow human beings, is beneficial, but running has rarely been a social activity for me. Even within the running community, I'd surely be regarded as decidedly off-centre. But, of course, I did run with my mate Jack.

I most likely have a psychological profile that suggests that I should've had extensive therapy during my life. But I've resisted the temptation, except for a short and very unproductive stint (I thought the psych was crazier than me and needed serious counselling), preferring my usual DIY approach in dealing with life's problems. I acknowledge that therapy is hugely beneficial to many people, but it's just not for me, despite admitting to enough deeply buried and disturbing neuroses to easily occupy a week-long psychologists' convention at a wellness retreat in Bali. A non-volcano-spewing week, preferably.

Instead of psychoanalysis, running has been my therapy of choice. Even if it may not have been entirely effective, at least I can rightly claim that it's been cheaper. For about $200, I can make a pair of running shoes last me a year. Each run is a free counselling session. And, for me, it has the same effect.

Running simply makes me feel like a better human being, more in control, when life is otherwise out of control, and with a greater sense of purpose. It's a wonderful restorer of self-respect and self-confidence, even if the rest of the day goes to shit.

There are days when running is just bloody hard work, though, particularly when the weather is less than ideal. Sometimes, it's a grind. Sometimes, a part of my ageing body (often one of my exceptionally bad-tempered Achilles tendons or uncooperative lower back) is aggravated to the point where my brain just says 'bugger off, forget it'. Thankfully, these days I've learned to slow down and run in a more relaxed state. I've learned to 'let it go', and the gruelling days are less frequent. (Except for those times when I've been totally consumed by Boston Marathon qualification, in which case brain and body give up communicating altogether.)

More and more, I find I simply enjoy the physical act of running, and the slower the better. It's most likely a chemical thing, endorphins and such like, though I haven't studied the science of it to any great extent. Some days it's pure pleasure. Almost meditative. Always at least mildly therapeutic. I hit a sweet spot and run in cruise control, my running rhythm is fluid and almost effortless, my cadence metronomic, my breathing even and light. I finish feeling pleasantly tired.

Some days, perversely, it's pleasurable to inflict on myself a fearsome hammering and drain my body of every drop of energy. For me, a total purge *can* be extremely gratifying and 'good for the soul'.

Running has helped me through some tough times. It's been a loyal and forgiving friend, despite my frequent neglect.

To me, running is the opposite of overindulgence, overconsumption, oversophistication, overcomplication and overreliance on technology, all of which I find somewhat troubling. For me, running is about core principles: simplicity, discipline, commitment, honesty, peeling back the layers and stripping back to the bare essentials, to a more natural state.

Running is time and location friendly.

I've run around Central Park in the middle of Manhattan. I've run around Lake Geneva and Lake Burley Griffin. I've run multiple laps of a concrete cycling velodrome in Rosebery (north-west Tasmania) in pitch darkness. I've run around the Bathurst Motor Racing circuit. I've run in the chaos of Bangkok and the tranquility of a Queensland rainforest. I've run on the Royal Canberra Golf Course, the MCG and Adelaide Oval. I've run over the Yorkshire moors in freezing sleet. I've run in Darwin in the middle of the monsoon season. I've run through snow in Vienna and Perisher Valley. In Tasmania, I've run to the 'edge of the world' and back.

* * *

I'm fascinated by what the human body can achieve, especially what an ageing body like mine might be capable of. I'm determined to explore my physical limits. Let's be clear, though, it's not a crusade. I'm simply curious to know. If it doesn't happen, so be it. If I fall short, it won't be the end of the world. Life will go on. I'll adjust my horizon and work within whatever limitations life dictates. In the physical world, surely exploring ultimate potential is all we can ask of ourselves as human beings, at whatever age we are or with whatever natural ability we have.

I have undying respect for a human being's innate resilience and ability to overcome adversity of whatever kind. Running is a great reflection of that basic and highly admirable human characteristic.

I have an aversion to image, veneer, spin and superficiality, all of which are, I regret to say, far too common in society these days. Surely, I'm not alone there. Running forces me to confront myself, to be brutally honest and, in an indirect way, it trains me to see things as they are and provides a welcome and regular reality check.

For me, facing reality reinforces resilience. Resilience fosters hope. Hope fosters survival.

Running is part of what I do on a day-to-day basis, apart from those times when I've gone missing in action. It's not the only part but it's an important one, an additional reference point if you like.

All this may seem like an over-analysis of an activity that is, inherently, very simple. Fair call. When it's all said and done, I'm simply far better off with it than I am without it.

Maybe, the Forrest Gump running philosophy says it all:

Reporter: *Forrest! Why are you running? Are you doing this for world peace? For the homeless? Are you running for women's rights? The environment?*

Forrest: *I just feel like running.*

7

GO WEST, OLD MAN!

In the space between stimulus (what happens) and response, lies our freedom to choose ... We can choose our thoughts, emotions, moods, our words, our actions; we can choose our values and our principles. It is the choice of acting or being acted upon.

Stephen Covey, '*The 7 Habits of Highly Effective People*'

The physical and emotional stress of the three years in Venus Bay from 2008 almost broke Diana and I in every way possible. We were doing our best to maintain the struggling café business (but fighting a losing battle), dealing with the fallout from the winding up of the legal practice (but fighting a losing battle) and otherwise trying to survive as functioning human beings and keep our faltering marriage together (winning that battle, but only marginally at times).

The destructive impact that those years had on our overall wellbeing can't be overstated. We'd transitioned to Venus Bay hoping, if not expecting, to find peace of mind, contentment, physical resto-ration and a reasonable dose of whatever the good life had to offer after years of hard slog.

Instead, we found ourselves up to our necks in more stress. We'd simply replaced one form of stress with several others — the only difference being that the recent versions proved more debilitating than the one that we thought we'd left far behind. By taking on another business, and suffering the trauma of events surrounding our Canberra practice, we repeated exactly what we had vowed we'd never do again.

The paradox is that Venus Bay is the kind of place where troubled or exhausted people come to heal, to recover from the hurt and pain of a previous life.

On a personal level, I was physically drained by the end of the summer holidays of January 2011. That wasn't unusual for that time of the year. Emotionally, though, I was also hurting from the cumulative effect of several years of stress, anxiety and heartache on a number of wretched levels, some of which are simply too personal and, in all honesty, can't be shared with you.

Towards the end of the summer holiday rush, I was at breaking point. It'll sound like a cliché, but there was 'no gas in the tank'. Sleeping long hours but never feeling physically restored. Always bone weary. At times, my heart would pound against my chest, my pulse would throb and I'd feel breathless. At other times, I'd sit motionless for long periods, as if frozen solid, and stare blankly at nothing. My brain was locked in neutral when it wasn't in reverse.

Many people wouldn't have reacted as badly as I did to the events that happened. But that adverse reaction was the reality for me and it couldn't be undone. In my own limited and ineffective way, I tried to fight it. Yet I lacked enough of the right physical and emotional strength to withstand the punishment or to rise above it.

I discovered what it was like to be at absolute rock bottom and still have a dangerous sense of slipping further away. And, sometimes scarily, almost willing myself to. It was terrifying. I shared my gut-level feelings with no one, though I know I should have.

In a way, I felt as though my spirit had been drained, as if a vacuum-cleaner nozzle had been rammed down my throat and had sucked the marrow from my bones. I'd experienced other suffocating 'black periods' throughout my life (more times than I'd ever admit), but nothing like this. I knew I'd lost control. Worse still was the strong conviction that, this time, I may be incapable of wrenching it back.

I can best explain it this way. If someone had said to me on the occasion of any one of my frequent dark moments, 'Enjoy the rest of the day. Chances are, you won't wake up tomorrow,' my initial response would've been one of total relief and comfort that the end was in sight. I'd lost the capacity to care, even about many of the things and people I should've cared about. I came to understand, at the most personal level, why people take their own lives.

The frantic summer holiday season almost tipped me over the edge. I'd drag myself out of bed barely in time to get to the café for the start of the gruelling working day. On particularly dark days, which became the rule rather than the exception, I'd force myself to flick an imaginary switch, drop into autopilot and steel myself to work through without a major meltdown. I wasn't always successful. The lid on the pressure cooker was never screwed on tightly enough.

I have no clinical explanation for what I was suffering at the time. Depression? PTSD? A breakdown of some kind? I chose not to have it diagnosed or professionally treated. I'd always taken the view that it's too convenient to place such readily available labels on what I thought were merely dark times. I had a gut-level belief that it would blow over in time. That, as with other life setbacks, it was a matter of sucking it up and soldiering on. I thought, mistakenly, that it would pass in time, particularly after the summer had ended.

It didn't, though, and it persists today, off and on. It lies in wait just below the surface, ready to grab me by the throat and squeeze hard when it judges that the time is right.

The effects have been deep-seated and long-lasting. Even now, I jump when I hear a phone ringing. Trips to the post office to collect mail fill me with dread. Email messages popping up on a computer screen or text messages on my mobile make my heart pound. I automatically associate these forms of communication with bad news, not as opportunities or things to look forward to. I have no desire to be easily accessible or reachable. From a wellbeing point of view, I simply can't afford to be. Anonymity is fine with me. I need it to thrive and survive, along with extended periods of solitude.

Worst of all, even though we were having our problems and I felt helpless to do much about it, deep down it hurt to see how much Diana had suffered through it all. There was no one less deserving of that suffering. To see this amazing person, the love of my life, being beaten up by circumstances not of her making was sickening. I hated being the source of more undeserved stress. And I couldn't be strong when she needed it most.

* * *

It'd be a vast overstatement to claim that running during those black days saved me, particularly as my efforts were spasmodic and barely above a slow trot, often no more than a walk. Nevertheless, it helped immeasurably during the infrequent times I could mobilise enough mental strength to push myself out the door. It broke the pattern of depression, if I'm entitled to use that term. It was my own self-help, my DIY version of much-needed therapy. I called on it for support when I needed it. Typically, it didn't let me down and I'll be forever grateful.

It enabled me to cling on to some degree of hope, even if flickering, of someday making it to Boston.

* * *

Once the summer of 2010–11 was finally and thankfully over, there were serious and soul-searching decisions to be tackled. I needed to pull myself together sufficiently to put a plan in place, as much as it hurt. It was reality-check time. If I'd wallowed any longer, I would've drowned. Staring reality in the face, and dealing with it, can never be put off indefinitely, no matter how downcast you feel. It can treat you cruelly if you don't get in first. I don't always get in first.

In some ways, we found ourselves confronted with the classic fight-or-flight dilemma. On the one hand, we could've sold up, cashed in and salvaged from the wreckage as much financial security as we could, then jumped in a van and done the grey nomad thing — this time for real — and driven off into the sunset for a couple of years, if not for good. We could have stopped the world and got off. That's such a mouth-watering prospect when I pause and contemplate it.

That could've been easily achieved and, in more vulnerable moments, we thought very seriously about doing just that. Maybe one day we will, but it just wasn't right then. It would've felt like waving the white flag. Capitulating. Rolling over and exposing a weak underbelly. That 'wasn't us'. It's not the way we do things.

On the other hand, we could fight back in any way we could to restore the security and self-respect we'd built up over many years. We could act rather than allow ourselves to be acted upon. But that would mean, in effect, going through the financial rebuilding process again. We certainly weren't up for *that* fight. We were both shattered physically and emotionally and our marriage needed some serious, ongoing repair. On the flip side, on a financial level, we needed income and fast.

It was obvious, and inevitable, that we'd be forced to pay for the past in more ways than one. But we couldn't allow things to drift. We needed to regain the control that had been taken from us — and which we'd thrown away ourselves.

As you may gather from the Stephen Covey quote, I firmly

LONG ROAD TO BOSTON

believe that every person, perhaps with some exceptions, has the freedom to choose which way they go in life. At the time, however, I honestly thought my choices were limited. The choices were there, but the range was paper thin. As much as I dreaded the prospect of getting back into legal practice — being at best a reluctant lawyer and strongly wishing to avoid this outcome — it seemed to be the best way, and was probably the only way, of scrambling back onto our feet.

And, let's be honest and face reality once more, setting myself up as a male escort, even with a funky website and heaps of clever photoshopping, was never going to be a pragmatic, or lucrative, option.

We were about to take a further, substantial financial flogging (it came to pass in the early part of 2012) and we needed a way to claw back what we were about to lose, or as much of it as possible. We needed to apply the brakes.

I'm sure most people vividly remember days, or specific moments in time, that have a significant impact on their lives. They remember exactly where they were and precisely what they were doing. These moments stand out. They stay with us. They're fixed in the memory, sometimes agonisingly, and our mental Rolodex recalls them readily.

I remember this particular day as if it were yesterday - a day in early February 2011 after the frantic summer holidays had passed. My habit was to sit at one end of the dining-room table in the living pod at the Venus Bay beach house, staring out over the front garden. That's where I did my most effective pondering, apart from when I was running. On that specific day, though, I was in no position to contemplate for long. The solution to our immediate problem was quite simple. It required no deep deliberation, inspiration or stroke of genius. Quite simply, I needed to get a 'real job' and earn some decent money.

Reluctantly, I polished up the CV (for me, this meant a complete reconstruction) and, at the not-so-ripe old age of 58 (in truth, I felt way past the ripe stage and more in an advanced state of decom-position), did what too many people of the same vintage had been forced to do post-GFC. I 'put myself out there'. You'll gather by now that putting myself out there is not a state of being that comes easily to me. I felt like a failure having to do it. After leaving Canberra three years earlier, I'd hoped that I'd put some distance between myself and the legal profession, and those goddam ties.

I hadn't anticipated that personal reinvention later in life, not that I wanted to embark on that course, meant effectively going backwards. Apart from that, the realisation that I'd have to be civil to clients again was counterintuitive (at best) and seemed almost impossible to bear (at worst).

I applied for legal jobs in random fashion, right across the country. After about six weeks, to my great surprise, a position arose in a mid-size law firm in Perth. The money was decent but not great. At least it'd put bread back on the table, though, even if it was the crappy, white-sliced home-brand variety. It was a start. A way to claw back. A toe in the door.

After a couple of telephone interviews, for which I was barely able to gather enough of my senses to sound vaguely competent, I accepted the job offer with great apprehension. The nasty little man in my head, with whom I battle periodically (and, quite often, lose out to), was his usual aggro, though convincing, self: 'You stupid old fart. What DO you think you're doing? What makes you think you're going to cope?'

I had grave doubts that I would. I'd co-run a private legal practice with Diana but had never been an employed lawyer in any other law firm, let alone one across the other side of the country. Another big learning curve was about to be undertaken, another character-building life challenge. Crap to that.

Towards the end of March 2011, two days before our 34th wedding anniversary, I flew to Perth and joined the firm as a senior commercial lawyer. I had a huge, and typical, attack of the guilts in 'abandoning' Diana to carry on at the café without me, but I still knew it was the best thing I could do to rescue our precarious financial position in the short term. We were desperate to establish a regular income again and, plainly, I felt obliged to take the first reasonable offer that came along.

Although we retained ownership of the building, we placed the bar/café/takeaway business on the market. If the business hadn't sold by the middle of the year, our plan was to close the doors and walk away. We wouldn't have been the first or the last business owners to take that heartbreaking course. Fortunately, we weren't forced to go down that road. The business was sold for a modest price a few months later and we leased the premises to the new owners.

Another chapter closed. Or so we thought.

Upon arriving in Perth, I rented a unit in the inner suburb of Nedlands, not far from the office where I was to work in Subiaco, and only a couple of streets away from Kings Park, which I figured would be a good place to convene my running renaissance / Boston crusade and undergo some further, much-needed therapy in the process.

The first few days at the firm were a complete blur, akin to the last few kilometres of a marathon. It's saying something, especially for me, but I'd rarely felt so out of place. I'd not been a paid employee of any kind for many years and it took some weeks to come to grips with the fact that I was just another cog in the wheel, albeit a quite senior one.

The feeling of having to start over again, at a relatively old age, was overwhelming. I felt mentally stale. My best-before date had long since passed. I was, at a pinch, only good enough to be fed to the chooks. But, right at that point, there was just no room for a misplaced sense of pride.

By the end of the second week, I was convinced I wouldn't last. I was a fish out of water, missing Di terribly and ready to jump on the next plane back east with my tail stuck fairly and squarely between my legs, if not firmly wedged up my backside. The only plus was running around Kings Park at 6am each morning. It's a tough slog up the roller-coaster hills on the north-western side of the park but for that same reason, it's a great place to train. It helped me navigate my way through those initial weeks and months. It created a diversion, although a physically testing one, and a different focus — something to help reinflate the self-esteem balloon, which had been punctured and only partially patched by a worn-out lump of Blu-tack.

Painstakingly, over a period of several months, I began to get more on top of things at work and felt I was making a contribution to the firm. My clients seemed happy, no doubt due substantially to my sparkling personality and witty repartee, and the work — a broad mix of commercial law matters — was varied and stimulating, though naturally not without its challenges. I was able to tap into my reserves of knowledge (the tap had to be sunk a long way down, mind you), put my solid legal drafting skills to good use and construct what I felt were high-quality commercial documents. Certainly, my boss seemed pleased with my efforts and their results.

As we know, perception is sadly everything these days, with substance hardly given much time or space. Thankfully, I was able to draw upon decades of legal experience to give the outward appearance of confidence and control. Inside, however, was a totally different story. Like the duck on the pond who looks calm and serene on the surface, but whose feet are going like the clappers under the water, I was struggling desperately to push back recurring emotional downturns and stomach-churning feelings of insecurity.

Surviving each day was a mini-victory and I celebrated as if it were. Upon arriving home, my habit was to kick my shoes off (no surprise there), chuck them in a corner of my bedroom (thank goodness for the very sane and sensible WA no-tie tradition), then head straight for the fridge for an ice-cold beer, which invariably disappeared within a few swigs.

* * *

My running progressed slowly over April and May, but I began to string together some quite decent training weeks. Towards the end of June, my overall mileage crept up to about 70 kilometres a week with my long Sunday run increasing to about 25 kilometres. All running was performed at a snail-like pace, but was still a far cry from my unexceptional efforts in Venus Bay several months before.

Apart from the physical improvement, the running effect continued to be almost life-saving therapy. I was slowly and laboriously emerging from the post-Venus Bay fog.

Despite the training progressing well, my original but tentative plan to run the July 2011 Gold Coast Marathon for a Boston 2012 qualifying time was looking remote. I was cutting it too fine to be ready in time, to be marathon fit.

You see, there's 'fit' and then there's 'marathon fit'. In reality, they're worlds apart. The beginning of July was just too close. I simply lacked the necessary stockpile of kilometres in my legs.

I looked around for an alternative qualifying race. Working backwards from Boston 2012, my best hopes were the Adelaide Marathon in August or the Chevron City to Surf Marathon in Perth at the end of that month. Adelaide didn't appeal, as it would mean taking time off work. The Perth race fell into place for several reasons. Obviously, there'd be no need to travel, and I'd also be able to train over at least part of the course and familiarise myself with it. It was also run at the end of August which allowed a few more valuable weeks of preparation.

So, that decision was straightforward. The Perth City to Surf Marathon, on 28 August 2011, would be where I expected to qualify for Boston 2012. That was the plan.

It became clear to me soon after I'd made the decision that I wasn't doing myself any favours. The City to Surf marathon is a tough course. To be fair, the first half is flat and easy going. It's the second half where the difficulties begin, precisely where you don't want them. The climb up William Street and the steep drag up St Georges Terrace to Kings Park is an energy-sapping stretch, as is the long, gradual climb out of the park to arrive at about the 30-kilometre mark. From there, the run along Hay Street is flat then another shortish climb takes you towards Perry Lakes before a longer uphill section along Oceanic Drive eventually takes you down to the finish line near the beach. It's a demanding course and I was fearful of it.

I drove the course, and ran parts of it as many times as I could to visualise the route and familiarise myself with its ups and downs and twists and turns. And there was a further catch. The Boston qualifying window effectively closed before the end of September 2011. For all intents and purposes, the Perth marathon was my last chance to qualify for Boston. All my eggs, several of which were already cracked and fragile, would be stacked in the one basket. I only had one shot at it. If it didn't work out on 28 August, it would be a case of: nice try, thanks for coming.

* * *

While the running was generally on track, I was, regrettably, becoming increasingly unsettled at work, despite having only been there for a relatively short time. The work itself was interesting and stimulating — solid commercial legal work, the kind I quite enjoy — but the nature of being a salaried lawyer was something I was wrestling with unsuccessfully. Another personal battle being fought and lost.

Most private law firms require their lawyers to record between six and eight 'billable hours' each day, made up of six-minute increments for each unit of work performed. That may sound easily achievable in a normal working day, but the reality is that unless you're super-efficient with your time, it takes many more hours to get even close to the required daily billable hours.

I found myself driven by the fear of not achieving my daily targets. It's a sad reflection on the legal profession, or maybe it just reflected badly on me, that the typical employed lawyer in a time-charging firm tends to compromise himself, or herself, to some extent just to survive. It wasn't for me. It became an added layer of unwanted stress and pressure which I didn't need and, in all honesty, wasn't at that point able to cope with.

Besides, I'd been hearing stories of high-paying opportunities in the mining industry in WA for people with my skills. The construction phase of the industry was booming and I was in the mode of looking around for the highest paying job possible. If I was going to be stressed at work, I might as well earn buckets of money in the process.

I was staggered at the salaries being thrown around, which were up to double what I could ever hope to earn as a reasonably senior commercial lawyer in a private legal firm. For someone in my financial position, it was, of course, not even debatable, not something that required even a millisecond of contemplation. I owed it to myself, and to our financial circumstances, to at least explore the possibility of a higher income, doing who cared what.

I learned that jobs were on offer for 'contracts specialists' working on mining construction projects up north in the Pilbara region of WA. I was unsure what that meant but didn't care much if the money, and lots of it, and regularly, somehow magically fell from the sky.

***

With Diana due to arrive in Perth towards the end of June, following the sale of the café business, I needed to find a house to rent that would be big enough for the two of us plus our beautiful Welsh springer spaniel, Taffy. Taff was our second springer, our first being Basil, named after the fantastically neurotic *Fawlty Towers* character and one of my few 'heroes'.

I knew the unit in Nedlands was only a temporary arrangement and that we needed to be somewhere more permanent. At first, I searched for the impossible, a fully furnished, dog-friendly house. But with Perth bursting at the seams, rental properties were at a premium. It was doubtless a landlord's market.

After weeks of false starts and disappointments, I secured a rental in Dalkeith, a leafy, fashionable suburb to the west of the CBD and close to the Swan River. The house was unfurnished but at least the landlord would accept pets. Dalkeith also looked to be a perfect base from which to run as the cycle path bordering the river was only a short jog away. I knew Di would love it. A beautiful place for her to paint and recover from the trauma of the previous years.

Diana finally made it over to Perth at the end of June. I met her at the airport with a bunch of flowers and a hug that I never wanted to end. She settled in quickly as I knew she would. I was determined that she reacquaint herself with the good life, in an environment where her creative juices could flow once more. I was incredibly glad to see her. We hadn't been together for over three months, the longest period we'd been apart in almost 35 years.

She'd been left to wind up the café business, with lots of help from Hamish and Peter, and to pack up the Venus Bay beach house. It was a huge amount of work and she handled it with her customary strength and resilience. The indestructible Mrs Burns wasn't born, she was honed and polished to create the most dazzling diamond. A stronger character I've yet to meet and, in any case, I doubt exists.

The Dalkeith house was a big, rambling barn of a place, an old art deco house whose best days had long since passed. But the location was ideal, just around the corner from the local shopping centre, which I knew Diana would enjoy fossicking around and only a short drive along the river's edge to trendy Claremont, which I knew she'd frequent even more often.

She joined a local artists' group and used a spare room at the back of the house as her studio. She seemed happy to have finally made the break from the stress of the café and could start afresh. Time to recharge the batteries and explore and experience a new part of Australia. It was an escape for both of us, but we saw it as a positive move and not as an act of defeat or surrender — somewhere to rebuild, regroup and recover. And, in our own way, to continue the financial fight back, however long it might take.

The move to Dalkeith also worked in well with my marathon preparation. An easy downhill jog of about 1.5 kilometres led to the start of the cycle path bordering the Swan River which then snaked its way past open playing fields, the Royal Perth Yacht Club, the University of Western Australia and, eventually, across Mounts Bay Road and on to Kings Park. (A few years later, Mounts Bay Road would be the scene of an accident in which I was, agonisingly, to play a major part.)

By early July, I'd increased the length of my Sunday long run to about 30 kilometres: down to the cycle path, through to Kings Park, and two laps around the outer edge of the park before retracing my steps back home. It was a three-hour run, a hard and draining slog.

The first time I attempted it, I finished totally exhausted, even though I'd built up to the extra distance gradually over several months. It took me back to that very first 20-mile effort two weeks before the Canberra Marathon back in 1979. But this time there was no dam close by to jump and splash hopelessly about in, and I certainly wasn't brave enough to jump into the Swan.

The two long climbs through the north-western side of the park were especially tough and only became marginally more comfortable after several weeks. Both Achilles tendons were also causing me grief. After a couple of time trials hammered out on the cycle path adjoining Riverside Drive and Mounts Bay Road, I was reduced to not much more than a slow plod.

Despite these minor setbacks, by the beginning of August, much of the hard training mileage had been safely tucked away. I was consciously easing back, tapering off and trying to freshen up before the 28th. I cut back the overall training volume and introduced some short 3-kilometre and 5-kilometre hit-outs to inject some speed into my legs. Although the Achilles tendons were tender to the touch, gentle stretching, ice and self-massage afforded some relief after each effort.

With less than two weeks to the race, I was to have my last hard session — a mid-week 3-kilometre time trial along the cycle path. The run was progressing well until I veered slightly left to negotiate a bend in the path. Being early morning, the sun was only just beginning to make an appearance and the light was still muted. In the half-light, I didn't see the pothole. At least, not until it was too late. It was a shallow one, not much more than an indentation, but still deep enough to catch my right leg and pull it sideways. The slight rip to the already vulnerable Achilles tendon didn't feel particularly severe at the time, but I knew it was serious enough.

I walked the rest of the way home. There were ten days to the marathon - adequate time, I thought, to rest up, ice the damaged leg and recover sufficiently. Why I chose not to book myself straight into a physiotherapist and decided instead to self-medicate (DIY as usual) is something I still can't fathom. I always know what's best for me, don't I? Big mistake this time.

On the morning of the race, the Achilles tendon felt quite comfortable. In hindsight, that was probably just adrenaline kicking in, but I was nevertheless hopeful that it'd withstand the 42.195 kilometres ahead. I lined up at the start to take in the usual pre-race pep talk, this time from Robert de Castella, who I'd long regarded as a true marathon legend.

The first 5 kilometres were easy going and I barely noticed a twinge. Then, very gradually after that point, it all began to fall apart. With each additional kilometre, it became increasingly difficult to land my right leg on the road and to push off with any degree of power or momentum, or without discomfort. A sharp pain shot up my leg and my right calf began to stiffen and tighten. I knew then that the cause was hopeless.

Even so, I managed to pass through the 10-kilometre mark in about 49 minutes which, for me at that early stage, meant that I was well on target for a comfortable Boston qualifying time.

The whole sorry episode ended just after the 15-kilometre point. I knew in my gut that I wasn't going to make it, especially with the tough hills in the second half of the race still to come. At least I bailed out at a stage where the hobble back home wasn't too far, but even that hurt.

Diana was visibly shocked to receive the knock on the door. I felt like crap. It was something I'd worked hard for, over a period spanning almost 18 months (despite the disruptions and occasional emotional meltdown), and it was over in an instant. Not with a bang but definitely with a bloody whimper.

No qualifying time. No Boston 2012. No memorable 60th birthday celebration. I felt shattered, but I also felt like an idiot. Whatever made me think I could do it in the first place? Deluded old fart. I was too old and too beaten up. I was kidding myself. Right?

* * *

A couple of weeks before the Perth marathon, I'd started work as a contracts specialist with Calibre Global, an engineering procurement and construction management company, an EPCM as they're known in the resources industry. Companies like Calibre effectively acted as project managers for many of the major mining and resources companies like BHP, Rio Tinto, Woodside and Fortescue Metals on large-scale construction projects in the Pilbara region of north-west WA.

I'd spent the first few weeks in the company's head office in Perth undertaking the various inductions and training courses. I barely had time to lick my wounds after the Perth race before being 'mobilised to site' only four days after the marathon. The Achilles tendon in my right leg railed against being encased in a steelcapped boot, but that small amount of discomfort meant nothing in the scheme of things. The important thing now was to head 'up north' and earn the big bucks on offer.

The time for self-indulgence was over, or at least it had to be placed on hold for the foreseeable future. The focus now was the next life form I was about to morph into. The life of a FIFO contractor.

Once again, I had no real sense (in truth, absolutely no bloody clue) of what I was about to launch myself into. I was continuing to make life up, DIY-style, as I went along - a fragmented, patch-up approach to the things that mattered most, without any long-term plan in mind. That was unusual for me, up until recent times.

It was unknown and untrodden territory. For someone pushing 60, it was also totally terrifying.

8

LIFE IN THE PILBARA

In the Pilbara, no-one can hear you scream.

(with apologies to the film *Alien*)

Like most blokes, I tend to keep my emotions bottled up and safely locked away. But, when I crack, I completely fall apart.

I hadn't appreciated how fragile my mental state was until I fronted my boss towards the end of July 2011 to deliver the news that I was leaving the Perth law firm. Without warning, the flimsy strand of fibre that'd kept all internal things miraculously together snapped. The floodgates burst open as I trawled over the events of the previous few years to explain why I couldn't pass up the opportunity to earn bigger money in a quicker timeframe.

The pent-up emotion that I'd successfully kept a lid on, apart from several manic meltdowns at The Fishy, rushed to the surface in that awkward, embarrassing moment. My unrehearsed and garbled explanation didn't help my cause. Nor did the sniffles or the dribbles or the coughs or the splutters, all of which spewed out at the same time.

No sympathy was forthcoming. A box of Kleenex would've been welcome. I guess it was fair enough in the circumstances. The firm had invested time, energy and money in me and I was giving it the flick after only about five months. My boss was pissed, to put it mildly, and almost as inconsolable as me.

I regretted ending the job on such a sour note but, quite simply, and as much as I dislike the sentiment, I'd been made a better offer. My decision to leave wasn't exactly a ruthless action by today's corporate world standards — in fact, it would've been seen as bland and routine — but it wasn't in my nature all the same.

The year had been a crazy ride to that point. I'd evolved from flinging flake in a coastal Victorian seafood café to working as a senior commercial lawyer in a Perth law firm and, then, in my latest reincarnation, becoming a so-called contracts specialist on a mega-sized construction project in the Pilbara. All within six months. I was changing direction more times than I was changing undies.

Personal reinvention of any description wasn't what I'd envisaged for my senior years. Learning to play the guitar was more what I'd had in mind, or an even less racy pursuit. Life hadn't worked out as planned, though. The carefully crafted life-schedule had to be dramatically revised. Personal reinvention had been thrust upon me in response to a radical change in circumstances. Directional change that caused me to swim with the tide, or my own peculiar flow again. Suck-it-up time once more. Crap to that.

* * *

I knew very little about the contracts role I was about to take up on site. What I *did* know was that it was, broadly speaking, a 'contracts management' position and, crucially, that it paid incredibly well. I could live with that. Nothing else mattered.

Taking on this new role was no career move. It wasn't a critical stage in a journey of self-discovery either. Stuff that. I was interested in nothing more than the dollars being thrown at me. I was in ka-ching mode, pure and simple.

The T155 Rail Duplication Project involved constructing a duplicate of the existing mine-to-port rail line operated by Fortescue Metals Group, the chairman of which is Andrew 'Twiggy' Forrest. The line ran from Fortescue's iron ore unloading facility just south-west of Port Hedland to its two mines, Cloudbreak, about 250 kilometres to the south-east, and Christmas Creek, a further 50 kilometres down the same line.

The project wasn't to construct a complete duplicate of the rail line. Rather, each duplication was to be built at a strategic location along the line. The new construction would include rail sidings along the rail network to allow the easy passage of ore trains. As well as the mainline duplication, the project comprised the construction of the 'Solomon Spur', a 150-kilometre length of completely new rail that would branch off the mainline at the 'chainage 195' point and travel south to Fortescue's two new mines, Kings and Firetail.

In total, the project aimed to triple Fortescue's production and export of iron ore from 45 million tonnes per annum to 155 million tonnes, hence the name 'T155'.

I arrived on site on 1 September.

The site office was located at the 6.2 chainage point on the rail line, 'chainage' being the name given to the distance in kilometres along the line from Fortescue's port unloading facility. Positioned neatly in a wire-fenced compound of six small, demountable buildings, the office sat near the junction of the rail line and the Great Northern Highway. For the most part, the office was an open-plan jumble of chairs, desks and computers separated by low-level partitioning. Somehow, though, I'd scored one of the few tiny, self-contained offices in the building.

None of the induction courses I'd attended in Perth remotely prepared me for my arrival on site. Nothing could. I discovered an entirely alien world light years from what I'd ever experienced or imagined, both in terms of the extraordinary physical landscape and the outmoded, black-and-white, one-size-fits-all office culture.

I had no understanding that such a world existed. Nor could I comprehend that, by some freakishly random act, I'd somehow been time-machined into it. I pleaded with Scottie to 'beam me up' in those first few days, but he must've been out of range.

Those early days and weeks on site were filled with almost overwhelming insecurity and dread. What else had I come to expect? True to form, I felt like a fish out of water. This was a major rail construction and engineering project and I knew nothing about either. Of course, the people I worked with were largely unaware of that and I needed to keep it that way for as long as possible. I'd also never worked on a construction site before, let alone a project of this scale. And, for good measure, I'd never set foot in the Pilbara. The site crew was full of Pilbara rail construction veterans in all aspects of which I was a complete novice.

To cap it off, I had no clear picture of what my role actually was. My marching orders were simple and direct, but nonetheless disconcerting: 'Just get your arse up to site Ross. You'll work it out when you get there.' So again, drawing on decades of professional experience, a large dose of survival instinct and a dash of rat cunning, I took a deep breath, shoved my arse into an appropriate gear (barely avoiding reverse) and invented a role tailored to my skills.

(Note for file: When you've absolutely no clue what to do next in a new job, just storm around the office looking very serious, with an almost permanent scowl, and shake your head a lot. You either look like you know what you're doing, or look important, or both, if you perform convincingly enough. It works a treat. It also helps if you carry a large wodge of paper around with you — doesn't matter what's on it or whether anything's on it — and mumble to yourself things like 'bunch of fucking cowboys!' At the very least, people leave you alone. That's always a plus for me. It's remarkable how many plainly intimidated souls, thereafter, approach you apologetically with the words: 'Sorry to bother you ….')

Regrettably, though, I couldn't fake it forever. I determined that the best way to make an impression and look semi-useful, to survive and keep my job, was to focus on what I *was* good at: research, analysis and written advice. If there was an opportunity to involve myself in something even vaguely 'contractual' or 'commercial', I jumped onto it without hesitation. I assessed contractor claims and liability, and prepared written advice and contractual correspondence for the site crew, and the project manager and project director back in Perth. I wasn't conscious of protocols or procedures. They hadn't been explained to me in the first place. I didn't give a toss anyway and just ploughed on regardless, chalking up as many points as I could with the people who mattered. Classic brown-nosing, and unashamedly so.

About 20 major contracts underpinned the project, ranging from the construction of earthworks, the delivery of the steel rail, and the welding and laying of the rail, to bridge building and the installation of incidental and complex infrastructure such as fibre optic cabling, signalling and communications. My job, as far as I could tell (and, in any case, as I moulded it to suit my skills) was to manage each of the contracts at site level. After just a few weeks, though, and partly at my initiative, the job quickly developed into an on-site, DIY, in-house legal counsel role. Lots of on-the-run, seat-of-the-pants legal/contractual advice (with or without fries) on a diverse range of legal and practical issues concerning the project. Over time, I became the resident expert in shitogramology. It's been included in my CV ever since.

By far the biggest learning curve for me was to wrap my tired brain around the engineering concepts and construction principles that I was compelled to deal with on a daily basis. The only engineering concept I'd ever mastered was how to physically haul Mrs Burns in and out of bed and around the maternity ward of the Royal Canberra Hospital (and the strategic positioning of a bedpan) during the birthing of our two kids. The only construction principles I had the faintest clue about (aside from my very ordinary barbecue building effort in Canberra) were learned during Hamish's short-lived Lego phase — when we acquired about 526,000 individual pieces, none of which slotted into any other but most of which were, nevertheless, welded together by congealed layers of vegemite or (crunchy) peanut butter.

In a previous life form, I'd had to coordinate the preparation and cooking of a seafood platter for two, one grilled whole snapper, one scallop mornay and a paella. Now, I had to come to grips with such weird and wonderful rail construction concepts as borrow pits (no, they're not banks), flashbutt welding (sounds painful but it's not what you think), turkey's nests (neither are they), ground disturbance permits (permits to dig holes, usually big ones), insulated rail joints (nothing at all to do with smoking dope) and sub-ballast capping (a fancy name for a special kind of very ordinary-looking dirt).

As well as struggling to cope with the work and the very average physical working conditions, a further enormous cultural hurdle to grapple with and overcome was dealing with camp life.

Our camp was blandly known as Camp 25, named by some incredibly intelligent type because of its location at the chainage 25 point on the Fortescue rail line. There were other camps along the line with equally unoriginal and gulag-esque names, like Camp 145 and Camp 195.

When I first laid eyes on Camp 25, on the afternoon of my first day on site, I was almost violently ill. I barely avoided spraying a projectile vomit on the windscreen of the ute in which I'd travelled to the camp. My countless 'beam me up Scotties' and the occasional 'please God, help me' (and I'm not at all religious, as you know) obviously fell on deaf ears.

The camp consisted of about eight rows of demountables. Each row contained eight buildings. Each building contained four 'dongas'. The standing, but hardly original joke, was that the camp was the only place in Australia where the dongas were all the same size.

The rooms were basic but reasonably comfortable, about 15 square metres in dimension. There were no mod cons of any description, unless you count a bed and a TV as conveniences. The most valued object in the room was the air-conditioner, which was literally *never* turned off apart from a period of about four to six weeks in the middle of winter.

Not by the longest stretch of the most fertile imagination could Camp 25 ever be described as Club Med Pilbara. Although newly built, I found the camp to be (even on a rare upbeat day) dismal, bleak and unwelcoming. Mind you, it didn't pretend to be anything else. Perched next to the rail line about 100 metres away, the camp was surrounded by vast, flat expanses of sparsely vegetated red-brown Pilbara desert, with the occasional mesa thrown in to break the horizontal monotony.

The dominant feature of the camp, and which afforded almost reverential respect, was the huge separate dining room and wet mess (bar) which, by choice, I visited only twice in the time I was there. The food was the usual, though above average standard, buffet/bistro style. No one could ever complain about the volume of food on offer — just one example of outrageous WA/FIFO/Pilbara 'bigness': generous food offerings, physically huge people, hefty pay packets, enormous machines, massively expensive projects, jaw-droppingly long ore trains, never-ending expanses of raw and spectacular desert. All aspects of site life were framed physically, yet surreally, in up-your-bum, in-your-face, over-the-top bigness.

I worked a 12-hour day 'camp to camp'. In other words, we'd leave for the office, in a four-wheel drive or minivan, by about 5.30am and were bussed back to camp by 5.30pm with a 30-minute lunch break sandwiched in between. The early start meant a 4.30am wake-up which took several weeks of adjustment. I worked a '3 and 1' roster. Three weeks on and one week off, with a rostered day off, always a Sunday, slotted somewhere in the middle of the swing.

The architecture, physical location and general design of Camp

25 reinforced the prison-like, almost *Shawshank Redemption*, atmosphere. The only items missing were the barbed wire and the guard towers which, in any case, would've been entirely useless and wasted additions. There was simply no need for any form of security. If you 'escaped', where would you go? You'd surely perish out there.

Whoever designed the camp had little or no imagination or sense of private space. Being a construction camp in the desert, it didn't strive to be anything that it wasn't. The catchcry was repeated often enough that you got the message loud and clear: 'It's a construction site. What do you expect?' It was a simple proposition, and got no arguments from me. I expected nothing and was rewarded with even less.

Put plainly, Camp 25 was a warts-and-all proposition. Take it or leave it. Most took it, largely because of the money on offer. Some left it, largely because of the massive culture shock. 'Massive' does little justice to the size of that shock. It was more tectonic. Earth moving. It was never a surprise to learn that a site crew member simply hadn't shown up for their next swing. It was no less of a surprise that some people bailed halfway through it.

I, too, wasn't expected to last beyond my first three-week swing. I was considered too old and too straitlaced, not one-of-the-boys, and too much of a nerd to cope with camp life and the unconventional office culture. (I turned up for work on day one with a briefcase. I abandoned it on day two). As a tough(ish) old coot but, admittedly, principally because of the money, I proved them wrong. And proved a few things to myself at the same time.

Anecdotally, it was claimed that Camp 25 was called a 'camp' and not a 'village', like other accommodation sites in the Pilbara, to discourage the expectation that living there could ever be regarded as a pleasant village-like experience. No such expectation was raised in me. On the contrary, the camp merely comprised row after row of featureless, dormitory-style rooms linked by a series of concrete footpaths and walkways. The rows of dongas faced one another and were positioned such that, if opened fully, the front doors were depressingly close, resulting in little or no privacy.

Although the 'wettie', the social focal point of the camp, was only a short walk away, many camp residents preferred to congregate in groups of four or more outside their dongas, have a few drinks and bang on for hours. Eventually the camp curfew (and security patrol) would kick in and force them to reluctantly scurry back to their rooms at about 9pm each evening.

The interior space of each donga was designed in such a way that the bed butted up against the one next door, separated only by the thinnest and flimsiest of walls, like how I imagine the paper walls of a Japanese teahouse. Consequently, if you copped a snorer in the adjoining room — invariably the case — drifting off to sleep and staying asleep were problematic.

Often, the snorer would've spent several hours in the wettie. He'd arrive back at his donga after curfew and way past my bedtime. He'd change out of his work gear and proceed to drop about $50 worth of coins on the floor, along with his steelcapped boots. He'd then shower, audibly carry out his ablutions, cough uncontrollably, fart ferociously (and giggle at how clever he was) or perform some other weird activity or ritual unknown to humankind or, for that matter, the rest of the animal kingdom. To cap the evening off nicely for himself, he'd then watch TV (at a volume fractionally below noise pollution level) and not uncommonly leave it on till the small hours if he'd passed out in the meantime.

Unhappily, I'd have the dubious honour of hearing all this in quadrophonic surround sound from the comfort of the adjacent room. And I knew for a cast-iron fact that my neighbour had enjoyed a blissful sleep, partly at my expense, because next morning he'd greet me with the heartiest, 'Morning, mate. Sleep well?'

Still, my fellow inmates were, almost universally, good-natured and decent souls who, despite diverse backgrounds (social, ethnic, cultural or otherwise), were tied together by a common thread.

They had zero enthusiasm for being where they were and surely wouldn't have been if it weren't for the money that magically fell from the sky like confetti on a wedding day.

But not my wedding day.

Not that it concerned me directly, but only four mid-strength beers per person per night was allowed. We were breathalysed each morning before work at our 'pre-start' meeting. If you 'blew numbers', you were given a second chance 30 minutes later. If you blew over again (which was more than likely after only 30 minutes), you were stood down for the day without pay. If you were daft enough to repeat the effort, and many simply couldn't help themselves, you were on your way home on the next available plane, having had your 'site access terminated'.

A regular 'treat' for the site crew was the spasmodic and very unwelcome visit by head office personnel from Fortescue and Calibre, both of which were headquartered in Perth. These creatures were not so affectionately known as 'seagulls'. Their irritating habit was to fly in, flap their wings, squawk and generally make a lot of unsettling noise, shit everywhere and then fly out again, often on the same day. At least they didn't pinch your chips.

You could spot a seagull a mile off. *Every* item of PPE was pristine, ironed, buttoned up and proudly on display. Discussions with them were succinct but, nevertheless, deeply message-filled:

Seagull: *What's your role here on site, Ross?*

Ross: *To somehow make it through each fucken day, mate.*
(Most times, I left out the 'mate'.)

My mission each day was uncomplicated and straightforward: as much as humanly possible, to fit in (tricky for me) but also to fly well below the radar (not so tricky for me). I figured from the outset that it was a smart move to do just enough to get by and not piss too many people off (trickier still), to contribute and be useful but not stick my head up to the extent where it could get chopped off without warning (trickiest of all).

It wasn't uncommon for a person to be chopped just for 'being a dickhead'.

* * *

The lease on the Dalkeith house was only short term. We knew that we when signed up. Apparently, the landlord was planning to renovate the house some time towards the end of 2011. The demolition phase would've been straightforward. The 'Fremantle Doctor' would certainly have done the job on a blowy day.

A decision had to be made on where we'd relocate to. Rents were ramping up at a rapid rate in Perth and we knew we'd be renting for the foreseeable future. Not by chance, the rental discussion drifted to thoughts of relocating out of Perth altogether. We talked about Margaret River as we'd enjoyed it so much when we stayed there on our trek through the south-west back in mid-2010.

It was the perfect choice: an ideal place for Diana to develop and promote her artwork, and somewhere relaxing for me to rest and recover from my FIFO swings. So, that was that. Di contacted a few real estate agents in the town and, on one of my breaks, we drove to Margaret River planning to spend a few days checking out likely rentals. We chose the third house we were shown, a four-bedroom house nestled in a newish development on the edge of the town at 16 Bottlebrush Drive. It was way too big for our needs but quite modern, comfortable and set in a quiet neighbourhood.

We eventually moved in on my R&R break in November, only a few days before the horrendous bushfires that wiped out thousands of hectares of bush and over 30 houses in the Margaret River / Prevelly / Gnarabup areas.

* * *

After the disappointment of the Perth marathon at the end of August, and still nursing a very sore Achilles tendon in my right leg, I did no running at all for the rest of 2011. The 70–80 hour working weeks put paid to that, even if I'd felt inclined.

I'd deserted my dear friend for the umpteenth time in our relationship without so much as a note stuck up on the fridge or a one-line, don't-call-me-I'll-call-you text message.

* * *

I returned to work in the early part of January 2012 after the Christmas / New Year break and almost immediately experienced my first cyclone. Tropical Cyclone Heidi was only a category 2, but nonetheless made a direct hit on Port Hedland. It bulldozed its way through Camp 25 one morning at about 3.30am. I woke to a deafening roar, much like the noise of a jet engine as it powers to full throttle prior to lift-off.

Except for the fact that they have their own season and generally confine themselves to northern parts of Australia, cyclones have no sense of timing or place and otherwise act entirely randomly. They're exceptionally nasty, thoughtless beasts, too.

There'd been much anxiety about the 'cyclone rating' at Camp 25. Fortescue had assured all concerned that the camp was cyclone-proof, yet there was huge scepticism about the camp's safety, especially given Fortescue's track record with Tropical Cyclone George in 2007. TC George had hit the same area in the March, pounding a rail camp not far from the Camp 25 site. Two people had been killed.

As an unfortunate consequence of Heidi's unwelcome gatecrash, one of the camp's three giant septic tanks was literally flattened to resemble an oversized tin pancake. Another had caved in on one side, and the third had somehow remained upright, though with a very pronounced Tower of Pisa-like lean. Not surprisingly, the contents of the squashed tanks had spilled onto the ground. Shit happened in mega proportions. Even I (a vastly experienced shit handler as you know) was overwhelmed. Cleaning up the contents was literally like pushing shit uphill with a pair of chopsticks but somehow a bunch of brave and dedicated souls managed to do just that. With shovels, though, not chopsticks.

In March, the second cyclone for the summer, Tropical Cyclone Lua, landed as a category 4, much larger, meaner and potentially more destructive than Heidi. At one point, it looked as though we'd suffer another direct hit but, as cyclones are prone to do, Lua swerved contrarily at the last minute as it approached land and ended up slamming into the small settlement of Wallal about 80 kilometres further up the coast. Port Hedland was spared the worst of the devastation but the rain from Lua still caused massive delays to the project.

* * *

I celebrated my 60th birthday in April, not in Boston as I'd hoped, but at work in the 6.2 office. I reckoned I'd done a first-rate job of concealing its arrival (I was the oldest site crew member by quite some distance) until I let slip the fact that I'd reached this milestone a couple of weeks after the actual date. I was quite touched that someone then went to the trouble of arranging a cake, until one of my 'colleagues' (my mate Carl, a mad Englishman) proudly, and publicly of course, announced that the '9' on the cake had been wrongly placed upside down.

One morning a short time later, I arrived at work to find that someone had stuck up on the office wall a picture of Grandpa

Munster, to whom I was supposed to bear a striking resemblance (can't see it myself). It was placed there by a guy who professed to be a friend. My mate Carl, again.

On more than one occasion, I was teasingly referred to as 'old timer', whereupon I'd smile and laugh along with the joke, while inwardly cringing at the same time, as you do – just that bit too close to the bone for someone continually flirting on the edge emotionally and, at times, barely hanging in. It was a standing joke that I was the only person on site who needed a walking frame as standard PPE - a joke to most but never to the person on the receiving end.

Still, over time, I proved my loyalty to the crew (essential) and demonstrated that I 'knew my shit' (optional). This was enough to drag me through, kicking and screaming, though having to develop a thickish construction-site skin came in exceptionally handy.

Lack of accommodation fast became a huge logistical problem on the project as construction work ramped up and more contractors arrived on site in the months after March 2012. Being further squeezed for space at the 6.2 office and at Camp 25, in May we relocated, this time further down the rail line to Camp 145.

Aside from Port Hedland, the nearest town to Camp 145 was Marble Bar, about 100 kilometres away to the north. The camp was perched on a small hill overlooking both the Fortescue and BHP rail lines which intersected at one point about 5 kilometres to the north-west.

Camp 145 was a compact, 200-person camp with a friendly atmosphere. The rooms were standard but, again, tired looking. One big plus was the food, which was, on the whole, excellent. Unlike my unexceptional efforts at The Fishy, those guys *could* cook. Surreally, we'd been thrown into the middle of the Pilbara desert, one of the remotest, most desolate and inhospitable places on the planet, and the food was top class - a paradox I could never quite come to terms with.

While the food was well above standard, our office accommodation was nothing less than dreadful and much more what you'd expect of a remote desert site. Two office dongas had been hastily relocated from an abandoned camp elsewhere, and were cramped and inadequate in every way imaginable. Each small, demountable building was about 20 by 15 metres in size and packed in about 20 people.

Roughly scissored, black plastic garbage bags had been sticky-taped over the windows as temporary blinds for protection against the hot morning sun. As is the habit with many things temporary, the bags were never replaced by real blinds.

I hadn't scored an office this time, which was no big deal. But my desk was jammed up against a wall in one corner within touching distance of a self-closing fire door on the windward, morning sun side of the office. The door slammed shut right next to my left ear all day as people came in and out. Some people were considerate, others really couldn't give a stuff, and one or two even took great pleasure in slamming the door shut knowing that the noise jangled my nerves and set me off, claiming that I was far too precious for my own good. But, that's what I came to expect. The level of respect for a person's time, personal space or modest level of comfort in this kind of working environment can, to put the best possible spin on it, be very ordinary.

Still, at one time or another, and in one form or another, most site crew members copped some 'stick'. It went with the territory. It was part of the deal. If you didn't like it, you could always leave and, if you did, there'd be someone more than ready to take your place and gratefully accept the good money that went with it, and which continued to miraculously fall from the sky.

The office, such as it was, would be my new home for the foreseeable future and I took up residence at the back of the room in what became known as Fossil Corner, affectionately named, of course, after myself and a good-natured soul, Michael, who also had the temerity and lack of foresight to be on the wrong side of early retirement age.

* * *

My mate Carl and I were, in many ways, complete opposites. Carl was English. I most certainly wasn't, and somewhat proud of the fact. Carl was a fanatical revhead. I most certainly wasn't, and more than somewhat proud of the fact. Carl lived on acreage, toted guns and thrashed motorbikes. I most certainly didn't. Yet, somehow, we gelled.

Carl was a Pilbara rail construction veteran. He'd worked on various projects prior to T155 and knew the country around Camp 145 like the back of his hand.

It was a Sunday afternoon, as I recall, with nothing much happening in the office. I swear it was Carl's idea to skive off. I'm not a natural skiver, but I caved in and skived off anyway. We borrowed one of the office utes for the afternoon joy ride / field visit. Nothing dramatic was intended, just a couple of hours wandering through the Pilbara desert bush, or so we thought. Just a bit of sightseeing. A mini outback tour.

Carl was a good driver, but a fast one, if it's possible to be both at the same time. Carl obviously thought so. For the most part, the roads around Camp 145 were nothing more than regularly intersecting dirt tracks: construction roads and rail maintenance tracks. Sometimes they were roughly smooth and sometimes smoothly rough, they were often potholed or at least mildly pockmarked. And they had dips. Lots of them. A stretch of several hundred metres commonly threw up six or seven dips in roller-coaster fashion.

It was apparent early on in our joy ride that Carl had a major problem with dips. They pissed him off in a huge way. They cramped his style. He was in free-range hoon territory and determined to flex his muscles. When it comes to driving, I'm not a muscle-flexer by nature, preferring cruise-control mode.

It mattered little to Carl that we were in enemy-occupied lands — BHP rail territory to be precise — not where we were supposed to be or entitled to be. I could tell his dip-agitation level was in Apollo 13 lift off proportions. His knuckles had turned a whiter shade of pale and three veins in his neck were about to rupture.

Finally, he'd had enough of this piss-ant, fart-arsing about. He was ready to rumble. At that point in time, Carl ceased being my mate Carl. He was now a *Mad Max* version of Evel Knievel, decked out in full-length white sequined suit, high-heeled cowboy boots and helmet. He spied his opportunity ahead. To the unpossessed like me, it wasn't remotely an opportunity, just a small dip in the track with a launch pad on the near side and a landing pad on the other, and a gaping chasm in between.

I've never witnessed the brain–accelerator pedal–foot interaction operate with such blinding speed. He gunned it, floored it and throttled it all at the same time. As it happened, however, he less than nailed it.

The next several seconds were a complete blur. As we approached the launch pad at DeLorean speed, time froze. As we hit the ramp, we turned and looked at each other, Thelma and Louise style. We stopped short of holding hands, though. Guys don't do that, no matter how desperate the circumstance.

Despite a successful launch, from the moment we were airborne, and I mean *completely* airborne, it was blindingly obvious that, yes, 'Houston, we have a problem'. The nose of the ute dipped well before it was programmed to and well short of the landing pad. Instead of gently caressing the top of the pad and rolling serenely down the other side, the shuttle hit the pad nose first with an almighty thump, smashing through a sizeable chunk of dirt, rocks and other debris and reducing the height of the pad by about half a metre.

We made it through the near-death experience and out the other side, but only just. For once, Carl was lost for words. Once his brain finally engaged with his mouth, all he could manage was a plaintive and somewhat pathetic 'Yee-ha', accompanied by a tragically unconvincing fist pump. We paid each subsequent dip the respect it deserved.

I understand BHP are still looking for us, with a substantial dirt road repair bill. Forget the state of the ute, and the flat tyre we got on the way back to camp.

* * *

The one plus that emerged from my stint at Camp 145, apart from the better food and not having to routinely travel anywhere with Carl, was that I started to run again.

At the beginning of June, Diana and I spent a week in Broome and I decided that I'd get stuck into running once more. By the end of the week, I'd managed a slow, 20-minute jog. It was a start even if an awkward one.

Like any good friend, running will give you a clip over the ear if it judges that you've been disrespectful and deserve it.

The running environment at Camp 145 at that time of the year, mid-winter, was almost ideal. I'd head off after work at about 5.15pm while there was still a trace of sun. Turning left out of the camp and onto the Marble Bar Road, I'd cross the Fortescue rail line before heading left again along the rail maintenance track. After the turnaround, the run back to the camp was usually in half-light as the sun receded from view behind the hills to the west.

The late-afternoon air was crisp and cool on the skin and the absolute silence was a soothing relief from the noise of the office and the day's general aggravation. The hush was broken only by the sound of squawking crows, the occasional small herd of cattle drifting across the road (an angry member of which chased me down the road on one particular day) or the 'singing' of the rail line that heralded an approaching ore train still some kilometres away.

I embraced the aloneness, solitude and beauty of this harsh and ancient landscape. I was on the verge of feeling at home. The bonus was that, over that short period, I began to feel a tiny amount of fitness returning.

* * *

A curious ritual was introduced, and institutionalised, at Camp 145. At the end of each pre-start meeting at 6am, all site crew members were dragooned into performing a set of stretching exercises conducted by the gorgeous camp gym instructor, 'Kiwi Bec', a young lass obviously plucked straight from a Jane Fonda cardio workout video.

Apart from the fact that the daily contortions she put us through were well beyond the capacity of my ageing and extremely inflexible body, the ritual was made a tad more difficult due to dear Bec having the thuckest Kiwi accent known to the Western world. If put to the test, Bec's voice (by the time the words had rolled around the back of her throat and emerged, excruciatingly, sideways through her nose) would, I'm convinced, have literally peeled paint.

'Stretch' became 'Strutch'.
'Back' became 'Beck' (maybe Bec's name was really 'Bac').
'Wrist' became 'Rust'.
'Flat' became 'Flet'.
'Skin' became 'Skun'.
'Pecs' became 'Pacs'.
'Abs' became 'Ebs'.

And so on. You get the picture.

In the course of this routine torture, I discovered, thanks to the adorable Bec/Bac, my 'core' for the first time. I had no idea that I possessed a core or what the hell it actually was, let alone glutes, quads and other apparently significant miscellaneous body parts.

Anyway, unlike some of my fellow reluctant devotees, at least my 'plank', also enthusiastically demonstrated to us by the outrageously lovely Bec/Bac, didn't go kaplonk in the middle of a morning workout. That *did* happen sometimes, with disastrous and embarrassing results, such as an inadvertent and very audible fart emanating from the he or she concerned and which resulted in the rest of the group writhing hysterically on the floor or hurriedly vacating the office for an unscheduled, but much-needed, toilet break.

This fascinating ritual was even more curiously concluded by the congregation giving itself a polite and modest clap/clep as if we'd accomplished something quite remarkable which, in my case, was no doubt true.

* * *

By mid-2012, the major players in the mining industry, such as Rio Tinto and BHP, were announcing cutbacks to several significant projects, particularly in the Pilbara. Worsening world economic conditions and the slowing of the Chinese economy had an inevitable ripple effect on the mining operations of the big Australian companies operating in the Pilbara and elsewhere.

Cutbacks across all sectors of the industry began to kick in almost immediately. On cue, Fortescue announced it was cutting several hundred of its Perth-based staff positions. The trickle-down effect would doubtless have an impact on us at site-level. I needed insurance. I polished up the CV again and began to circulate it, including to a contact in Calibre who'd moved sideways to a similar rail construction project, this time for Rio Tinto.

The events over the next week proceeded rapidly. Calibre site management announced that about 20 site jobs would be axed. I approached my site boss asking for a release. His reply was swift and predictable: 'No way, get fucked, fuck off.' Luckily though, he phoned me the next day to say that Perth had reluctantly agreed. Some strings had been pulled on my behalf. I lined up an interview with the Calibre senior contracts manager on the Rio project. That afternoon, I flew to Perth, where I stayed over the weekend and then, on the Monday, interviewed for the position of senior contracts engineer on the Rio project.

My stint with Fortescue came to an end at the beginning of September. My last night at Camp 145 was memorable. Although I'd never been to the wet mess before, it was compulsory to front up this time and pay my 'departure tax'. I duly deposited $100 on the bar to rev up the celebration.

For someone who rarely drinks, and who literally only drank a few times at any wet mess while up north, I held my own and accounted for myself admirably. While I didn't exactly make it onto the table (in true Mrs Burns fashion), some of the more reckless types made it under the table. Nevertheless, I was nursing enough of a hangover the next morning to guarantee that I must've had a good night.

* * *

While this was happening, Diana had scheduled a trip to Melbourne to look after Jess's dog, Rupert, while she was trekking in Nepal. The plan was to mind Rupert, and when Jess returned, for Diana and I to fly to Tasmania for a driving holiday for a week or so.

The day after the job interview, I was waiting at Perth airport to board the plane to Melbourne. Then the phone rang. It was Di in a terrible state. She'd been walking Rupert and Taffy near Albert Park Lake, blacked out and performed a swan dive and then face plant onto the road. She'd managed to drive home to Jess's place in Richmond and had called me from there.

I arrived later that night to find her sprawled on the lounge, cradling her left arm across her chest and obviously in dreadful pain. We did what we could that night to make her more comfortable and Di pumped herself full of painkillers but with little effect.

The next morning, after an initial consultation with a GP, we attended a doctor's surgery at the orthopaedic department of the Epworth Hospital for follow-up X-rays. The result: Diana's arm and shoulder were broken in four places and needed immediate surgery. That happened a few days later with pins and plates being inserted into the severely smashed wing.

Bizzarely, this single physical mishap triggered a cascade of significant medical problems for Diana that played out over the next several years. Related to each other or merely isolated and random, this chain of events would change her life forever.

Needless to say, the Tassie trip was abandoned.

Maybe, some other day?

9

I GO TO RIO

I got the sand in my collar
Got the sand in my hair
Got it in my pockets
Got it everywhere
I got sand in my shirt
Got it in my shoes
Got them low-down,
dried-out desert blues

The Allman Brothers Band, 'Desert Blues'

In early October 2012, I flew back to Perth, spent a week there undergoing the obligatory Rio inductions and HR courses, and mobilised to site later in the month.

Because Di needed follow-up visits with surgeons, doctors and physiotherapists, she'd decided to make the trip back to WA in late November when she could travel with Brendan, Denis, Julie and Jacinta, who'd already planned to spend several days with us in Margaret River.

My first stint on the new Rio job was 30 days, a week longer than the brutal roster I'd signed up for — a 23/5 swing: 23 working days (again, with a rostered day off somewhere in the middle) and five days R&R.

The Rio project was similar to T155 — constructing a rail duplication from a major junction on the Rio rail network to one of its main port facilities at Cape Lambert near Karratha. In total, the RCE (Rail Capacity Enhancement) 353 Project was expected to cost Rio more than $3 billion and, when completed, would increase its capacity to export iron ore annually to 353 million tonnes.

The office and accommodation were part of the one camp (Northern Link), which of course meant no travel. Or, so I believed at the time. Northern Link Camp was located about 70 kilometres south-east of Karratha along the 'Deepdale' arm of Rio's rail network.

At the outset, I was determined to progress my running after I'd churned through some decent mileage over the previous several months. While in Melbourne helping Diana with her shoulder recovery, I'd had some solid hit-outs, chasing the convoy of immensely annoying but obviously incredibly clever yummy mummies, two or three abreast, power-pramming their designer babies around Melbourne's Tan Track. (Jess's house in Dover Street, Cremorne, is so close to the 'G you can hear a wicket fall.)

A few days after arriving at Northern Link, I was shown a dirt track suitable for running. From a gate at the north-west corner of the camp, the track travelled for about a kilometre before looping through a rock pile where oversize rock from the construction of the camp had been 'spoiled'. The loop then linked back to the gate from where it headed south along another track on the outside of the camp to a 'laydown' area, where I'd turn around and head back to the gate. The circuit, only taking about 15 minutes of easy running, was flat except for a very small bump on the way back from the rock pile. The road surface — finely crushed gravel — was near perfect for running and hardly ever used by vehicles.

The major drawback was the blinding Pilbara heat. Even at 5.30 in the afternoon, the temperature was commonly in the high thirties or low forties, even in late spring. Being 70 kilometres inland from Karratha and Dampier, the temperature at Northern Link was regularly several degrees hotter than what was recorded in either of the two towns. Invariably, a strong, hot wind barrelled in from the desert to the east on the trek out to the rock pile.

Unimaginably worse were the dreaded Pilbara flies: swarms of them, literally in their hundreds, even when I doused myself with Desert Dweller, one of the insect repellents of choice up north. It was never entirely effective and masses of them would still buzz around my face, even if they were more reluctant to land.

The only advantage to running into the oppressive desert wind was that the flies were repelled for a short time, only to reacquaint themselves on the tailwind return leg. By the time I returned to my donga after each run, my face, neck and arms would be caked in a sticky blend of red-brown desert dirt, drenching sweat, insect repellent and insects of varying sizes and shapes that had stuck solidly to me. Much like the blotchy patches of tissue paper that dotted Norman Gunston's pallid phiz.

My daily run, by necessity, took me past a long row of dongas on the western side of the camp. At that time of day, it was common to find groups of people, mostly men, assembled in twos, threes and fours enjoying an after-work cold beer.

In the first week or so after my arrival at the camp, I was greeted by each group with a moderate amount of heckling, the odd un-friendly comment or, occasionally, with a generous dose of derision. They seemed to be in competition to see who could deliver the smartest and loudest roasting. Obviously, the madness of running in such atrocious conditions wouldn't last, would it? I was an idiot, wasn't I? Well, let's be honest, there might have been an element of truth there.

After about three or four weeks, most of the groups had grown quieter but still gawked, probably with a greater sense of disbelief. After a few months, even as the daily temperature commonly rose well into the forties during the day, those who could be bothered merely acknowledged me with a wave. Some even raised their drinks, which I took to be a half-respectful salute.

* * *

In early February 2013, the familiar problems associated with Pilbara construction camp accommodation surfaced again and forced several site crew members, including me, to relocate to Kangaroo Hill Village, located on the WA coast about 5 kilometres north-east of Dampier and 15 kilometres south-west of Karratha. The village, really no more than a camp like all the others, was perched on top of a steep hill overlooking Rio's iron ore port operations facility and Woodside's North West Shelf Gas Project.

The layout of the village followed a common design. Concrete paths ingrained with a red-brown mixture of ore dust and Pilbara desert dirt linked the dozens of rows of drab and featureless dongas.

The bitumen road leading into the camp from the Dampier Highway wound its way up a steep hill for several hundred metres before dropping down sharply to the security hut and boom gate just before the camp car park. Signing in and out at the security hut was mandatory, as was the vehicle driver's bretho test on the way in. I even had to negotiate the sign in/out process on my afternoon runs from the camp and back. Occasionally, a sympathetic security guard would take pity on me and wave me through, but that happened rarely.

Past the car park rose a short, steep footpath heading into the camp. The 'poo farm' was positioned at the entrance to the camp and the sea breeze always blew in such a direction that you'd be greeted at the start and end of the day by plumes of unpleasant stench wafting up from the tanks.

Kangaroo Hill was a large and well spread-out camp, enveloped by somewhat lush and tropical vegetation. The view out across the Indian Ocean was spectacular.

But that's where the pluses ended. The dongas were old and tired looking (like me by then) and gave a sense of having gone well past their use-by date (even more like me by then). The worn-out vinyl floor in my room was so heavily ingrained with splatterings of red dirt that nothing short of a bucket of bleach would've made a blind bit of difference to the colour which, at a time long since gone, may well have been an insipid lime green.

The floor had a distinct lean to it so that the three footsteps from the door to the bathroom or the bed were gently uphill. Easy going in the morning as I bolted out the door but mountain-like after each afternoon run. The lighting was dim and the bathroom in poor shape. The lining on the walls was peeling off in several places.

* * *

It was a toss-up whether the running conditions were better at Northern Link or Kangaroo Hill.

The heat at Northern Link was baking and the humidity at Kangaroo Hill was suffocating. The dirt tracks at Northern Link were a better surface to run on, much easier on the legs. But the heat and flies at Northern Link were horrendous and there was a greater chance of a snake encounter of the worst kind, especially when winding through the rock pile. Strangely, though, my only close encounters with snakes happened on runs from Kangaroo Hill — they enjoyed sunning themselves on the hot bitumen roads — and not at Northern Link.

On the other hand, although it was marginally cooler at Kangaroo Hill due to a regular afternoon cooling sea breeze, the humidity was a killer. At the end of each run, I'd stand outside my room, strip down to my undies (modesty counts for nothing in a remote construction camp) and wring out my singlet, containing enough sweat to half-fill a plastic cup. Every item of clothing was sopping wet, including my 20-year-old blue cap and running shorts, which I'd wring out into the toilet bowl in my room before hanging them up to dry. Every inch of me and my gear — socks, jocks and locks — was drenched in a sticky film of sweat.

The run from Kangaroo Hill started from the camp carpark after the compulsory sign out at the security hut. The road then rose up a short, steep hill before dropping down and levelling out for a couple of kilometres until it reached the Dampier Highway. From there, I could either turn around, climb another hill to the entrance to Rio's port operations facility or turn right and run into Dampier, past the monument to Red Dog, who became the subject of an Australian movie of the same name in 2012.

If I was forced to make a choice, I'd have to say that I preferred the Northern Link runs, despite the flies. The crunch-crunch of a dirt road is always for me more aesthetically pleasing than the slap-slap of the bitumen. Somehow, dirt is more forgiving. It treats you kindly. I like the smell of it, especially after rain. Beaches are better still.

Irrespective of whether it was Northern Link or Kangaroo Hill, I found running difficult and the toughest conditions I'd ever faced. The heat and humidity over the spring and summer were nothing short of wretched. I managed about five runs per week. Each run was anything from 6 to 9 kilometres and exceptionally slow. No one could have enjoyed the end-of-run shower more than me, except for the fact that it was always in hot water. Although I'd only run the cold-water tap, the water in the pipes was still so hot from the day's blistering sun that a cold shower was never an option.

* * *

I don't like snakes, and I'm not at all embarrassed to admit that they terrify the bejesus out of me.

Snakes were prevalent in and around Northern Link, though as mentioned I had no direct encounters myself. As their habit was to emerge at night to graze on local delicacies such as frogs, mice and lizards, they were commonly caught by the camp's night security patrol, who would thoughtfully dispatch them into a green garbage bin. The bin was then left in our office for us to discover the next morning.

On one particular morning, one of our unsuspecting crew members removed the lid of the bin to deposit some wastepaper only to be welcomed by an irritable, and more than sufficiently venomous, Pilbara death adder. Mutual greetings were hurriedly exchanged, but with no handshake, and certainly no conventional cheek-smooch/bump. At that point, it was unanimously agreed that, henceforth, the bin would be labelled. Nonetheless, it was always disconcerting to find the bin placed in the way, most likely on purpose, as you walked in the door in the morning.

The contents of the snake bin would usually be emptied by one of the brave female environmental advisers during the day. The 190-centimetre, 120-kilo beefies in the office would always be too shit scared. Me too.

* * *

By the beginning of 2013, it was apparent that we'd clawed back a small chunk of the loss we'd suffered from the Canberra fallout. We'd achieved a degree of equilibrium; the ship had been righted, though still wasn't completely stable and still leaking in places. The damaging financial and psychological impact we'd endured was beginning to fade, even if very slowly and ever so slightly.

Diana was falling in love with Margaret River at breakneck speed. Tentatively, we dipped our toes in the Margaret River real estate water, but ended up diving in headfirst and purchasing a 5000-square-metre block of land in Mansfield Avenue, barely a mile from the centre of town.

* * *

On a construction site of the magnitude of the Rio project, there's always an enormous importance placed on safety. More so than on any other single issue. That's understandable. To have a major injury or, far worse, a fatality occur on a project is not a good look for a construction company or, for that matter, a project manager like Calibre, whose responsibility it is to safely oversee and manage the site.

Within a couple of weeks, two of our site crew were independently involved in dirt road or highway rollovers, one of which was witnessed by a few of us in another vehicle several hundred metres away as we drove back to Kangaroo Hill. The driver had obviously dozed off in the afternoon sun and we watched helplessly as he sailed off into the sunset (Carl-like) and finished, up-ended, in a ditch by the side of the road.

Luckily, moments before, I'd declined his offer of a lift. My mate Noddy acquired his nickname for a very good reason. He'd succumb to fatigue more readily than most. He'd regularly face plant his desk at about three o'clock each afternoon. Consequently, he always travelled alone.

He was 'removed from the project' a few days later.

No major injuries had resulted from the two incidents (apart from my heart palpitations at the thought of my Noddy-near-miss) but it looked less than impressive on our collective resumé. Predictably, senior management at Rio went ballistic when news of the second of the two incidents was reported back to Perth.

We were immediately stood down and confined to camp. No problems for me on that score. New driving rules were introduced immediately. Only a small fraction of the site crew was permitted to drive. Henceforth, all those staying at Kangaroo Hill were required to commute to work each day at Northern Link by way of an 18-seater commuter bus arranged by Rio.

In true fashion, the whinges, moans and bellyaches began within seconds of entering the 18-seater and didn't ease up until most of the little treasures had blissfully dozed off in the baking afternoon sun. I didn't much like it either but chose to keep my grizzles to myself.

Human nature being what it is, each reluctant commuter was quick to claim their favourite seat as if they owned it and got extremely pissed off if any of their fellow travellers even innocently assumed adverse possession.

My mate Stan was a classic. Very early on, he took permanent possession of a seat at the front of the bus just behind the driver. Fair enough, too. Stan was about six foot six in the old scale and needed the extra leg room. He took great delight in passing judgment on the technical skills of our female bus driver. Either by shaking his head in total disbelief when she performed some routine bus-driving manoeuvre that annoyed him or, not being able to contain himself, by bleating out unfriendly words of advice, or other uncomplimentary chirps, even on how and when she should change gears.

Stan's philosophy on life was simple, straightforward and unambiguous: 'unfuckingbelievable' was his usual assessment of anything that happened to displease (or even please) him, and the means by which he commenced (and even ended) every utterance no matter the topic of conversation.

'*Morning Stan. How'd ya sleep?*'
'*Unfuckingbelievable.*'
'*What'd you think of the cricket?*'
'*Unfuckingbelievable.*'
'*How's the boil on your bum?*'
'*Unfuckingbelievable.*'

* * *

In mid-January 2013, Tropical Cyclone Peta landed on the Pilbara coast. Only a category 1 and causing minimal havoc, it did dump a fair amount of rain in the area and, of course, resulted in several days delay to the project. Much worse was to come in the form of TC Rusty (category 4), which hit the coast about 100 kilometres from Port Hedland at the end of February. As well as sending wind gusts of over 200 kilometres per hour, Rusty dumped over several hundred millimetres of rain over the Pilbara region in super-quick time.

By early March 2013, it'd become obvious that the office was fast becoming an unsettled and unhappy workplace. Morale was low, bordering on subterranean: not exactly toxic but at least mildly gastric. In my experience, that's not uncommon on construction sites up north where the conditions are tough to begin with, and exacerbated by extreme levels of fatigue. People get pissed off reasonably easily and often — like every second day, or every second hour. It's written into each job description: your capacity to remain in an un-pissed off state is a crucial key performance indicator.

I too was becoming crapped off with work by that stage. The body was becoming increasingly weary. Making it through the summer in the Pilbara was not without challenge. Although my choice, running five days each week after a long workday inevitably took its toll. In all honesty, though, it simply came down to one thing. I'd had enough. I hated the idea of being away from home for 300 days of the year. Although it'd served its purpose to an extent, and I was thankful to have had the opportunity, I needed to put the whole FIFO experience behind me.

I was also more than faintly aware that my use-by date was fast approaching. Job security was never guaranteed in the construction industry up north. No one was safe, particularly the older crew members who, whether it was deliberate or not, seemed to be the first ones to go. The same question played over and over in my head: 'How much more time do I need to "serve" before we have enough money to survive?'

Old age doesn't bother me (except for the internal bladder/ brain hostilities, which the bladder most definitely wins — usually around 2.29.42 am each morning), but poverty does. As does the closely linked loss of personal control.

It was always a great tragedy to me that when my father died, one of the very few 'legacies' he left behind was a nondescript brown vinyl bag that contained a small number of personal items he'd collected over his lifetime. One such item was a pewter beer mug 'awarded' to him by a group of drinking mates and inscribed with the words 'A Good Bloke'.

Don't get me wrong. There's nothing negative about living your life as a good bloke. Surely, there are worse epitaphs than that. It's a decent and honest legacy, isn't it? Yet the relative insignificance of that legacy was an impression that never escaped me. Should that be the sum of a person's life? Is that all there is? Is that all we leave behind us? Should we, in any case, expect more?

It was my perception, even as a young kid growing up, that my dad was a deeply troubled soul who'd had his spirit crushed by life, or by his inability to cope with it, after he left the Baptist ministry at a relatively young age. He never seemed to recover or, for that matter, want to recover.

My memory recalls an incident involving my father when I was in my early teens. It was the aftermath of an almighty blue with my mother. That wasn't uncommon. The house was in total turmoil. That wasn't uncommon either. I hadn't escaped as usual with a cricket ball or golf club. I waited around. I needed to know that things would be okay. They clearly weren't. The atmosphere inside the house suddenly turned deathly quiet. I heard the faint sounds of my mother sobbing in her bedroom. I needed to find my father. I walked into the bathroom. He was wearing shorts and a T-shirt.

Solid build. Barefooted. Crouched over the bath with his left arm extended over the edge. Between the thumb and the first finger of his right hand, he held a razor blade. The hand was visibly shaking but still poised to strike. He turned his head slightly to the right. He said nothing, but gave me an anguished look that indicated everything. I said nothing, too frozen to move. He stopped. He didn't carry it through. Maybe I'd broken his concentration. I have no recollection of what happened after that split second. Unusually, my memory shut down, and the incident was never spoken of.

To me, my father didn't appear whole. There was something missing. There was an obvious void. You could see it in his eyes. That frightening, empty, 'dead' male stare. He was reclusive, withdrawn and insular and I felt I might've inherited that from him. Maybe it was in the genes?

I can't say I really knew him well. Few people did. How well do we truly know anyone, even the people we're closest to? I could never explain to myself why I felt so sad for him. In hindsight, I see things in me that I saw in him. Like long periods of almost total silence when you'd never know what he was thinking. That scares me mostly because, if it is in any way genetic (and I have no idea whether it is), I'd be shattered to think that I might've passed it on to my kids.

My father was great mates with my Uncle Bruce and they were, from an early age, more like blood brothers than brothers-in-law. In addition to Uncle Bruce, I had two other uncles on my mother's side. Don, who I knew throughout my childhood and growing-up years, and Charles, or 'Dick', as he was known.

I never knew my Uncle Dick. He'd enlisted in the army in his late twenties and died a dreadful death in the Japanese prisoner-of-war camp, at Sandakan, northern Borneo, in early 1945, only a few days before the commencement of the infamous Death Marches. From all accounts, Uncle Dick was a decent, 'solid' young man. My mother told me many times that he and I were very much alike.

I'm sorry that I know very little about his life, his hellish time as a Sandakan POW or about his tragic death.

I *will* find out one day. It's unfinished business. For some reason unknown to me, I feel I owe it to him.

10

15 APRIL 2013

We are one
We are strong
We are Boston
We are Boston strong

(Announcement just before the start of a Major League baseball match at Fenway Park, the home ground of the Boston Red Sox, five days after the Boston Marathon bombings)

The issue was simple. Did we have enough financial security for me to quit work?

Sadly, retirement, or 'transitioning out of full-time work', 'making a lifestyle change', 'going on extended gardening leave' — call it what you will — too often simply involves a mathematical calculation of how much your income and assets are worth, divided by how many years you think you'll live for. In other words, retirement is often governed by a large amount of arithmetical guess work.

Regardless of what they say, or pretend, I'll wager that many people in the same position, secretly and maybe chillingly, 'do the math'. I know I did — increasingly so during the early months of 2013.

On hearing the news of the Boston bombings and their grotesque and tragic consequences (in the Northern Link office on the morning of 16 April), my plan to run the Boston Marathon in 2015 had been effectively ditched. Because of my strong personal connection with the race, the qualification timeframe was hurriedly brought forwards by a year. But there were logistical and other challenges to confront and overcome.

Problem No. 1: How would I qualify in time? Entries for Boston opened on 22 September and closed a couple of weeks later. Looking at the Australian marathon calendar for the year, the only realistic qualifying chances were, as was the case back in 2011, at the Gold Coast Airport (4 July), Perth (25 August) or Adelaide (25 August) marathons.

Although run on a fast course, the Gold Coast Airport race was too close. Perth was also out. I needed to give myself every opportunity to qualify and the Perth course was just too tough. That left Adelaide. I googled the race and saw that it was a reasonably flat course. That decision, then, required little internal debate.

Problem No. 2: How could I schedule enough long runs to be marathon fit? The straightforward answer was: I couldn't. There were 18 weeks before the Adelaide race. Pragmatically, that meant about 16 training weeks, more than adequate on the face of it but my 23/5 roster and 70–80 hour working weeks left very few available long run days.

Practically speaking, it came down to this: eight long runs over the 16-week period — two runs of 20 kilometres, two runs of 25 kilometres and four runs of 30 kilometres. A little on the light side by normal marathon standards, but it would have to do. In any case, all I wanted was a qualifying time, a time of 3 hours 55 minutes or better (the qualifying time for the 60–64 age group had been reduced by 5 minutes from 4 hours some years earlier).

Problem No. 3: I was scheduled to have a double hernia operation in the coming months.

Problem No. 4: I'd developed severe lower back pain and some days I was reduced to little more than a hobble until the soreness had eased sufficiently.

So, the situation was far from ideal.

The changed plan meant that I had to shift into serious training mode, and quickly — regardless of the obstacles. An extra training day would need to be added. The weekly kilometres required cranking up as quickly as possible but managed so that I wasn't left overtired or broken down with injury or illness.

I devised a 16-week schedule aiming to finish the training phase on 11 August to allow for a two-week 'taper'. I'd increase the training volume to 60 kilometres for the first week and gradually add extra kilometres over the following weeks with a maximum training week of 80 kilometres.

The bread-and-butter daily run from Kangaroo Hill would be 10 kilometres. I'd only be able to tackle a long run every two weeks, either on my rostered day off or on my five-day break back in Margaret River.

A logistically tricky plan, but a plan nevertheless.

* * *

At the end of April, I was landed with a double dose of slightly unnerving medical news. My back problem was diagnosed as a 'strained piriformis muscle in the right buttock'. In other words, literally, a pain in the arse. The recommended treatment was an assortment of contortions, which my inflexible and ageing body had trouble even picturing, let alone performing, and even more gruelling and impossible than those inflicted on us at Camp 145 by the adorably gorgeous Bec/Bac.

Physios love me and I swear I can see the dollar signs light up in their eyes whenever I crawl crab-like into their consultation rooms. The same goes for dermatologists and, as I was about to discover, surgeons.

A few days after the torture inflicted by the physio, I attended an appointment with a surgeon. In extremely graphic detail, he explained to me (and the medically savvy Mrs Burns, who foamed at the mouth in anticipation) how he was going to slice and dice me to repair, much as a mechanic would repair a punctured tyre, my increasingly bulging right groin, which by then had assumed the size and shape of a duck egg. He added, 'Why don't I do the left-hand side at the same time?' as it was bound to 'go' sometime in the future anyway.

It was on the tip of my tongue to enquire whether this two-for-the-price-of-one special deal came with fries, a set of steak knives or a family-size bucket of KFC. I stopped short, though, anxious not to upset the very person who would soon be hovering above me with scalpel in hand as I lay comatose on the operating table, ready to 'do me' like a side of beef in an abattoir. Mrs Burns would've booked ringside seats for the gloriously gory show if she could've.

So, there it was. If I chose to defer or not have the surgery and endure the pain and discomfort, I could continue my marathon preparation in the blissful knowledge that I'd magically grown a lump in my groin so big that I bore a striking resemblance to the Three-Testicled Lady in the circus and had a lower back so stiff that I could barely manage the turning circle of the *Titanic*.

Otherwise okay? At least the Achilles tendons weren't playing up. Yet.

* * *

Apart from the tragedy of Boston 2013, other significant events occurred in May of that year that would change life again, even my revamped marathon preparation.

One such incident stands out very graphically and painfully. On 21 May, I experienced what many people, including those of my vintage, would label a 'defining moment'.

What is it about advancing years and defining moments? It's as if the closer you get to eventually departing this life, the closer you get to the 'truth'. What a bloody waste of time that is. Why can't the wisdom and clarity bestowed upon a person later in life be included in a how-to instruction manual that comes with you when you're born? If IKEA can do it, why can't it happen naturally, as a standard part of the birthing/flatpacking process?

In any case, at my age, defining moments are, more often than not, reality checks dressed up as something more profound and life-changing. We call them defining moments to give them sex appeal when, let's be honest, they're really 'oh shit!' or 'what the fuck have I done?' moments. But this defining moment was a genuine block-buster.

Diana called.

She'd had a routine mammogram and the results had come back. A small lump had been detected in her left breast and required further investigation.

If I'm honest, I was, to some extent, looking for an excuse to quit work. Irrespective of my real motives, though, I just couldn't stay on in the circumstances. I hadn't been there for Diana (at least emotionally) at crucial times in the recent past. I needed to be there with her this time and lend my support. I gave my notice to the site construction manager and area manager. Tearfully, I confess. I sooked up again.

Twenty minutes later, I was on my way back to clear out my room at Kangaroo Hill. Fifteen minutes after a quick pack, I was sitting in Karratha airport waiting to board a flight to Perth, most likely for the last time.

As happens so often in FIFO world, events fell into place with lightning speed once the decision had been made. I had no time at all to take it in. I was, for all intents and purposes, finally out. No fuss, very little notice, very little drama. No farewells. No wet mess night and no hangover to nurse from the night before.

I wasn't the least bit sad about leaving. It was an experience I wouldn't, couldn't, forget. Financially, it had provided, even if short-term, a get-out-of-jail-free card. It meant we were able to reclaim some of the financial security we'd built up, and then lost, over previous years. It enabled us to buy the block in Margaret River and to commence the build. I didn't for one minute regret the decision to live and work the FIFO lifestyle, but I also had no qualms in seeing the end of it. It'd been gruelling and draining and had taken a hefty personal toll: stress on stress, physical and otherwise, after the Venus Bay café and Canberra fallout years.

Surely, I could now move on with a feeling that I'd recovered at least some measure of self-respect and, vitally for me, a sense of personal control. Surely, no more false starts. Surely, the good life (and inching closer to discovering its true meaning!) were now within reach.

Time now for straw hard hats and steelcapped sandals.

11

NEW AGE HIPPIE WANKER

At 70 years old if I could give my younger self one piece of advice, it would be to use the words 'fuck off' much more frequently.

Dame Helen Mirren

It must be the new age hippie wanker in me but, like many, I suspect, I've always craved a return to a simpler life. Looking back, I got to live it as a kid (as we all do) until I was forced to grow up (as we all are). I was determined to have a slice of the good life this time around. And I figured Margaret River was an ideal place as any to achieve just that.

My gut tried to convince me that by the end of my FIFO life I'd earned a measure of redemption. That I'd done my time and could walk away with my self-esteem intact, even if that lump of Blu-tack was still sticking around for extra protection. I wanted it to be my contribution to getting things back on track financially. I also saw it as a way of regaining Diana's respect, which my ever-reliable gut also told me had slipped to some extent in the post-Canberra years when, for a short time at least, I fell apart and couldn't cope.

For reasons I've given up trying to rationalise, I regularly feel the need to inflict a certain amount of physical punishment on myself. Maybe that's partly what attracts me to long-distance running. It sounds crazy but it's as if the only time I'm content is when I'm in physical discomfort. That, for some perverse reason, I *deserve* to do it tough. Maybe I'm a stoic in the truest sense – patiently enduring stiff backs, depressingly painful Achilles tendons and duck eggs in the groin.

By about mid-2013, though, the pennies had dropped — just a handful, not in Malcolm Turnbull's spare-change jar proportions. It wasn't a dramatic light-bulb moment, but a slowly dawning realisation that I should beat myself up on a less regular basis.

After she'd had a couple of falls, and had suffered recurring medical setbacks like the most recent breast cancer news, I also needed to be on hand for Diana in a physical sense, to devote some time to be together doing the things we enjoyed in common. Growing our own food, for instance, and travelling to parts of Australia we hadn't seen. Both of us staying fit and healthy. Just enjoying life as simply as possible in a peaceful and restorative physical environment.

Sounds all very Darby and Joan but, so what? We'd battled the hard yards together, which would have broken some people and would have broken more than a few marriages. It almost broke ours. But we'd survived it and had come out the other end relatively intact. Somewhat twisted, banged up and bent out of shape but at least hanging in there.

Now it was our time. Time also for me to become a fair dinkum, new age hippie wanker, perhaps? Like, maybe, grow a few carrots, a chia crop or the odd mung bean. Make the switch to tofu burgers and one of the gazillion varieties of herbal tea. Go totally quinoa and almost gluten free. Grow a beard. Shave my head. Have some assorted rings and studs stapled onto various protruding body parts — except one perhaps.

While it was very likely I had no creative talents at all, I felt that

I owed it to myself to at least explore the possibilities. A completely new life was within sniffing and touching distance: collecting spoons, ballroom dancing, cake decorating, taxidermy, frisbee golf, learning to play the ukulele, becoming a weekend Viking. Such salivating prospects. Maybe even write a book.

Diana had tapped into her considerable creative talents and was thoroughly enjoying her new life, apart from the regular physical mishaps and the most recent adverse medical news. It was time for me to do the same or, at least, have a go. Though the thought of death doesn't concern me in the slightest, I couldn't die wondering.

I know some people find it immensely difficult to walk away from the trade or profession that they'd devoted their entire working life to. Not me. I couldn't wait. I'd done the career thing, several times over as it happened. I'd achieved a measure of professional success. I'd cut my fair share of ribbons.

In some respects, I wish I'd been a more successful lawyer. I have great admiration and respect for those people, like my good friends Brendan and Denis, who make it to the top of their profession or who are recognised as having achieved the highest level of competence and proficiency. They're the real deal. They have exceptional talent and are rightly recognised as such. I, too, had developed some decent legal skills over four decades of professional life. I was certainly no dill. But on the reality-check test, I wasn't among the very best at what I'd practised, either.

Fear not. I wasn't going through a midlife crisis. That had come and gone decades before and, from memory, had only lasted about 48 hours. There was simply no time for the Full Monty back then. In any case, there's no sense of finality with a midlife crisis. After all, the key element is that it's 'mid'. If you stuff it up, you've still got time to regroup, carry on and try again.

For someone of my age, it was, if anything, more like an end-of-life crisis. If you stuff it up at my age, there's no coming back, is there? It's not so much that I was apprehensive about the future, I was more mindful of the possibility that there may not be much of it left. After all, both my father and grandfather had died in their late sixties. Not such a wonderful pedigree there. No great scope to wait around for the avocados to ripen in the bowl.

I've also heard it said that at my age you should embrace every moment with renewed vigour. Not me. I just wanted to do my own thing at my own pace. I simply needed to live the life of a reasonably fit and healthy 60-plus year old. I didn't need to suck the marrow out of life. I was quite content to chew on the bone for a time before handballing it to the nearest dog.

The course Diana and I took and the response we made to the trauma of the previous several years was, to a considerable extent, of our own making. I had deep regrets about the situation we'd fallen headfirst into, but I had no regrets about how we attempted to dig ourselves out. The past is just that. It will inevitably shape the kind of people we are. But it needn't control our future or determine who we are, or define us, for evermore.

In hindsight, we probably should've sought more professional help with our faltering marriage. But we soldiered on, as many people do, in the mistaken belief that we could work through the crisis and survive without external intervention.

We're that kind of couple. We just do what we think needs to be done, more times than not without too much regret. Often without regard for our own wellbeing and, certainly, without undue sentiment. In some ways, our marriage has been more of a partnership in the strict business sense. Maybe that's because we were business partners for so many years.

In any case, I guess we're not always the most romantic of couples and I strongly doubt we'll be renewing our wedding vows on a beach in Bali any time soon, on a non-volcano-spewing day or otherwise.

* * *

As chance would have it, Day 1 of my new-found freedom, Day 1 of the 'good life', happened to coincide with Mrs Burns's visit to Perth to attend the opening day of the 2013 Craft & Quilt Fair.

Originally, we'd planned to meet up after Di had attended the fair on her own and then drive back to Margaret River for my R&R break. But, my sudden work departure, following Diana's troubling medical news, changed all that and I was now able to attend as well. What joy.

Typically, Mrs Burns had the day carefully planned for me and my personal attendance at the fair was demanded and, therefore, guaranteed. In the event, it was a terrifying and traumatic experience and one that would scar me for life.

I was a little old man cast adrift in a sea of little old ladies.

Crossing over the threshold into no-man's-land (literally) was like stepping into a cross between the Tardis and the Narnia wardrobe. I was an outsider, an intruder in their secret world. It was obvious they wanted me *out*. I would've gladly obliged. But, alas, Mrs Burns wanted me *in*, largely as her human shopping trolley and inexhaustible money supply. So, that was the end of it.

I'd been introduced to the mystical world of arts and crafts many times decades before, but had no need for it in recent times. There's little call for it on rail construction sites in the Pilbara.

From the outset, Mrs Burns was in her element. Upon entering the vast exhibition centre, she instantly made 746 new besties. She was like a giddy schoolgirl at her first Beatles concert. In her eyes, each of her crafty brethren was a rock star in her own right. The idolatry was palpable and frightening at the same time, as idolatry of any kind usually is.

She tackled the day's activities with the speed and flamboyance of a whirling dervish. My standing, more like marching, orders were clear and unambiguous: 'Where's your credit card?' and 'Move on!' when the all too frequent purchase had been made. That was our only form of communication for the day. She was clearly on a mission from the Craft God.

The good Mrs B dutifully, almost religiously, attended many of the countless craft workshops conducted during the day. I refrained, as respectfully as possible, preferring to observe from the outer edge rather than risk being sucked into the vortex from which there'd be no return. Occasionally, I sought refuge in one of the aptly named Rest & Recharge booths. Regrettably, the relative tranquillity was short-lived, and I'd soon be summoned once more to do battle.

And battle it was. In the course of the day, I'd be cross-stitched, appliqued, quilted, wire-worked, embroidered, embossed and embellished. And I felt every painful bit of it.

As if the physical brutality wasn't enough, after we'd escaped outside at lunchtime for a bowl of pumpkin soup with crusty sourdough roll (what else?), upon re-entry into the vast auditorium, we were greeted by one of the attendants with: 'Thank you ladies!' There we had it: we were no longer husband and wife. We were now craft 'sisters', twin souls, as if by virtue of my attendance I'd undergone a weird, unintentional, *Silence of the Lambs*, patchwork sex change.

At least I wasn't as badly off as the only other male in attendance that day. Like me, the poor sod had walked in at the start of the day chirpy and fresh-faced. When I observed him by mid-afternoon, however, I swear he'd aged at least 30 years and now resembled Dorian Gray's grotesque alter ego. He looked like how I felt. At one stage, as we passed, I attempted to 'reach out' to him (I rarely reach out, as you'd appreciate) with a not too hopeful, 'How's it going mate?' Sadly, the response was such garbled and incoherent gibberish that I knew instantly that the world had lost him forever.

For me and my mate Dorian, the only plus for the day was that there was no queue for the men's toilet.

Then, even more mysteriously, the grand event suddenly came

to an abrupt, almost cataclysmic, end. No doubt brought on by the universal need for an afternoon nap, the vast, cavernous auditorium emptied as fast as it'd filled. As dramatic as the aftermath of a summer Pilbara cyclone.

Miraculously, somehow I'd made it out the other side. I'd survived to tell the tale. I conquered my own Mount Everest that day — severely bruised and bloodied, but not bowed. After this, qualifying for the Boston Marathon would be like a walk in the park.

It'd been an exhausting experience and, at the end of it, I was totally Pfaffed.

* * *

Day 2 of the good life: See Day 1.

12

BOSTON BOUND?

Distance runners are experts at pain, discomfort and fear. You're not coming away feeling good. It's a matter of how much pain you can deal with on those days. It's not a strategy. It's just a callousing of the mind and body to deal with discomfort. Any serious runner bounces back. That's the nature of their game. Taking pain.

Mark Wetmore

Margaret River is nothing short of a runner's paradise. There are literally hundreds of kilometres of dirt trails and tracks within easy reach of the town and criss-crossing the town itself.

Although by mid-2013 I'd been settled in the town for over 18 months, I couldn't really say I knew it well, having spent no more than a week at a time there because of my FIFO roster.

Within a few days of what I expected would be the start of my brand-new life (post Craft & Quilt Fair trauma), I'd completely rejigged my training schedule and geared it, once again, to a Boston qualification. And, I'd be able to train for the race without having to combine it with a full-time job, a luxury unknown to me before then.

Since moving to 'Margs' in November 2011, we'd lived about two kilometres to the south of the town, just off the Bussell Highway, at 16 Bottlebrush Drive.

For the first few weeks, I increased my usual weekday run to about 12 kilometres. From home, I'd jog for a few minutes through a large, heavily treed reserve only a couple of doors from the front of our rental before crossing over the highway. From there, it was a short run along a dirt path that bisected nearby farmhouses before hitting the 'Rails to Trail' (now known as the Wadandi Track), a purpose-built dirt and gravel track for walkers, runners and off-road cyclists. These days the track runs from Witchcliffe, about 8 kilometres south of Margaret River, all the way to Cowaramup, or Cow Town, as it's known to the locals, 15 kilometres to the north. It's a near perfect trail for running, especially when it meanders its way through forest and across the Margaret River itself.

I used the same track for my long Sunday run, which I increased to 25 kilometres early in June. My total weekly training reached 80 kilometres by that time and, ambitiously, I planned to increase it further to over 90 kilometres during the second half of June, and also for July.

***

By early June, our plans to build on the Mansfield Avenue block were well under way. Not uncommonly, though, we encountered several obstacles — natural and bureaucratic — before building could commence in earnest.

The first hurdle concerned the physical nature of the block itself. It was enormous by average standards — over 5000 square metres — and covered in a dense planting of enormous trees: salmon gums, karri and other species of eucalypt. To compound the problem, the block was bordered on two sides by council or state-owned or con-trolled forest.

As mentioned earlier, Margaret River had suffered a devastating bushfire in November 2011 when a controlled burn-off to the north of the town had gone horribly wrong, quickly raged out of control, and leapt across the river mouth. As well as devastating parts of Margaret River itself, the blaze slammed into the beachside villages of Prevelly and Gnarabup, wiping out over 30 homes.

As a consequence, new bushfire mitigation rules were introduced by the local council that required new building blocks to be largely cleared to minimise potential bushfire fuel. In effect, that meant stripping our block of much of its vegetation and, hence, much of its original attraction. As gut-wrenching as that prospect was, we had no alternative if we wanted to build. In total, the block was cleared of at least 50 percent of its trees - unavoidable, but an environmental tragedy nevertheless.

The architecturally gifted Mrs Burns had, characteristically, conjured up a great design for the new pad, though not 'pad' so much as 'pod', three of them to be precise. She'd taken the idea from the Venus Bay beach house she'd designed years before.

One pod would contain three bedrooms and a bathroom, another featured an open-plan kitchen and lounge-room area, along with the now customary (if not compulsory) 'reading nook'. The two pods would be linked by a single roof over both and separated only by the equally stock-standard 'alfresco living area' which, though originally intended to hold small, intimate gatherings of like-minded locals, inevitably (due to Mrs Burns's bigger-than-Ben-Hur approach to life) magically transformed into a venue large enough to take in the annual AFL grand final. And, possibly, a Test cricket match at the same time.

The third pod, separated from the other two by a few metres, corner to corner, and located closer to the back of the block, would be the 'studio' in which Mrs Burns would paint and craft away to her heart's content and where I would, well, 'do my own thing', whatever that was supposed to mean.

I failed to score my own man cave, however, which was fine by me as I would most likely have just wandered aimlessly around in it anyway. Which is most likely what men really do in them if the truth be told — apart from hide. I don't tinker. I don't potter (though I took up pottery at one time). I don't mend or repair things. I don't whittle or gadget fiddle. I don't even strum the banjo, play the flute or engage in power yoga. I'm not in the slightest way mechanically minded. I have no concept of how machines work. No wonder I can't navigate my way around a simple can-opener or, needless to say, a new-fangled espresso machine. In short, I'm the sort of person who, for the safety of others and especially small children, should never be allowed to have a hammer in his hand or be within 100 metres of anything with moving parts.

Mrs Burns, the Energizer bunny on peptides, flew into project management mode with warp speed as soon as the building plans had been approved and the build could commence. She had more balls in the air than a circus juggler, some of which notionally belonged to a few poor males of the species who were brave enough, or stupid enough, to cross her. Woe betide anyone foolish enough to get her nose out of joint or stand in her way. (Take it from someone who knows.) Instantly, the he or she concerned (no gender bias for Mrs B) would receive the sharp end of her tongue delivered in an ice-chilled 'tone'. Smoke would billow from her ears. Laser death rays would shoot from her eye sockets (Jules Bishop is a rank amateur by comparison) and she'd rain down upon this poor wretch fire and brimstone of volcanic proportions in a Carrie-like display of shock and awe.

When in such a mood, which soon became the norm rather than the exception, my one great sadness was that I couldn't hook her up to the WA power grid and haul in some serious cash.

For the previous couple of years, I'd kept a safe and respectful distance, observing her comings and goings from afar, at least for about 300 days of the year. Up until then, she'd pretty much laid dormant, ominously biding her time, bubbling with toil and trouble under the surface.

But now, kickstarted by the new build, she'd gotten her mojo back big time much to the horror and deep regret of the Australasian medical profession, the building industry, the artist community, the local council and especially the local post office, as well as the usual, miscellaneous corporate suspects, such as banks, insurance companies and, of course, Telstra. And, the new mojo was the all-improved model, complete with power steering, sleek exterior and heaps of grunt.

* * *

But even the indefatigable Mrs Burns was stopped, or at least slowed, in her tracks to a degree by her latest unfavourable medical news.

After a follow-up mammogram and a visit to our wonderful local GP, Dr Louise Marsh, we were referred to the oncology centre at the Mount Hospital in Perth for a specialist diagnosis. The news was mixed. The cancer in her left breast was confirmed but, thankfully, diagnosed as relatively low grade and likely to be treated without removing the breast.

After the day on which the diagnosis was confirmed, events progressed rapidly. A week later, we met with Di's surgeon, the highly skilled and professional Dr Diana Hastrich, and surgery was booked for the last week in June.

The procedure was straightforward. During the surgery, a small number of lymph nodes would be removed and taken for testing. While the tests were being carried out, the lump in the breast would be removed. If the tests returned positive, further lymph nodes would be removed to lessen the risk of the disease spreading to other parts of the body.

That's exactly what happened. Having multiple lymph nodes removed meant extensive physiotherapy was needed on Di's left arm. It also meant she'd need both chemotherapy and radiotherapy. For the first stage, we were referred to Professor Arlene Chan, a well-respected specialist oncologist in Perth. We met with Professor Chan in early July and she mapped out a course of treatment for the next several months. Of course, the treatment had to revolve around Di's many activities. It could never be the reverse.

First, there was an art exhibition she'd scheduled in Perth in early August which was to run for several weeks. The operation and its aftermath hardly slowed Diana down at all. She promised about 50 paintings for the exhibition and didn't disappoint. As well as those she'd already created, she produced several other works to complete the portfolio. The exhibition was a huge success in showcasing her work in WA and was made more memorable by being opened by Dr Hastrich. Di also donated a painting that was hung in the care room at the Breast Cancer Clinic at the Mount. It hangs there to this day.

* * *

In early July, another defining (oh shit) moment presented itself. This time, for me, it was a big one that I regretted almost immediately after it occurred.

My training had progressed well over the weeks since finishing work at the end of May, even with the frequent trips to Perth for Di's operation and ongoing treatment. The overall mileage had increased steadily to about 80 kilometres, as had the long Sunday run.

To have a more accurate measure of my progress, I'd bought a training watch with a GPS function to record distance accurately and monitor my actual training pace.

On the second Sunday in July, I scheduled a 30-kilometre run along the Wadandi Track, as usual. It'd been an incredibly wet winter to that point and for several days during the week the rain had pelted down. It was a crucial run in my preparation, and I couldn't run the risk of reaching part of the way along the trail and being forced to turn back or cut the run short if the trail was impassable. I decided that a safer bet was to run multiple laps of Darch Road, a dirt road not far from home.

Not once did the rain let up during the run. I'd never run in such a deluge. The encouraging news was that, despite the conditions and being buggered at the end, I'd managed the run at a pace of about five minutes 30 seconds per kilometre. If I could run that pace in a training run in such horrendous conditions, I knew that a qualifying time in Adelaide was well within reach. For the next day or so, I was, unusually for me, almost euphoric. While by no means a formality, I knew deep down that I was well on track to achieving that elusive Boston qualifying time.

Then something happened that to this day I've struggled to rationalise. In the space of about four days, my mood inexplicably plummeted from great anticipation to absolute despair. The stark realisation hit me that the timetable we'd set for ourselves over the next several weeks was nothing short of crazy, including multiple weekly trips to Perth for Di's treatment, a trip to Melbourne to visit Jess before she left for overseas (to walk the Camino de Santiago), Di's art exhibition in Perth in early August, her chemotherapy treatment starting straight after the exhibition. All the while I would try to juggle my training in and around everything that was happening, and even planned a couple of races, requiring more travel to Perth.

For a fateful split second, it all seemed unmanageable and unachievable. I panicked, and then I froze, neither of which is conducive to rational decision-making. The rubber band that had been holding everything together snapped. The timing wasn't right. Logistically, it wasn't stacking up. There was simply too much to do and a scarily tight timeframe to cram it all into. For better or worse — and mostly for worse, as it happened — I determined that it just wasn't possible to do the training I needed to do in the weeks remaining before the Adelaide race.

By then, I'd missed almost a week's running while I tossed over in my mind whether to continue. Finally, on 16 July, I entered in my training diary: 'Marathon "plan" officially abandoned!'

Almost immediately after the decision had been made, and for several weeks and months after (and, if I'm truthful, even to this day), I deeply regretted what I'd done. Surely, I could've found a way through it. If you want something badly enough, as I thought I did with the Boston qualification, you can generally find a way around most obstacles. Maybe my irrational cave-in proved that I hadn't wanted it badly enough in the first place. I'd let outside influences, important as they may've been, determine my path and dictate my actions. I'd lost control again and I was resentful of it. I'd surrendered and taken the softer option. I'd quit, pure and simple.

Running is a time-forgiving and travel-friendly sport. I should've been able to work through it. I chose to walk away from something I thought I was desperate to achieve. I'd deserted my good friend once more, in a dismissive act of disrespect. Worse still, I'd disrespected myself.

There was only one positive to emerge from such a shambles. After several weeks, once I'd absorbed the impact of the decision and the disappointment had taken hold, I vowed I'd NEVER let the same thing happen again. In future, if there was something I wanted to do badly enough, like try yet again to qualify for Boston, I promised myself that I'd NEVER, EVER let anything, or anyone, stand in the way.

* * *

Meanwhile, back at Mansfield Avenue, the wet winter had slowed the building progress on the block to a crawl, and at times to a complete shutdown. Finally in early August, three sand pads were laid and concrete poured as foundations for the pods. At least the building process had begun in earnest.

At the same time, Di's chemotherapy treatment had begun, just after her art exhibition in Maylands. The treatment didn't progress to script. In hindsight, we should've seen it coming. The outcome was preordained:

1. *Take one extremely driven human being with a strong tendency to hyperactivity.*
2. *Add a pinch of anxiety and a generous helping of stress.*
3. *Place carefully in a confined hospital environment.*
4. *Blend with an incredibly strong will and an unhealthy disrespect for authority, especially that held by the medical profession.*
5. *Slowly bring to the boil.*
6. *Before serving, add copious amounts of drugs, particularly steroids.*

The result was inevitable, and not pretty — a cyclonic reaction to chemotherapy. The treatment was meant to be administered over a five-week period with a week between each session. Di's physical reaction to the first dose was so off the charts that Professor Chan suspended the rest of the program for several weeks to enable Di's condition to stabilise.

The patient's response was Krakatoa-like, a not-happy-Jan moment of biblical proportions. Di wasn't annoyed just because it postponed her treatment. She was more pissed by the likelihood that it would derail her plans for another Margaret River art exhibition in September and, more importantly, our forthcoming November trip on a cruise ship in Europe.

The cruise was advertised in a European art magazine that Di subscribed to. It was a five-day trip setting off from Venice with stopovers in Bari, Corfu, Valetta and Naples and ending in Nice. Included in the cruise was all-day painting tuition from an eminent Australian watercolour artist living in Belgium, Janine Gallizia.

Even without the setback of her treatment being postponed for a few weeks, cramming in all the remaining sessions before the

November cruise was always going to be extremely tight. But the redoubtable Mrs Burns flew through the next four sessions with characteristic courage. The side effects of the chemotherapy were, not surprisingly, totally debilitating. It was painful to see Di endure so much sickness and discomfort, though of course infinitely worse for her. Still, endure it she did, and without so much as the faintest whinge or grizzle.

Taking the always-look-on-the-bright-side approach, as she does with all life events (you may wonder, as I do regularly, how we *ever* got together), she was genuinely grateful that the disease had been discovered at an early stage and could be treated successfully.

* * *

In late November, we left for our European vacation, our first trip to Europe together since our backpacking adventure almost 40 years before. By then, Di had only just finished her chemotherapy treatment and was still recovering enough strength to deal with normal day-to-day activities. The prospect of adding a whirlwind overseas trip to that with all the usual stresses and hassles was too scary to contemplate.

We arranged a couple of stopovers on our way to Paris to ease the travel stress as much as possible. After the flight from Paris and an overnight stop in Venice, we met up with our tour group, almost all of whom were French speaking. They were a kind and generous group who instantly spotted Di's condition. Her one wig and vast assortment of hats were a dead giveaway, and the group went out of their way to make us feel welcome and included.

After spending the morning's *en plein aire* painting session around the streets and canals of Venice, we travelled by bus to Trieste and boarded the cruise ship, the *Costa Fascinosa*, 'sister' ship to the ill-fated *Costa Concordia*. The ship was enormous and held well over 3000 passengers and 1100 crew. There were 18 bars and restaurants.

The gym was on the 11th floor.

In all my years as a runner, I've only occasionally ventured into a gym and it's not something I enjoy, for very good reason. I've already referred to the sad fact that I'm painfully accident-prone. Arguably, I should never have emerged from the bubble. Part of the explanation is that I'm not well coordinated. I'm serially clumsy. I drop things (though strangely, I was quite a good wicket keeper in my cricket-playing days) and bump into things. Even large and obvious objects such as telegraph poles and street signs. I fall down or trip over gutters. And we all know how well I handle potholes. Consequently, asking me to negotiate a narrow treadmill while running is like insisting that I perform a high-wire act over Niagara Falls.

Nevertheless, I *did* venture into the ship's gym, and onto a treadmill, but only once as it happened.

Instead of being able to zone out and enjoy the sea view out the window of the gym or plug into music and while away the time like all the trendy thirty-something Euros prancing and preening on their personal conveyor belts, I was left forlornly hanging on by whatever slim thread of balance I could muster.

The required concentration was obviously too great. At one point, my right foot landed on the outer edge of the treadmill and threw my balance out totally. Just before being launched into the stratosphere, or being catapulted out of the one and only open window and thence into the Mediterranean Sea, I was saved by a quick-thinking gym instructor who slammed the machine's off button and brought me to a grinding stop.

The young dickhead Euros thought it was a monumental joke. Crap to them.

I never returned to the gym, considering it much safer, not to mention far more pleasurable, to continue my training in any one of the ship's 8 bars.

* * *

By early 2014, I'd been home for about seven months. In that time, with all of Diana's medical treatment and the expenses involved in our frequent trips to Perth for follow-up consultations, as well as the overseas cruise, of course, our finances had taken a hefty whack.

As much as I dreaded the prospect, the scheduled 'good life' would have to be placed on hold once more. My 'early retirement' plan had been way too premature. I knew I'd have to bite the bullet and find a job, most likely another FIFO job up north.

After about four weeks of sending my CV out as far and wide as possible, I scored an interview with Civmec, a large construction and engineering company based about 15 kilometres south of Fremantle in the Australian Marine Complex at Henderson.

Almost immediately after I'd accepted the job offer, the deal I'd signed on for changed, and more than once. I'd originally been recruited to work on a Rio Tinto project, the Nammuldi Below Water Table Project, up north near the Brockman 4 mine site, about 60 kilometres north-west of Tom Price. The day after I'd accepted the offer, I was told that I'd instead be moving onto the Mungari Project, the construction of a gold-processing plant about 25 kilometres from Kalgoorlie. Instead of the 21/7 roster I'd been offered for Nammuldi, the Mungari roster was 23/5 which I knew from previous Pilbara jobs to be a tough swing.

During induction at the Henderson office, I received the further news that I'd most likely stay on the Mungari job for several months while the contract was being closed out. Then, the day I arrived back on site from my first R&R break, I was given marching orders to return immediately to the Henderson office where I was to close the contract out, rather than continue on site.

I wasn't disappointed to only last one swing in Kalgoorlie. The accommodation and food were up to scratch by most standards, at the Overland Motel about 2 kilometres from the centre of town.

But the site office was the worst I'd experienced. It was cramped and dirty and I scrambled to find a desk in the tiny room I shared with two engineers, one from Malaysia and the other from Ireland, and an extremely noisy air con.

* * *

At about the same time, Mrs Burns was doing her best to single-handedly prop up the Australian medical profession by planning to have a hip replacement operation in June. She'd had her right hip 'done' in Sydney many years before. After the left shoulder surgery and this latest effort, there were few original body parts left, or at least very few that hadn't been prosthetically enhanced or otherwise tampered with.

Nevertheless, she'd been able to squeeze in yet another art exhibition and an open studio held in the customised pod now constructed on the Mansfield Avenue block. It'd been an enormous effort to have the studio finished in time. She'd had a huge amount of help from some incredible people, not the least of whom were Hamish (who had moved over from the east to help with the build) and Pete McCartney, our builder. But still amazing when you consider she was only just shuffling about for many weeks on one good leg.

* * *

Over the next several months, running for me was virtually non-existent. Up until I'd returned to work in about mid-February, I'd had about three months of reasonably solid running and regularly clocked up 60-kilometre weeks after the European cruise was over and Diana's treatment had moderated. But the three months straight after that were the complete opposite. I did almost no running at all, in fact, only one day. The 2014 Boston Marathon had come and gone in April and, despite feeling crap at not being there, I was able to brush the disappointment aside with the knowledge that I was earning again and able to pay for the inevitable extras that the building project had thrown up.

In the middle of May I mobilised to Nammuldi. For Civmec, the project involved the construction of a train load-out facility and conveyor system. The camp, the West Pilbara Village, or Brockman 4 as it was known, was enormous and by far the biggest I'd stayed at to that point. The facilities were excellent: gym, swimming pool, tennis court and a decent dining room.

My room at the camp was the usual Rio issue, plain and simple but comfortable enough. If I closed my eyes, I could've been at any of the other Rio camps I'd stayed in. It had the same configuration, the same fawn-coloured bedsheets, the same hideous multicoloured doona cover, the same vinyl floor ingrained with a generous helping of red Pilbara desert dirt — in fact, the same everything.

However, I was earning again and nothing else mattered.

I'd only been on site at Brockman for a few months when I received a phone call from a job agency recruiter enquiring whether I'd be interested in a position as contracts manager for Ansaldo STS, an Italian rail-signalling and communications company, and the 'sigs and comms' contractor on Gina Rinehart's Roy Hill iron ore project in the Pilbara.

I jumped at the chance to leave the Civmec job. The office environment on site was becoming mildly toxic and people were leaving or being sacked at a rapid rate, even by the usual ruthless FIFO standards. The other advantage of the Ansaldo position was that it was Perth-based, meaning I could live in Perth and commute back to Margaret River on the weekends.

After a couple of searching interviews, I accepted the job and started at Ansaldo's Canning Vale office at the beginning of July 2014. The office was a giant open-plan, barn-like room of about 20 by 30 metres, and housed up to 30 people: engineers, project managers, contracts specialists, planners, cost controllers, rail system designers and various administrative staff.

The office had the ambience of what I imagine a Philippines call centre to be like. If you farted, there was no place to hide. With the odd exception, the troops were a good-hearted, and immensely talented, bunch but enormously crazy at the same time. Sigs and comms is an inherently complex and technical area. Add to that the fact that daily communication from the mostly Italian engineers was delivered in very rough English, accompanied by a barrage of wild hand gestures, some of which were not altogether polite, and it's not hard to get a sense of the general chaos. A good day was one of mild dysfunction. What to my excitable Italian colleagues was a *bazic engineeerrring principale* was double Dutch, and totally incomprehensible, to me.

Right across the project, contractual rights and obligations between the parties were being enforced ruthlessly and to the letter. There was little of the usual, and practical, commercial give-and-take, and in my experience, minimal goodwill at many levels. The commercial relationships between some of the major contractors and the Roy Hill joint venture, and Samsung, its EPCM, were often sour, and contractual negotiations were conducted on a 'take no prisoners' basis. It was bound to end in the shedding of many tears, commercially speaking. And so it did.

I have few details of how the Ansaldo component of the project turned out, and I'm not particularly interested to know, to be honest. However, it's common knowledge that the project generated a significant amount of contractual angst.

My love affair with Ansaldo ended abruptly at the beginning of November. I didn't give them a chance to file for divorce. I jumped in first, citing irreconcilable differences. The marriage was over before it'd been consummated. It was a blessing there were no kids involved.

At that point, after another year in the trenches, I was hopeful that my working life was finally drawing to a close, despite the intermittent Dame Nellie Melba comebacks.

It was time to blow the dust off the straw hard hat and the steelcapped sandals, and give the pursuit of the good life yet another, hopefully final, crack.

13

FIFO WORLD

Mate, the first thing you need to understand is that 'FIFO' doesn't mean 'fly in, fly out'. It really stands for 'fit in or fuck off'. Get that into your head and you won't have any problems.

My mate Carl, offering a small but insightful piece of practical advice, free of charge, on my arrival in Port Hedland, 1 September 2011, Day 1 of my life as a FIFO contractor.

Let me make the point straight up.

My experience as a FIFO contractor, so far as this book is concerned, involved working on construction projects in the Pilbara region of north-west WA, as well as a short stint in Kalgoorlie, from September 2011 to November 2014. (I'm leaving Darwin aside here [and several other subsequent FIFO stints], which I'll come to briefly, but later.) And it's only *my* take on FIFO life during that period. Others may well have a different perspective on what life's like 'up north', or in 'FIFO World' generally.

As basic and crude as it is, the 'fit in or fuck off' sentiment was the prevailing and underlying 'philosophy' at the remote construction sites on which I lived and worked. The expression sounds hostile and threatening but it's merely stating a fact. If the lifestyle was distasteful to you or you couldn't otherwise cope, you left, or were strongly encouraged to do so. That's the culture, and it reflected reality. The money was so good, at least during the time I worked up north during the mining construction boom, that there was no shortage of people lining up to take your job if you couldn't handle it. And many people couldn't, despite the money.

Ironically, the huge money on offer was the source of a problem in itself. Many people became trapped by the 'golden handcuffs'. The lure of the big dollars was, to many, a virtual addiction.

For me, the whole remote site FIFO experience exposed a curious paradox, and I have mixed feelings about it as a result.

On the one hand, the lifestyle was physically demanding and, more surprising to me, emotionally draining. The 80 hour working weeks, the tough rosters and the extreme physical environment, particularly in the summer months, were unrelenting. Construction sites anywhere are inherently challenging workplaces. The isolation and working conditions of a construction site in the Pilbara, or any remote site, added a further layer of difficulty to that.

On the other hand, at times I felt at home in the remoteness, especially when running on the red dirt tracks to and from the various camps in which I lived. The aloneness was strangely appealing. An environment where oddballs aren't so odd — where, excuse the contradiction, eccentricity is almost conventional and accepted, where 'you don't have to be crazy but it helps' holds a measure of truth. Ironically, I almost found myself fitting in which, when I pause and process it, wasn't ironic at all.

It's a major understatement to say that the FIFO lifestyle isn't for everyone. I met very few people who wanted to be where they were. Resilience, both physical and mental, is in high demand. 'When are you out next?' immediately followed 'Good morning'. Sometimes, it was in the reverse order.

Sadly, no induction course conducted in a capital city hundreds of kilometres away prepares you for life in a remote-site camp which is, I've heard it said, no more than a five-star prison. (I was never convinced about the five-star claim.) You'd imagine that someone with my unusual, essentially insular, personality wouldn't have coped with the testosterone-charged, blokey atmosphere on rough and tough remote construction sites. There was at times a subtle but perceptible pressure to conform. The wet mess effectively acts as the focal point for social activity and connection. If you didn't conform (drink), or didn't have the personality that *allowed* you to conform (me), you had little choice but to overcompensate by proving your competence in your field. Once I'd achieved that, and had demonstrated in my own way my loyalty to the group — that I was tight in the peloton — I gained a degree of recognition and respect and just became 'the contracts guy who knows his shit and runs like a bloody lunatic'.

I was accepted as a member of the tribe, even if I'd pitched my tent on the outer fringe of the village and not been permitted to plonk it somewhere in the inner, purple circle. I could live with that if it meant survival, especially survival roughly on my own terms and without having to compromise myself to any great degree. In any case, don't you often gain a clearer perspective from the outside than you do from the inner sanctum?

On one site, I became known by the crew, including those at higher management levels, as 'Captain'. Nothing else, just Captain. When I queried why I'd been given this tag, the response was that I was the one person who most people looked up to and who injected a measure of sanity and common sense into the madness. A father figure, and occasionally a father confessor.

I could live with that, too, even if it was weird to be identified as someone who possessed an aura of sanity — me, of all people! Of course, this may have said more about the emotional wellbeing of others around me. It was a good example of all things being relative, but rarely equal.

I may be overstating it, but it was a further paradox and almost fitting that I'd 'do time' in remote camps. We'd made mistakes in our winding up of the Canberra legal practice and 'punishment' had to be meted out and suffered by someone. It was a further irony that camp life up north was in some ways prison-like — as if enduring the hardship was part of my 'sentence'.

* * *

As I've indicated, FIFO life presents a strange bundle of contradictions. Make no mistake, I saw, and experienced personally, many acts of kindness, but I also witnessed, and occasionally experienced personally, awful acts of psychological cruelty and bullying. At times, camaraderie was demonstrated at a true and personal level — sometimes the 'brother' tag was heartfelt and genuine. At other times, though, the 'look after your mates' mentality cynically operated only on the surface.

For the most part, you were left to your own devices and your innate capacity to survive. I did, but many didn't. If, in a terrible moment of weakness or vulnerability, a person dared to be a touch 'precious' (that is, human) the common retort was: 'Take a spoonful of concrete, princess, and harden the fuck up.'

I could never accept that little nugget of FIFO wisdom. I found it dismissive, simplistic and lazy. I preferred the message on the poster that, for a short time at least, made its way onto an office wall: 'Telling me to toughen up doesn't help. Talking does.'

Tough love may be the order of the day on a construction site where the constant expectation is that you 'man up', and it may work for some people, but it's not a helpful or appropriate response for everyone. Used in the wrong context and in the wrong circumstances, it can be devastating and crushing.

I've never believed in the philosophy that you need to be cruel to be kind. Just being kind will do it most times. If you want someone to walk alongside you and be part of a team, and not just pay lip-service to the notion, it's counterproductive, and just plain dumb, to squash them in the process. There's a monumental difference between having a strong and forceful personality and being a complete arse. Often, people on site at all levels and who should've known better were incapable of appreciating the distinction, let alone putting it into practice.

Some individuals had the people skills of a cane toad.

Though it's not surprising when you dig deep and analyse it, an individual's entire persona could transform the moment he or she donned the hard hat and the steelcapped boots. Some people seemed to 'arc up' the instant they buttoned up the high-vis shirt. Catch them in the airport bar in their civvies and they'd be as meek as lambs - the psychology and power of the uniform.

Nothing prepares you for the culture shock of life as a FIFO contractor. I certainly wasn't prepared when I landed in Port Hedland for my first swing in September 2011. I'd spent a few weeks in Perth being inducted into the project before being mobilised. But all that guaranteed was having the right certificates and authorities to allow me to go to site. It didn't in any way 'orientate' me, or condition me, to living and working on site, especially with respect to camp life.

It wasn't unknown for new recruits to arrive on site only to last a couple of swings before chucking it in, despite the money on offer. Very few people in 'human resources' (burrowed in a comfy Perth head office) took the time to adequately brief new recruits on what life is like on remote sites. Part of the reason is that, in my experience, very few HR people ever set foot on site themselves and, therefore, had no idea what site life was like.

Being a FIFO contractor takes a significant personal toll. You pay a price for being paid the big dollars. High rates of relationship breakdown were common; the 4 weeks on / 1 week off roster — though thankfully rarer these days — was referred to as the 'divorce swing' or, for good reason, the 'suicide swing'. In too many cases,

FIFO life contributes to the disintegration of family life and features significant rates of alcohol abuse, higher than average smoking rates, instances of sexual harassment and higher than average levels of mental distress.

We regularly congratulated ourselves on site about the number of injury-free days that had been accumulated on a project. Yet, FIFO sites have, ironically and tragically, often been burdened with higher-than-average suicide rates, particularly in the 25–45 age bracket.

Although I can't verify it medically, I just don't believe that the human body is well enough equipped to endure the stresses of FIFO life, at least not on a long-term basis. The body is thrown out of balance. Its equilibrium is disturbed. Sometimes the body just can't cope and breaks down, and I'd make the same, or an even stronger claim for a person's emotional wellbeing. The 'human system', at all levels, is simply overstretched.

It may be a broad generalisation, but it seemed to me that long hours and tough rosters created two distinct categories of people: those who spent much of their downtime 'recovering' in the wettie, and those, like me, who buried themselves in their rooms. Neither option is healthy. Yes, there are gyms, swimming pools and tennis courts in the better camps, but they tended to be popular with only a small bunch of hardy souls who weren't the norm.

The FIFO worker is taken away from his or her home, family and broader community, subjected to extreme fatigue and isolation in a remote and alienating working environment, and is then expected to return to an everyday life and function as a normal human being on their R&R break. That's simply not possible. Especially when all you desperately need to do is catch up on lost sleep. And, it's not exactly conducive to a happy home life or meaningful, and long-lasting, personal relationships.

A remote construction site can be a ruthless and uncompromising working environment. Expendability is an understatement.

I'd seen it happen many times. People were flicked on a regular basis.

Not uncommonly, a bean counter sitting at a desk in the bowels of head office in Perth (or, say, a pissed off site manager) would do the numbers and make arbitrary decisions on what positions should be cut from the site's org. chart. It wasn't inflicted on a 'no hard feelings' basis; indeed it gave the impression of being carried out with no feeling at all. Having firmly planted in the back of your mind the notion that 'this could be my last swing' is unsettling, but realistic and useful emotional insulation. Announcements would sometimes be made at pre-starts that a crew member had been removed from the project or had their site access terminated. Rather like, 'Elvis has left the building'.

It could happen to anyone at any level. It was usually enforced in a not-so-subtle fashion. It could come from nowhere and without warning. When someone was being given the heave ho, the bad news was often delivered with the half-joke: 'Do you want a window seat or an aisle seat?'

That's the nature of the life of FIFO contractors in my experience. They came and went, often in rapid succession, and most times with barely an acknowledgement or recognition of either occurrence. No quarter was given and none taken. A FIFO contractor is pretty much a hired gun — a mercenary who'll take the best offer going, with little sense of sentimentality or regret. Loyalty is given fleetingly and with little conviction. If a FIFO contractor is made a better offer, he or she usually won't hesitate to bolt for the nearest exit with only a cursory 'cheers mate, all the best'.

And, that 'better offer' is more often than not accepted on a 'same shit different shirt' basis.

This isn't taking a cynical perspective, just one based in reality. Truth be known, I adopted the practice myself on a few occasions, and had no misgivings in doing so.

After several years in the Pilbara, I'd become familiar with much of the 'construction site speak' that was, regrettably, part of everyday life. Some of it no doubt would be common to all workplaces. Other expressions were vintage FIFO construction site gems:

> 'I'm not trying to screw you over' = 'I'm just about to screw you over.'
> 'What happens on site, stays on site' = 'Normal rules of acceptable behaviour don't apply. You have virtually free rein to do anything you please, just don't get caught.'
> 'It's a construction camp, not a holiday camp' = 'It's a virtual prison — deal with it.'
> 'Do I look like I give a crap?' = 'I don't give a crap.'
> 'Talk to someone who cares' = 'I don't give a crap.'
> 'He's a senior member of the site crew' = 'He's a cranky, broken-down old fart who people barely tolerate' (I was referred to as a senior member of the site crew on a few occasions. I got the message.)
> 'I'll bend over backwards for this job but I won't bend over forwards' = 'I think I'm just about to be screwed over.'
> 'Good pick up' = 'You just avoided being screwed over.'
> 'Shit rolls downhill' = 'I've just had my head ripped off by a dickhead in head office, so I'm going to stick the boot into you, brother.'
> 'Window seat or aisle seat?' = 'You've just been screwed over and you're on the next plane back to Perth … bro.'

Despite the many negatives, would I do it again? Definitely. The money was too good to pass up, and kept falling out of the sky miraculously and at regular intervals. It dug us out of a huge financial hole.

Do I regret my time as a FIFO contractor? No, not for a split second, apart from the persistent feelings of extreme fatigue and emotional stress. That's the price you pay. Would I go back again if I had the chance? If I had to, yes. But it would only be for the obvious financial rewards. I certainly wouldn't do it for my physical health or mental wellbeing.

Or as a soul-cleansing search for my sensitive inner self.

14

ORCHID RAMBLINGS

I'd rather laugh with the sinners
Than cry with the saints
The sinners are much more fun
You know that only the good die young

Billy Joel, 'Only the Good Die Young'

In early November 2014 (five days after leaving Ansaldo), and while driving on my way to pick up Diana from a medical appointment in Perth, I was cleaned up by a 5-tonne truck on Mounts Bay Road near Kings Park.

Shit happened. Right on cue.

Coincidentally, the crash occurred only metres up the road from where I'd trodden in a pothole and torn my vulnerable Achilles tendon prior to my failed Boston Marathon qualification attempt in 2011.

Lightning may not strike in the same place twice. But shit, apparently, can.

The truck hit me side on, T-bone style, fortunately on the passenger's side. The force of the crash spun the car around 180 degrees.

By the time my car came to a stop, it faced the oncoming traffic, forcing other drivers to swerve to avoid a head-on collision or brake to a screeching halt in the middle of the road.

I managed to dodgem-car my way to the side of the road, despite much of the rubber being shredded from two of the wheels. I crawled out on all fours, staggered to the footpath and propped myself up against a brick wall. The boofhead truck driver was completely unscathed. All he could bleat was: 'Didn't see ya, mate.' No shit?

My initial recollection was of a sharp pain in my neck and ribs. Once the ambulance arrived, my neck was placed in a brace and I was hauled off to Sir Charles Gairdner Hospital. All I remember from that point was being jumped on by a team of doctors and other hospital staff in the emergency department. My clothes were scissored off and tubes and other assorted gadgets were attached to, or inserted into, various body parts. For some weird reason, I enjoyed the attention.

To cut short a long and painful story, I was discharged four days later with a few fractured vertebrae in my neck, several cracked ribs and miscellaneous plumbing issues. I considered myself lucky; it could've been much worse. If events had turned out only slightly differently (the odd few centimetres here or there), I may've succeeded in writing only half a book, perhaps just the prologue. Someone else would've had to finish it off, plus pen the 'In Memoriam'.

Despite an initial diagnosis that I'd be confined to the neck brace for several weeks or even months, I was free of it just before Christmas and by then well on the way to a quickish recovery.

Mrs Burns, who was particularly pissed at her car being totalled, seemed only incidentally miffed that its single occupant had been somewhat banged up as well. That reaction may've had something to do with the projectile vomit I showered her with at one point during my hospital stay.

Please don't mention the 'c word' here, though — 'catheter', that is. For many weeks after the crash, I could still see the horrible wee pee tube whenever I closed my eyes. That reaction might've had something to do with the Nurse Ratched who gleefully inserted it into me on a couple of occasions when I couldn't 'perform' without her rough handling, as it were. The least she could've done would've been to enquire whether it'd been good for me too.

It hadn't. And I continue to be wary of hospitals. And nurses with glints in their eyes, especially those who reassuringly chirp 'this won't hurt a bit'. Or who casually throw in the double-meaning 'just a little prick' comment seconds before they do just that.

Of course, the accident did nothing to advance my fitness level which, after leaving Ansaldo, I had vowed to improve. Still, by mid-January 2015, I'd taken the first tentative steps to resurrecting my on-again-off-again-on-again running 'career', yet again, the pursuit of which seemed increasingly pointless due to galloping old age and an incredibly stiff and sore neck, courtesy of the crash.

I ran/walked three or four times a week for the second half of January, and by April I'd started to string together some 40-kilometre training weeks. The weekly kilometres increased throughout May and June and by about mid-July I'd also occasionally pushed the weekly long run to 20 kilometres.

Inevitably, my thoughts again turned to Boston. It may come as no surprise that I simply couldn't shake it free. As soon as I recommenced any kind of even semi-serious running, the thought would pop back into my head and gnaw away at my brain without respite.

Although four years that had passed since I'd had the somewhat offbeat idea to qualify at the 2011 Perth marathon for Boston 2012, on turning 60, it seemed like only yesterday. Injury had forced me to abandon the plan back then. I'd tried again in 2013. Again, there'd been another disappointment but this time it was largely self-inflicted.

Why go through it all again? WTF? I can only put it down to the idea of unfinished business, a notion that regularly looms large in my psyche. Boston for me certainly wasn't a 'bucket list' item. (I wonder sometimes whether the real thrill for people is to proudly announce at dinner parties or barbecues that they've crossed the bucket list item off the list, rather than experiencing the joy of the event itself.)

No, it'd always just been something I'd stubbornly clung on to for decades and which wouldn't let me rest until I'd achieved it or, at least, given it a red-hot go. Much like how writing this book eventually became. There are some things in life that are impossible to let go. They stick to you, and won't let you be, like a plague of pesky Pilbara flies.

Again, timing and logistics were major concerns. Realistically, I'd have to attempt a qualifying race in 2016 to qualify for Boston 2017, on 17 April, four days after my 65th birthday. At least the qualifying time for the 65–69 age group wasn't looking too daunting: 4 hours 10 minutes. It'd been so long since my first attempt several years before that I'd fallen over the line into the next age group!

So, yet another tentative Boston plan had been hatched. It meant a slow build-up for the rest of 2015, gradually increasing the kilometres in the early part of 2016 before going flat out for three to four months and running the Gold Coast Airport Marathon on 3 July. And, hopefully qualifying to run Boston 2017.

Here we go again. Time for the brain and body to re-engage once more, to reacquaint themselves, if not become bosom pals.

* * *

From the early months of 2015, I was placed on full-time gardening leave under the watchful eye of the horticulturally gifted Mrs Burns. She allowed me sufficient time to recover from the accident — just. As soon as I'd been unshackled from the neck brace, it was full steam ahead on the good ship Orchid Ramble — the name she'd bestowed upon our not-so-humble abode in Mansfield Avenue and which had been prominently positioned on a rock wall at the entrance to the driveway.

The construction of the rock wall which, naturally, I nicknamed 'Hadrian', was undertaken (not by me) with such painstaking care that, from go to whoa, it seemed to take longer to complete than any of the rail projects I'd worked on in the Pilbara. The cost of construction proved only marginally less expensive, too. My mate Hadrian is now a permanent fixture on the Margaret River landscape and attracts busloads of tourists — local, interstate and overseas.

I understand it can be seen from space.

The garden at Orchid Ramble has always been Mrs Burns's pride and joy. It is, without doubt, a credit to her amazing determination, endurance and horticultural skills. Far be it from me to describe the garden in my own words. It's fitting to let Mrs Burns have free rein. So, here it is in all its glory:

'Brick wall entrance. Red and yellow roses line the driveway to reflect the Orchid Ramble glass panel on the rock wall. Left-hand side planted out. Right-hand side tall eucalypts and wattle trees to the creek bed. Closer to the main house, large deciduous trees: ginkgo, maple, crepe myrtle. Nut trees: pistachio, macadamia, pecan. Oak trees inoculated with fungus for future truffle production. Natives of many varieties and wattles along the boundary to the creek bed. Creepers and climbers planted to cover all fences. The driveway turns left to the "farm gates". The forest is beyond the gateway — Boston ivies, Japanese maples, clematis and more wattles are planted along the boundary. Each of the three 'pods' has a bank of concrete planters stacked five high, each block weighing 23 kilograms. There are 583 of these concrete blocks and all are filled with self-propagating fuchsias, natives, buddleias, various bulbs, diosma and other shade-loving plants. Each bank always has some plant or shrub in bloom. Between the *pods (alfresco area), ferns, begonias, cyclamen and bulbs are planted around a water feature. The two house pods and archway are fenced with climbing roses and creepers. There are two circular herb gardens at the back of the main house surrounded by ground covers and natives. The studio garden has a circular seat surrounding a weeping cherry, lots of irises, alliums, ground covers, bulbs and boronia. Bottlebrush (pink, red, white and yellow) also fill the garden. Orchids bloom constantly near the studio and around tree peonies and water bowls for the birds. Behind the studio near the large veggie garden is a native garden with South African plants, tall salmon gums and assorted fruit trees — mandarin, orange, lemon, lime, apricot, avocado, quince and pomegranate. Also near the veggie garden are three mature olive trees and two fig trees. A bank of hellebores, ground covers and daisies protect the circular driveway around the studio. Outside the studio — Japanese maples, two lime acacias, striped pink and white crepe myrtle, a flowering quince and more buddleias.'*

Very Mrs Burns. It took her about three minutes to write it — all from memory. She wasn't even in Margaret River at the time. Typically, she didn't draw breath, not even once. My only contribution was a quick, and much-needed, spell check. Mrs B and decent grammar aren't the closest of friends. That's probably why she enjoys using the F-bomb so much these days. Short, sharp, direct and leaving the recipient in no state of confusion, especially when it's combined with equally simple words, like 'shut', 'the', 'up', 'go' and 'yourself'.

By the way, if the property sounds mildly appealing to you, I'm open to any reasonable offer. It needs to have a substantial number of zeros in it, though. Please negotiate direct with me.

As you'll know well by now, Mrs Burns does nothing by halves. In fact, she does everything in full mega doses. A minimalist she most surely isn't.

The veggie patch, tucked away in the left-hand corner of the 'top paddock' at Orchid Ramble, is more like a market garden. It comprises four raised beds each about 15 metres by one, and one bed of about 10 metres by one. I'm convinced the patch is not too far short of the total size of our first house in Canberra. A casual stroll between the rows to pick a few goodies for the evening meal often develops into a serious workout involving running shoes and a wheelbarrow.

Mrs B isn't content with mere self-sufficiency. The bounty from the patch is so plentiful it borders on commercial production. Of course, this vast expanse of veg comes with its own dedicated and sophisticated watering system that's well equipped to make even a scorched Pilbara desert bloom. When in full flow, it's certain to reduce the Margaret River water table by a significant percentage. The patch is aerially cropdusted twice weekly.

Aside from the usual suspects like carrots, tomatoes, pumpkins, broccoli, peas, cauliflowers and potatoes, a favourite of Mrs Burns is the humble broad bean. She plants them anywhere and everywhere and they grow prolifically. Consequently, they're indiscriminately added to every dish — soups, stews, salads and, when I'm not looking, blended into drinks, muesli and all manner of dips and spreads.

Now, for someone who already has a robust constitution and is as regular as clockwork (we're talking twice a day here, folks), over-dosing on broad beans, particularly when mixed with gravel-like muesli interspersed with even more broad beans, doesn't sit well with me. Actually, 'sit' isn't quite the right word. The nuggety little buggers don't sit at all. They travel straight through me at a rapid rate, like a juiced-up, out-of-control Ferrari.

I'm the one who does the sitting, so regularly the clock can't keep up. I positively percolate with a proliferation of prodigiously potent pulses. Poo to that!

If I'm not running, sleeping or working in the garden, you know where to find me.

* * *

You might recall that, before we moved to Mansfield Avenue, Diana and I lived blissfully together (as blissful as a marriage can be — that is, at times with little or no bliss) in a four-bedroom rental in Bottlebrush Drive. Having four bedrooms, the house was spacious enough to warehouse most, but not all, of Di's many handcrafts and other miscellaneous hobby interests.

Bedroom 1 was dedicated entirely to her life-long craft favourite: wool. Mrs Burns could knit by the time she was five and, since that time (I won't say how long ago but I imagine that most of her knitting then was carried out Florence Nightingale-style under the glow of a kerosene lamp), she's most likely knitted her way through the equivalent of an entire outback sheep station, or two. Her hand speed with the needles is so fast it would reduce to tears even the slickest 13-year-old gamer. Mrs Burns can produce a jumper with matching gloves, scarf and beanie during a return car trip between Perth and Margaret River. If put to the test, she'd be well able to knit directly from the sheep's back.

Bedroom 2 was her artist's studio, where she magically created some of the most beautiful watercolour paintings imaginable. She's gifted in many ways but none more so than in her watercolour artwork. Seriously, her work is truly special, and she deserves the highest praise and recognition. She prefers truckloads of cash, though, but will accept any form of crypto currency and/or crowdfunding.

Bedroom 3 was the 'textile room', which housed silk paintings, quilt covers and cushions, patchwork, embroidery and all manner of textile garments at various stages of construction.

The covered outdoor pergola area was turned over to mosaics, plant propagation and a plant nursery. Her love of art and handcrafts is equalled only by her love of plants. In Diana World, they're all in a dead-heat for first place.

For many years, I beseeched the multitalented Mrs Burns to

learn to paint with her feet so that she could knit and paint at the same time. Though sorely tempted, this feat has sadly never come to pass, but I'm sure it's by no means beyond her remarkable skill set.

Out of the four-bedroom house with double garage, I was offered, and dutifully accepted, one smallish half of the bed in bedroom 4 and about 10 per cent of the hanging space in the walk-in wardrobe. That's standard issue for most males, I expect. Of course, I should've been grateful and, of course, I was and expressed my gratitude, humbly, many times over.

You'll understand then my state of high anxiety, not to mention sheer panic, at the prospect of housing all of Mrs Burns's arts and crafts treasures in the new pad at Mansfield Avenue. I conjured up what I thought was a brilliant scheme to install a shed grand enough to warehouse the considerable volume of 'stuff' she'd made, acquired, looted, requisitioned, blatantly stolen or otherwise accumulated over many years, including the piles of bric-a-brac gathered lovingly from the monthly Lions Club shed sales. Obviously, it couldn't just be a dinky little garden shed big enough for a lawn mower and two shovels. We needed a 'Taj Ma-shed' of DFO proportions. And that's exactly what we got. An 80-square-metre whopper.

It cost a small fortune, almost half the entire cost of our Kaleen house back in 1978, but it did the trick. If the time ever comes when it's not occupied, highly unlikely as that may be, I'm sure we could hire it out as an indoor cricket centre, a roughish bogan-pleasing wedding reception venue or as a temporary hanger for an Airbus A380.

Although of gargantuan proportions, 'The Taj' is way too important to hold humble garden tools. At Mrs B's insistence, they must remain, and rust, outside.

* * *

The location of the new house put me within easy range of several excellent running tracks. Heading out the back gate, each route led me about 600 metres along a bush track to the intersection with Terry Road. If I turned left, I could go a further 500 metres and pick up the Wadandi Track and run as far as my fitness permitted, either north in the direction of Cow Town or south towards Witchcliffe. The track either way was great running.

If I turned right at Terry Road, I could, via dirt road, cycle path and beach track, run past the back of Cape Mentelle and Xanadu wineries to Prevelly Beach, where I'd meet Di after her early morning swim. This she'd do more often than not with the Prevelly Penguins, a fit and hardy bunch of dedicated ocean swimmers who take the plunge all year round. I rarely passed up an opportunity to meet her there as it meant a favourite 10-kilometre run followed by a banana and honey smoothie at the popular Elephant Café overlooking the beach.

* * *

It wouldn't be surprising for you to learn that the good Mrs Burns isn't fond of people even coming close to encroaching on her patch at Orchid Ramble. Right from day one of her occupation of Castillo del Diana, the highly combative Mrs B waged an ongoing, one-person war (not me, I'm too chicken shit) against many of the local dog walkers whose daily bush trek takes them within spitting distance of our western boundary which, despite my never voiced (of course) but real concerns, remains unfenced.

She had no highly aggressive wombat to wage hostilities against, so she took it out on the exceptionally passive two-legged human variety. She laid out an elaborate obstacle course with the occasional booby trap to prevent each responsible dog owner from enjoying their daily constitutional with their beloved pooch. I'm half expecting the resourceful Mrs Burns to set up a machine-gun nest in the Orchid Ramble alfresco area. Thankfully, she's held back — so far.

She thrives on confrontation does the good Mrs B, while I avoid it like the plague. She's no pale-faced, talentless, wishy washy 'influencer'. She's a born, in-your-face, what-you-see-is-what-you-get 'disruptor', even before the concept became well known, fashionable and, of course, overused.

She makes a great attack dog whenever I need someone to do the heavy lifting. We tend to divide up life duties on a 'best use of resources' basis. Anything requiring a heavy-duty bulldozer approach, copious quantities of aggression or a lump of 4 x 2, Mrs Burns gets the gig. Anything requiring subtlety, careful consideration, the filling out of forms or a dustpan and brush after the bulldozer has crashed and burned, I'm the man, so called. Less good cop, bad cop, more Oscar and Felix.

* * *

Ever been to Fiji?

Many Australians have, no doubt, but not me, and not even the-up-for-just-about-anything Mrs Burns. Not until July 2015, that is. We'd eyed a cheapish package deal earlier in the year and looked forward to escaping the chilly Margaret River winter for a week or so at the fabulous Outrigger Beach Resort on Viti Levu. As it happened, on the plane trip over, Mrs Burns picked up not just some common garden variety sniffle but a full-blown virus that gave every indication of being a cross between Ebola and the bubonic plague. Being the wonderfully generous person that she is, Mrs Burns happily shared the bug with me.

Despite the mild inconvenience of being at death's door, the incredibly robust Mrs Burns was hell-bent on engaging in every activity the resort had to offer: personalised garden tours, handcraft workshops, full body massages, aerobics classes in the main pool (where she terrorised most of the other resort guests, especially the children) and the many and varied activities of the resort's 'hilltop spa', the steep uphill climb to which was made effortless for Mrs B by dint of the personal chauffeur-driven buggy she commandeered for the purpose. She was also quite chuffed at having a 'Talai butler' service deliver her afternoon cocktail to our room at 4pm each day.

The only glitch for the week was her insistence on having a crack at snorkelling on the reef adjoining the resort. Mrs Burns loves all things animal, especially all things aquatic animal. If she's ever to be reincarnated — now there's a terrifying thought — she insists on returning as Sir David Attenborough or an ancient, grumpy, but still hyperactive tortoise on the Galapagos Islands.

Anyway, being prone to overdoing things, the wonderfully watery Mrs B overstayed her welcome on the reef that fateful afternoon and, to her horror, found herself temporarily marooned when she finally surfaced after seemingly holding her breath for two and a half hours. The last remaining tropical fish had long since given up and gone home to bed. So had the very uncooperative tide. However, Mrs Burns, the intrepid pioneer that she is, wasn't at all fazed by the realisation that she'd now have to literally walk over the reef to get back to shore, some several hundred metres away.

At first, progress was slow, due to the fact that she was battling the distance to the beach in a full-body wetsuit and flippers the size of palm trees. Still puffing away through her snorkel, and uncannily resembling the Creature from the Black Lagoon, she waded, waddled, flopped, floundered and otherwise steamrolled her way ever onwards, trying desperately not to destroy great chunks of coral reef that lay in her path. Massive fail on that one.

But make it she did, somewhat tuckered out, still in one piece and ready for the next challenge that life would soon throw her way. Sadly, though, she was too late for that afternoon's Talai butler service.

At least she was the unintentional source of high entertainment for several resort guests on the beach when she emerged from the water, backwards. The pennies had finally dropped that going backwards in flippers is decidedly easier than proceeding, and stumbling, face first.

For me, much of the week was spent flat on my back unsuccessfully negotiating my way through the dreaded lurgy that Mrs Burns had graciously handballed to me.

Although our island adventure was memorable, I must confess I found the local's use of the word *bula* a bit troubling. It seemed to be used, universally, as a greeting, even at times as a farewell, and would otherwise be dropped indiscriminately into any other manner of conversation. Even when the bula-giver was obviously over it and not feeling in a bula-bequeathing mood. By the third day, I was 'bula-ed out'. I was tempted to ask the resort management whether I could just deliver an all-embracing, catch-all, cover-all, once-and-for-all 'omni bula' to all guests and staff via the resort's PA system to cover the whole of the week.

But I thought that might just sound a trifle unfriendly and not in the true Outrigger spirit.

15

DRIVING MS DIANA

Many men go fishing all of their lives without knowing that it is not fish they are after.

Henry David Thoreau

By the time I'd recovered from the Fiji flu episode (and finally stopped automatically greeting people with my own throwaway *bula*), I'd lost six weeks of running. I hadn't run a step in the whole of that time. On top of that, even through September and into the early part of October I'd only managed to average 20 to 30 kilometres each week. I was way behind where I should've been at that stage. Surely not another abandoned Boston attempt!

On the positive side, Mrs Burns and I did make a rather momentous decision for the 628th time in our married life. It was one of those coulda/shoulda/woulda moments when you look back at life and beat yourself up for not doing half the things that you know in your gut you should have. We all do it, don't we? Some of us more than most.

Part of the pent-up frustration, at least on my part, was not being able to land a job since leaving Ansaldo. I wasn't, if the truth be known, done with working at that point. I had little choice. I'd been kidding myself to think otherwise. I'd even created a website to market a contracts management consultancy I'd established. But the mining construction industry was suffering a major downturn at the time (it had effectively died in the bum) and the glory days, when jobs were relatively easy to pick up, had long since passed.

I'd had a few interviews, but no job offers. I'd even tried overseas, particularly the Middle East, where prospects looked more positive. However, again, nothing came of my efforts. Needless to say, I was moderately cheesed off. I think it was me who turned to Diana during a mutual grizzle session one afternoon and blurted: 'You know what we should do? We should just pack up a few clothes, buy a second-hand campervan and bugger off around Australia.'

I held my breath and left the room, quickly, to allow Mrs B sufficient time to digest the magnitude of what I'd had the audacity to suggest. One thing I'd come to expect from Mrs Burns in more recent times was the unexpected. Life was never dull. Ever. True to form, a hyper-quick response shot back from the adjoining room: 'When do we leave?'

To say this reaction threw me would be a massive understatement. I hadn't anticipated for one minute that Diana would buy it. She was rusted on to Margaret River and the new house and garden, which were a source of great joy and comfort to her, and deservedly so, after several unsettling and troubling years.

But buy it she did. Swallowed the idea hook, line and sinker. By the next morning, she'd completely replanned and restructured our lives - for the 629th time. In truth, the only plan was to have no plan or structure at all. We decided to have no preconceived ideas of where we might travel or how long we'd be away. When people asked about our intentions, we simply said that we'd trek all the way around Australia, and when we reached the end we'd turn around and trek back the other way. That very loose arrangement appealed to us. We wanted the absolute freedom to go anywhere. If we enjoyed a particular place, we'd stay. If not, we'd move on.

We gave ourselves a month to pack up the house and move our personal stuff to the Taj Ma-shed, intending to rent out the house semi-furnished. Diana flew to Melbourne in the second week of October 2015 and I followed a few days later after tidying up some loose ends and generally squaring things away.

We planned to camp with Jess in Richmond for several weeks and then leave early in the new year for Tassie, via the *Spirit of Tasmania*.

* * *

In the months leading up to Christmas 2015, my volume of running increased steadily and, by the time the year was out, I'd managed to string together a few 60-kilometre weeks. Best of all, I'd been able to clock up several 20-kilometre runs, which gave me some reassurance that serious marathon training was within reach in the new year.

* * *

In the last week before Christmas, we bit the bullet and bought a second-hand campervan from a tour operator in Melbourne. To describe the van as 'second-hand' is to pay it the highest and most unjustified compliment possible. No vehicle could seriously be regarded as merely 'second-hand' if it had already clocked up almost 750,000 kilometres and had undergone the campervan equivalent of a quadruple bypass. It came with its own portable life support system. At least, we figured, the poor old dear knew its way around Australia and was unlikely to get lost. That would always be a bonus, given my very average sense of direction.

Being the clever people we are, we named the van 'The Van', mainly because that's what it was — a Toyota Hitop. It contained sleeping for two (just), a small fridge, a small two-burner stove, two small upright cupboards, two small overhead storage spaces and two small floor-level storage bins. Every item in The Van was Lilliputian in size. (By the way, we travelled 'plus dog'.)

But small is often handy, as I discovered by sheer accident that I could lie in bed and open and close the fridge with my left big toe. Retrieving and putting back actual fridge items and cooking a three-course meal with the same big toe arrangement proved a trifle more difficult to master, notwithstanding my vast professional restaurant experience.

Despite its limitations, size by no means being the only one, The Van suited our purposes and was to be our transport and home for the foreseeable future.

We made an overnight crossing from Melbourne to Devonport on 11 January 2016. I'd never been to Tasmania, but Diana had travelled there for work in the 1980s when she was an advocate with the Department of Veterans' Affairs on veterans' entitlements claims.

We spent a few days in Devonport touring around the local sites, including the Maritime Museum, which was very special. From there, we travelled through Ulverstone and on to the small town of Penguin and then to Burnie, where we camped for a week at the Somerset Caravan Park about 10 kilometres out of town. We intended to use caravan parks as much as possible and to 'free camp' when we could to make our tight budget stretch a bit further.

The first few weeks were spent hugging the north coast of the island, hopping from Burnie to Turner's Beach, Wynyard and Stanley before we were forced back to Port Sorrel by the bushfires raging on the north-west coast. But we did manage a short stay in Latrobe, where Di was in her element touring around private gardens and nurseries in the area.

I was able to squeeze in some satisfying runs during the remainder of January, including the Postman's Track loop at Three

Sisters Beach, several longish, gentle beach runs at beautiful Turner's Beach, a 15-kilometre bush run from Port Sorell to Squeaking Point and back, and runs along the Launceston waterfront.

* * *

Our Tassie travels were interrupted at the beginning of February when I flew back to Canberra to appear in the ACT Supreme Court in a long-running legal battle — another unwanted legacy of our former Canberra legal practice.

Just before we left the practice, and Canberra, in February 2008, we received a phone call from a former client advising us that he and four other related parties intended to commence a legal action against the practice for negligence allegedly committed by me back in 2002. Gee, thanks.

I'd acted for these clients in their purchase of serviced apartments in a unit complex in Sydney. Their claim was that alleged negligent conduct on my part had caused them monetary and other 'damage'. Over the years, four of these actions had been settled through the firm's professional indemnity insurer with no admission of liability on my part, which I'd always strenuously argued.

But one of the litigants held out and refused to settle, and his action against the practice had dragged on over the intervening eight years. At various times I'd provided comments, statements and other evidence in the ongoing saga. I'd also travelled back to Canberra several times to provide further follow-up briefing.

The action was set down for a five-day hearing commencing on 1 February. It ran the full distance and was even adjourned at the end of the week to a continuation (another five days) in mid-May.

The week was stressful. To say the least, it's disconcerting to hear your name mentioned disparagingly again and again in a courtroom and have your honesty, integrity and competence called into question. The action taken against me had been nagging at me off and on over the eight years. At least it had now come to a head, for better or worse.

I did no running that week.

Around the same time, we also settled our own claim against the former tenants of The Fishy who'd failed to pay rent over many months during 2014 and had to be forcibly evicted from the premises, leaving considerable damage and a costly repair bill. The claim was settled after a protracted, stressful and costly legal process.

* * *

The week after Canberra was a good running (de-stress) week for me in Launceston, mostly along the West Tamar Trail, Cataract Gorge and the gut-busting Zig Zag Trail, a steep climb up one side of the gorge. It was the best week's running I'd had for a few months and by the end of it I calculated that I had about 18 weeks of serious training before the Gold Coast Airport Marathon on 3 July. Time enough to flick the switch and launch into serious running mode, but no time to waste.

On her return from medical appointments in Perth at the end of that week, Di and I took off immediately for Greens Beach on the north coast. We stayed almost a full week, visiting the Beacons-field mine and museum. We also stopped off at Sea Horse World near Beauty Point. Mrs B had fallen hopelessly in love with the tiny critters and spent countless hours scouring beautiful Tassie beaches for any that may have washed up.

Lots more easy beach running for me at Greens Beach.

By the middle of February, the days were following a familiar pattern. We'd wake up early, around 5.00am, with first light, and a couple of coffees would make us feel semi-human again. Every so often, we lapsed into a three-cup morning if we felt especially feral. I'd then head off for a run, mostly on the beach where I'd meet up with Diana after she'd taken Taff for a walk and collected all sorts of random objects, or taken countless numbers of photos as subjects for her paintings. We'd then usually plan the rest of the day to take in local sites and places of interest, particularly anything to do with the history of the region we happened to be in.

By about 4pm each day, our self-proclaimed happy hour, we'd zero in on the best local pub we could find. Sometimes it was a golf, RSL or bowls club — anywhere really, that we could grab a beer for me and a glass of wine (or two) for Diana.

It was no surprise to us that we took to campervan life like ducks to water. No teething problems at all. We made it up as we went along, and that was half the fun. We quickly became familiar with The Van and all its quirky features. We fumbled our way through the first couple of weeks, but after that we felt like serious, veteran roadies. It's not for everyone but we coped with the confined space and the lack of creature comforts without much inconvenience and with little discomfort.

At times we'd 'free camp', either in a designated free camping ground or in an open paddock-like area adjacent to a country pub or club. These sites weren't exactly free, though. Some would charge a token fee of, say, $5 or $10, or even sometimes just a gold coin donation. In each case, the money would go to a local volunteer group, such as the Country Fire Authority. The only issue with these sites was that the battery power in The Van was only good enough to last for a few days, after which we'd have to scurry off to the nearest caravan park and power up again, and polish ourselves up as well.

Still, we managed. We managed back in the early Graduate House days in Canberra, we managed on our overseas backpacking trip to Europe in the mid-1970s and we were coping again in similar circumstances 40 years later.

After Greens Beach, we headed for St Helens on Tassie's east coast. We stayed at the Hillcrest Tourist Park, using it as our base for the following week.

St Helens was a good running week for me. The bitumen road from the park meandered for about 8 kilometres to St Helens Point, Burns Bay and the entrance to Georges Basin. The week centred around runs out to the point, taking in, at different times, Steiglitz Beach, Blanche Beach and the spectacular Beer Barrel Beach on the southern side of the point.

The stay in St Helens was special in another way. I reacquainted myself with my boyhood love of fishing. I remembered enough to buy some reasonably decent gear, nothing flash, and set off for Steiglitz Beach early one morning, a non-running day, to try my luck. No luck at all.

A few days later, I ran out to the breakwater that adjoined Blanche Beach at the entrance to Georges Basin and met Diana and Taff there. Within minutes, I'd hooked my first mackerel for the day which, by the time I'd finished a couple of hours later, had swelled to eight in total. They were all decent-sized, too. I was over the moon. I loved it. The most enjoyable day I'd had in years.

Now, some people will happily advise that mackerel aren't the greatest table fish going around. Don't believe it. We crumbed some of the fillets and cooked them in a shallow frypan with a drizzle of butter and olive oil, accompanied by a fresh mixed salad with a light dressing. Very simple, just how fish is meant to be cooked. Uncomplicated and delicious.

* * *

At most caravan parks, an area is set aside for permanent residents. The standard of homes varies greatly. Some are incredibly elaborate. Others are bland and nondescript, more likely than not reflecting the humble financial circumstances of their occupants. Some even display the Australian flag. But they all have one thing in common: their owners are genuinely proud of their homes, and they're almost universally neat, tidy and well kept.

At Hillcrest, one such permanent park resident was an elderly Irishman, Brendan (in truth, probably no more elderly than me), whose daily ritual was to sit outside his home in the early part of the evening and befriend a rather large glass of Irish whiskey, which he'd cuddle up to very warmly. He was a nice old guy (in truth, probably much nicer than me) who always had a pat for Taffy whenever we'd wander past his home and say hello.

I gave Brendan a few mackerel fillets. When I handed them over, he accepted them as if they were gold, in a way that suggested he hadn't been on the receiving end of too many even modest acts of kindness in his lifetime. He was on the verge of tears. Being the big sook that I am, so was I. I saw him briefly the next day. He nodded and half smiled, just enough to indicate, in his own quiet way, that he'd enjoyed his supper the night before.

Some days, it feels particularly good to be alive and, even I must admit, to be a part of the human race.

* * *

By this stage of the trip, Diana had well and truly sussed life on the road. Riding shotgun high up at the front of The Van, she surveyed all before her in the manner of the late Queen during a royal parade. I'm sure I detected the occasional 'royal wave'. But, maybe in Mrs B's case, it was the 'royal piss off'. That right regal image is well suited to Mrs Burns as, truth be known, she's a closet monarchist from way back. We part company on that topic I have to say. A monarchist I most surely am not. Vive la Republique, I say!

True to form, Mrs Burns thoroughly embraced her new-found happy camper status. In fact, during our many camp stopovers, she took up the unofficial and self-imposed responsibility of Camp Commandant with great relish and gusto. Mrs Burns (aka Colonel Klink-ette) was in her element as she regularly doled out extremely helpful, some would say 'gratuitous', advice to all those within earshot concerning park rules (about which she knew very little) and protocols (about which she knew even less and, without fail, refused to follow herself) on such matters as:

- *Noise.*
- *The behaviour of children, for whom Mrs Burns doesn't exactly have a warm and fuzzy feeling. (Her theory is that all children should, from about the age of 14, be dispatched to the Pilbara [I know just the place] and only be permitted to return when they've reached their mid-forties.)*
- *The behaviour of dogs, except Taffy.*
- *Park curfew hours.*
- *The use of the camp kitchen fridge.*
- *The use of the camp kitchen (generally).*
- *The use and cleanliness of the park amenities block.*
- *The parking of vehicles.*
- *How other campers should treat Taffy, even when he wasn't on a lead — which was most of the time if he was in her 'care'.*

She continued to insist that she could control Taff purely by 'voice command', which, to put it as politely as possible, is quoting liberally from the Little Book of Bullshit. On one not so memorable day, I spied her having a crack at an innocent and unsuspecting dog owner about camp dog rules while Taff was (off the lead) cocking his leg on the prized possessions of some other equally innocent and unsuspecting camp guest.

***

After Bicheno, Binalong Bay and Scamander, we free camped at Moulting Lagoon, about 10 kilometres north of Coles Bay and the Freycinet National Park. We had no choice this time as the Coles Bay Caravan Park had a 'no dogs' policy and we certainly couldn't camp in the national park.

I caught more fish from the lagoon, this time a decent haul of mullet, which were filleted, smeared with a dob of butter, some mixed herbs and a dash of lemon juice, wrapped in foil and thrown on the open fire near our camp site.

The running highlight for me was a 14-kilometre round trip from the Freycinet car park, via a steep climb to the lookout over Wine Glass Bay, an equally steep and treacherous descent to the beach, along a narrow, winding and bumpy bush track to Hazards Beach and then back to the car park.

In early March, we drove south to Orford where we stayed for about a week, near Prosser Bay and close to the Prosser River. Great fishing again, at the junction of the river and the bay — this time a good catch of bream. All were cooked in the same way, pan-fried in oil and butter, sometimes dusted in a thin coating of flour or, more often, just lightly pan-fried as they were.

There was more solid running for me on the Orford Foreshore Track — then only recently constructed, so the crushed and compacted gravel surface was near perfect under foot.

Following a short stop at Dunalley, and free camping in the paddock next to the Dunalley Hotel, we headed south again and free camped once more, this time at Nubeena in the grounds adjoining the Nubeena Bowls Club.

It's difficult to do justice to the convict settlement at Port Arthur, which was for me the best of many highlights during our Tassie trip. We visited around the time of the twenty-year anniversary of the Port Arthur massacre. The brutal history and the shocking memories of this most recent tragedy combined to leave us with a deep sense of sadness and sorrow. The memorials were represented tastefully, sympathetically and with much respect – a truly historic and memorable site.

* * *

Seven Mile Beach got its name, not by chance, but from the fact that the beach is about seven miles long from the western end near the village of Seven Mile Beach to the entrance to Frederick Henry Bay and Pitt Water. I can vouch for the accuracy of the distance, because on our second day there I ran from the Seven Mile Beach Caravan Park to the entrance and back and extended the run to a total of 24 kilometres.

It wasn't the last time I'd venture to the point. I figured that the spot where the ocean met the estuary would be a prime place to fish. I couldn't extract much information from the locals, mostly because the only way you could get there was by boat (which I didn't have) or on foot (which, happily, I did have). I learned that it was possible to drive part of the way there via a car park adjoining the beach. I woke up early on 21 March, a scheduled non-running day, intending to make a day of it.

A long beach walk was inevitable, which is never a chore. In fact, it's always been for me one of life's great pleasures. I figured that the walk from the car park along the beach to the point would take about an hour. In the end it took almost 90 minutes, and I don't muck around when I walk.

The weather that day was perfect. Windless. Cool with brilliant sunshine. The walk to the point was blissful. It was low tide and the walking was on flat, hard sand. The silence was broken only by the occasional squawking seagull or the crunch of my footsteps on the crusty sand. I could've been on another planet. It was the next best thing. The solitude was soothing and incredibly relaxing. It was obvious that few people had ever ventured this far up the beach, though regular hoofprints confirmed local advice that this part of the beach was commonly used for horse training. I arrived at the point at about 7.30am, just as the tide had turned and was on its way back in. Great timing, so I thought.

On my third cast, I hooked an undersized whiting which I promptly returned to the water without so much as a smooch on the cheek. And, well, that was it for the rest of the day. Not a nibble or a tickle or a tap on the line.

By about 4pm I was ready to pack it in. While I'm a firm believer in the philosophy that 'there's no such thing as a bad day's fishing', this day's non-event was bordering on the ridiculously annoying. I knew I had a long walk back to the car park to reach The Van and that the light would be fading by around 5.30pm. Still time for one last cast. All fishermen go through the same forlorn ritual, and more than just one final cast, too (if I'm any guide).

Bang! One very decent flathead. And that bang was repeated another 11 times over the next hour or so. I'd bagged a dozen extremely keepable fish. They must've all been coming home from the pub and were half cut and suffering the post-pub munchies. Virtually every time I cast, they would bite. It was going off, and so was I, big time, though I'd not quite gone viral by that stage.

(I even started performing a little jig up and down on the spot, much like how sporting teams irritatingly celebrate after they've won some major championship. I reckon it looks ridiculous, especially when some members of the team refuse to jig at the same time, thereby disturbing the team's jig-sync, or remain jigless and glued to the spot.)

By now it was just after five o'clock. It's my practice to gut and scale my catch before leaving a fishing spot – it's much less messy than performing this irksome task at home, especially when 'home' is The Van.

I've never scaled and gutted fish with such ferocity, though with such a lack of dexterity. Scales and guts flew everywhere. The spectacle would've looked appalling to most fair-minded people. The sheer fury of the attack and the whirling of the knife blade, Edward Scissorhands style, was even too much for the usually impatient seagulls and other assorted sea birds. Wisely, they kept a safe distance for fear of mistakenly being gutted and de-feathered themselves.

Once I'd regained my composure — that was a big ask as I was now well and truly, if uncharacteristically, pumped — and the blood had returned to my brain, I was faced with the realisation that I had to negotiate a 90-minute trudge back along the beach in semi-darkness. The problem with semi-darkness is that it's only a matter of time before it crosses over into pitch blackness.

What do you do if you have a long beach walk ahead of you and no time to stuff around? Well, you run, of course. So it was that, with pack on back, a rod in one hand and a bucket (half filled with water) of gutted and scaled flathead in the other, I set out to run on my designated 'run-free' day. A 50-year-old déjà vu moment: minus the heavily bleeding foot, but plus a bucket of fish.

I was soon to discover that the issue with pitch blackness is that you can see very little. Especially when, inconveniently, beaches aren't dotted with illuminated light poles. Nor was the track from the beach leading to the car park and the relative comfort and safety of The Van.

As it happened, I was out by several kilometres and made my right-hand turn from the beach through the dunes way too soon. I had no idea where I was as I scrambled my way to a track, but not *the* track that led to the car park, and safety. Up until that moment, I had little concept of how scary total darkness is.

So I just kept running in true Forrest Gump fashion, fully aware that if life *is* a box of chocolates, I really had no clue at all what I was going to get or, for that matter, whether I was going to end up with any kind of chockie at all. Truth be known, I was getting a smidge concerned when I turned left and headed back to the beach in utter desperation. Then the going got tougher - nothing but powdery sand that I sunk into up to my shins, as if it were actually quicksand.

In pitch darkness, and by sheer accident, I stumbled upon The Van at about 7.30pm. If it wasn't for the clear night and fullish moon, I'd still be out there on a nameless track, or swimming in the general direction of Antarctica.

By the time I casually — but, in fact, scared witless — walked in the door of our cabin at about 8pm, Mrs Burns was having a conniption on a grand scale. She had come within the proverbial bee's eyelash of dispatching the cavalry to scour the countryside for me.

I don't do nonchalance very well. I think it was the terrified look on my face and the three litres of sweat still clinging to my body that caught me out. Was the highly inflammable Mrs Burns pissed? She shirt-fronted me in the manner that Tony was too shit-scared to shirt-front Vlad. Was she pacified even slightly by my catch of the day? Not a friggin' chance. So, as any red-blooded husband/male would do in the circumstances (well, maybe those, like me, whose blood is more of a pinkish hue), I just stood there, switched off and copped it, basking secretly in the afterglow of one of the best days ever.

One I'll never forget and one I'd give anything to repeat, even if it meant another bollocking from the missus.

* * *

Running for me during our Seven Mile Beach stay provided some further reassurance that the training was on target. As well as the gentler beach runs, I managed a 28-kilometre Sunday road run at a pace of 5 minutes 23 seconds per kilometre.

After Seven Mile Beach, we headed for Bruny Island and stayed for a few days at Adventure Bay. The small but fascinating Bligh Museum of Pacific Exploration is well worth a visit and the tiny entry fee. It showcases a collection of manuscripts and other artefacts from the explorations of Tasman, Cook, Bligh (who loved his fishing, apparently — couldn't have been all bad, then), D'Entrecasteaux, Furneaux and Baudin who, incidentally, is said to have named Venus Bay after George Bass's trading ship, the *Venus*.

If there was one thing I learned very quickly during our travels, it was that touring around in a van, whether *The* Van or any other, is not compatible with serious marathon preparation. Apart from the fact that being squashed into a tight, tin-can-like space for several hours each day (sleeping, cooking, reading, writing) can cause a dickie lower back to become even dickier, running logistics prove to be even trickier.

There were no problems when we'd decide to camp at the one location for, say, a week or so, like we'd done at Seven Mile Beach and Launceston. That gave plenty of time to suss out reasonable places to run each day. But if we landed in an unfamiliar town in the late afternoon only planning a stopover for a night, or even two, there was little option for me but to head out the next morning and just follow my nose, improvise and hope for the best.

Sometimes, this led to quite interesting runs. Other times, running was a hit-and-miss affair and I had to be satisfied with just clocking up time. Snug Beach (adjacent to the local caravan park) was a case in point. In reality, the beach was more than just snug. It was positively skin-tight, so much so that I was forced to run 20 laps just to pen some reasonable distance into the training diary for that day. Word spread quickly among the locals. I attracted quite a crowd. Some greeted me with a cheer at the end of each lap. Some, apparently, even took bets on the number of laps I'd run.

For me, one of the great joys of campervanning was the confirmation of how little you need to live in this world. Being a staunch anti-junk, anti-consumption, anti-indulgence advocate (except, of course, for the occasional trip to Fiji or luxury Mediterranean cruise!), I found it fantastically liberating.

The Van provided shelter, accommodation and transport. It was where we cooked, ate, slept and spent our spare time reading or, in Diana's case, knitting, painting or doing other handcrafts. Our meals were simple but nutritious — whatever we could fit into a single frypan and cook stir-fry style — lots of veggies, some meat, fish, chicken, pasta, rice. We slept in sleeping bags in the back of The

Van. It was a bit tight at times but still comfortable enough. We had very few creature comforts but found we missed none.

We had music wherever we travelled, the kind we enjoy: Billy Joel, Carol King, Crosby, Stills & Nash, Neil Young, Joe Cocker, The Allman Brothers, Joni Mitchell, Eric Clapton, The Moody Blues, Santana, BB King, Carly Simon and, of course, Bob Dylan.

If The Van played up at any given moment, we wouldn't have known it. If it started to cough and splutter, or gave the slightest indication that it was experiencing the campervan equivalent of a heart attack, in time-honoured fashion, we simply cranked the music up and forgot about it.

Our philosophy, if you like, was to travel light and to free ourselves from the trappings of conventional living. If the idea is to break free from the clutter of contemporary life, we didn't see the point in dragging half of it with us. Aren't we supposed to get away from it all by getting away from it all?

Every so often I'd grab a newspaper if there was one lying about in a camp kitchen, but never bought one. If there was something significant happening in the world, of which we were totally and de-lightfully oblivious, we figured we'd find out about it soon enough. If the end of the world was thrust upon us, we were as ready as we needed to be.

Did we feel we were missing out through not being 'connected'? Not for a single moment. Did we feel deprived by not being part of a 'national conversation' on matters that arguably have no enduring importance to anyone and represent only a tiny fraction of the 15-minute news cycle anyway? Not a chance.

We ate well, slept well, travelled well and saw and experienced as much as we could fit in. Need there be more to the good life than that? Not for me.

* * *

On one Saturday morning while in Hobart, we took ourselves to the Salamanca Markets near Constitution Dock. I rarely buy 'stuff' but can never resist an opportunity to browse second-hand book stalls.

At first, I was more attracted to the name of the author of the book I'd stumbled upon than its subject matter — Christobel Mattingley — who I'd met many years before during my time in the copyright area of the Attorney-General's Department. I hadn't known her well but I did remember Christobel to be a prominent, and well-published, Australian author. The book — *King of the Wilderness: The Life of Deny King* — caught my attention the moment I'd read the blurb on the back cover.

It's a fascinating and thoroughly enjoyable read. Deny King was the quintessential Aussie pioneer, without ever intending to be. Internationally recognised for his deep, practical knowledge of wildlife and the natural heritage of the rugged south-west region of Tasmania, he was a self-taught sailor, environmentalist, tin miner, artist and engineer - a man completely comfortable with himself and with the physical world around him. As one guest wrote in the visitors' book at Deny's Melaleuca house, he was a 'prime example of how men should live'.

I agree. Living the essence of the simple life on a real and practical level — honest, humble, unassuming, unpretentious — and leaving the smallest possible footprint, but making a real and practical difference. He was in tune with, and an intimate part of, the natural world around him.

As a runner, I wanted to run like Abebe Bikila. As a human being, I wanted to live a simple and meaningful life like Deny King.

Sadly, I'd missed the boat on both. That's okay, though. No tears need to be shed. No, or only a few, regrets. That's how life had panned out to that point.

I can still shut my eyes, take a temporary time out, jump back in the bubble and imagine.

That'll do, for now.

16

BOSTON OR BUST (YET AGAIN)

I think I get addicted to the feelings associated with the end of a long run. I love feeling empty, clean, worn out, and sweat-purged. I love that good ache of the muscles that have done me proud.

Kristin Armstrong

We arrived back in Melbourne on 15 April 2016 after an overnighter on the *Spirit of Tasmania*.

Since about October the year before, Diana had suffered from a nasty leg ulcer which had developed after she'd been bitten by a mosquito in Venus Bay. Despite visits to doctors in Melbourne and throughout Tassie, the ulcer hadn't healed and at times even appeared to be worsening.

I've made it plain already that Mrs Burns, with a few exceptions, isn't rapturously in love with the medical profession. Being a pharmacist before she became a lawyer doesn't help, as she's well able to second-guess what most of the population just takes 'as advised', including me. She isn't mystified in the slightest by any mystique surrounding the delivery of health care in any form.

If *I* have to go to the doctor, she comes with me as my attack dog to be unleashed and unmuzzled as and when necessary. If *she* has to go, I remain in the waiting room as my good wife needs no such support from the likes of me. Typically, Mrs B's appointments are 'triples', allowing sufficient time for the doctor to canvas the breadth and depth of her considerable medical issues and, more significantly, for *her* to canvas in graphic detail how the practice could, and should, be run more efficiently.

Anyway, the ulcer persisted well beyond the expected timeframe, so much so that the best medical advice was that Diana needed consistent and regular care from the one local team. That, in her case, meant twice-weekly visits to the Korumburra Medical Centre for treatment. This effectively grounded us at the Venus Bay beach house from about mid-April.

There were pluses and minuses to this forced hibernation. On the one hand, it was good news that Diana would receive the treatment she needed from the one medical team. It was also good that we'd be able to hunker down in a comfortable home in a peaceful coastal environment.

However, it wasn't so good that we'd been stopped in our tracks and wouldn't be able to continue our road trip for the foreseeable future. It was even worse that we'd have to negotiate a South Gippsland late autumn-into-winter, which is invariably cold and bleak. The late autumn and winter of 2016 in South Gippsland were, indeed, exceptionally cold and bleak.

The big plus for me, though, was that I'd be able to get some solid running under my belt in the one location and in the crucial weeks leading up to the July race on the Gold Coast.

Having run there many times over the preceding years, I knew the Venus Bay roads well. I measured out a 2.65-kilometre circuit from home using the GPS function on my Garmin runner's watch: left out of the front gate onto Jupiter Boulevard, right at Mercury Drive, left at Mars Street, right at Pandora Avenue, right at Echo

Street, left back onto Mercury, left at Pluto Drive, left at Paris Crescent, a final left at Jupiter and back home. (You'll gather from this description that the good folk of the Victorian Department of Road and Street Naming dined out on an astrological theme for the streets and roads of Venus Bay.)

Except for a stretch of about 250 metres from our front gate, the circuit was all dirt and gravel. Especially during the week, it was peaceful and quiet with only an occasional car and an even less common dog walker. Most times I ran straight down the middle of the road with no safety concerns at all. It was to be my principal, almost private, training track for the next 11 weeks.

Overall, those 11 weeks went incredibly well, certainly as smoothly as I could've hoped. For six to eight weeks, I averaged about 80 kilometres. Not mega mileage by most marathon standards but as much as I could manage without running the risk of injury or illness. The length of each daily run followed a familiar pattern. Three or four laps of the circuit, with an extra loop tacked on to the four-lap run to lengthen it to 11 kilometres, once again taking me past the possible gravesite of Margaret Clement.

In those 11 weeks, I became well acquainted with almost every physical detail of the circuit. Every bend, every 90-degree turn (all nine of them), where the soft sand was, every patch of rough and loose gravel and, of course, the exact location of every pothole.

The weekly long run was 12 laps of the circuit. It sounds boring, but as you may imagine I do boring very well. It also gave me the additional option of easily cutting the run short if I was particularly stuffed. That happened.

By the time I'd reached the taper phase of the build-up, about two to three weeks from race day, I'd worked several better-quality runs into my preparation. These 'tempo' or 'rhythm' runs of 8–10 kilometres were run at about marathon race pace or sometimes even quicker — anything between 5:00 and 5:20 per kilometre. I threw in a few time trials of 3–5 kilometres and these, too, had produced solid results. No rogue potholes this time around.

My weekly long runs hadn't progressed as I'd hoped, however, and were around the same pace as the long runs I'd done in Tassie. The best I could manage was about 5:20–5:25 pace. This was troubling. The long runs had stagnated for no apparent reason.

Determined to learn from the Perth Marathon disaster several years before, I consistently began the run slowly, easing into the first few kilometres at no better than about 5:45–5:50 pace, then gradually winding it up so that some of the middle and later kilometres were being run at about 5:15–5:20. But by about 28 kilometres into each run, my energy level had flagged and the last 5 kilometres of a 30–32-kilometre run were tough going. I wasn't panicking just yet but, all the same, I was uneasy about how I'd handle the last 10 kilometres of the marathon.

With few exceptions, the weather over the 11 weeks of training in Venus Bay was nothing short of atrocious. On average, I ran in decent conditions on only about two or maybe three of the six training days each week. By far the worst element was the cold and biting wind. The partial protection from the giant sand dunes to the south did little to temper the prevailing winds that almost always blustered in from the west or north-west and commonly reached about 30-35 kilometres per hour. At times, the wind was mixed with rain and, occasionally, sleet. Some days I'd finish chilled to the bone, bordering on hypothermic. A few of the weekly long runs, usually those on a Sunday, had to be postponed to another day during the week because the conditions were just too horrendous. Even back in the Canberra days, I rarely needed to rug up as much: long leggings, long-sleeved top, a short-sleeved T-shirt over that and a beanie.

The last left-hand turn into Jupiter Boulevard and the 500-metre run past home, or ending there, depending on how many laps I'd planned, was consistently run into a howling gale. It may've been relatively short (unless you run it 12 times, of course!) but that last 500 metres felt distinctly like running the wrong way in a wind tunnel.

Most running coaches recommend a two to three week 'taper' period in which the weekly mileage is progressively cut back and some shorter, sharper runs introduced to 'freshen' up the body after the grind of a large volume of running in the lead-up weeks. Again, that went well and, by the last week before the race, I knew I'd done as much as possible to be ready.

Before leaving for the Gold Coast, I fixed on a plan for the race:

0–10 km — 55 minutes

10–20 km — 53 minutes

20–30 km — 54 minutes

30–40 km — 54 minutes

40–42.195 km — 12 minutes (but hang on as best I could)

Predicted time = 3:48:00 (approx.)

Having trained so well, I thought that time was very achievable. In fact, I felt my prediction was even slightly conservative. Regardless, I convinced myself that I couldn't have prepared better.

Now it was only a matter of how I handled race day. Now it was all down to me.

No pressure. What could possibly go wrong?

17

BLISTERED TOES AND BLEEDING NIPPLES

We are different, in essence, from other men. If you want to win something, run 100 metres. If you want to experience something, run a marathon.

Emil Zatopek, three-time Olympic gold medallist and winner of the 1952 Olympic Marathon

I left for the Gold Coast on 30 June. After several years of disappointments and false starts, it looked distinctly possible that I'd at least make it to the starting line. Unless, of course, I found myself on the wrong end of another 5-tonne truck in the meantime.

There'd been some speed bumps along the way, even apart from uncooperative Achilles tendons, a dickie lower back, rapidly advancing years and, of course, a duck egg in the groin.

2011: Failed attempt at the Perth Marathon (pothole problems).

2013: Aborted attempt. Didn't make the starting line at the Adelaide Marathon, as planned, after I'd dummy spat the idea several weeks before.

Instead of running Boston 2012 to 'celebrate' my 60th birthday, I'd have to settle for Boston 2017 a few days after my 65th. If, indeed, I was able to qualify.

No excuses or regrets, it was what it was. Notwithstanding life's giant hairy bum constantly obstructing my way.

Race day morning unfolded like this:

3am: Intended to wake up at 4am but I'd tossed and turned during the night and was wide awake by 3. Nibbled on two slices of toast with honey and sipped a glass of electrolyte drink.

4am: Wake-up call from Diana. She was my back-up in case I'd slept in. No real chance of that happening.

6am: Left the hotel and walked up Cavill Avenue to the light rail stop. Hundreds of runners packed in like sardines for the 20-minute commute to the race start 'precinct' at Southport.

6.30am: Arrived at Southport station and walked about 500 metres to the race start area. Dumped my gear at the bag drop and did a slow warm-up jog with a few, quicker run-throughs. Ambled up to the starting line and positioned myself roughly where I thought was an appropriate place for me among the other 5000–6000 other runners.

7–7.20am: Waited in the crowd of runners, proudly sporting my 1980 Nike International Marathon singlet, trying to stay calm and loose but, in fact, progressively tensing up. Negotiated a couple of nervous dry retches and grossed out a few other runners in the process.

7.20am: The starting gun.

I settled into what I felt was a relaxed, comfortable pace. I eased through the 1 km mark in 5:22 and the 2 km in 10:47, much quicker than my planned race schedule. I hit the 10 km mark in 52:18.

Ever had that terrible sinking feeling that you've stuffed something up spectacularly even when you're only fractionally into it? And, worse, that there's no going back? I felt reasonable but not as comfortable as I should have. Not straining, but not cruising. I consciously worked to slow down and thought I had. I was wrong.

I reached the 20 km mark in 1:44:02, having covered the second 10 km in 51:44. Panic kicked in. I knew I'd raced far too quickly from the gun but, at that stage, it was too late to do anything about it. The deed had been done and couldn't be undone. You simply can't rectify a pacing miscalculation mid-marathon.

A wardrobe malfunction just before halfway didn't help. My shorts were unravelling, much like me. While straining to maintain an acceptable pace, I was forced to untie the cord that kept my shorts up and then wrench them violently skywards — which I overdid to the point where I closely resembled Baby Huey in a nappy. I then yanked the cord as tight as possible and retied it. The realisation that I'd pretty much given myself a full-on atomic wedgie (and had cut off the blood flow to my brain) did nothing to ease my increasingly fragile state of mind. Not something you wish for mid-marathon.

('Believe it or not moment': In 1984, I ran the same Gold Coast race but, that time, the half marathon. From the start, it poured relentlessly. My pants became so sodden they began to slip. I had to carry out the *same* gear rearrangement that I'd perform 32 years later — the only difference being that, in 1984, there was no cord to re-tie. So, while continuing to run, I unclipped one of the safety pins that secured my race number to my shirt and skewered it through my pants, desperately seeking to avoid inflicting a totally unnecessary second vasectomy. I managed to place third that day, despite the mishaps. My trophy? A slab. True story.)

The next 10 km split was run in 54:58. Not a dramatic slowdown but, by about the 28 km mark, I could clearly sense that I was in a crapload of bother. Kilometre 31 threw up the only serious hill on the course, which I crawled up in slow motion. It also coincided with the run back past the start/finish line. Not what you want to see when you're already struggling and you realise, for a cast iron certainty, that you're going to die over the next 11 kilometres.

That's precisely what happened.

The last 10 kilometres of the race were a blur. At times, I felt as if I was jogging up and down on the spot. Kilometres 30–40 were horrendous — 'run' in the snail-like time of 64 minutes. From about the 35 km mark, I stopped at every drinks station and took in any kind of liquid I could get my hands on. I grabbed every lolly available from the kids who lined the edge of the road and passed out sweet treats to flagging runners. I even occasionally stopped to a walk, something I'd never done in a race before. Ever.

Kilometre 41 was run/staggered in a woeful 7:02. I can't remember much about the last few kilometres, except that I felt completely destroyed and desperate to see the finish line. I lifted the crawl pace to run a still very slow 6:07 final kilometre.

I finished in 3:56:59.

Out on my feet, absolutely knackered, I felt like a grossly over-cooked dim sim. I was so delirious with fatigue that I almost performed a full-on 'Pheidippides Face Plant'.

(Ancient Greek history has it that at the conclusion of the Battle of Marathon in 490 BC [and from where the legend of the marathon began], Pheidippides, who'd run about 40 kilometres from Marathon to Athens to announce the news of the Athenian victory over the Persians, proclaimed on arrival something along the lines of: 'Rejoice, we conquer!' Whereupon, he collapsed and died.)

I must've looked very ordinary as a fellow finisher grabbed me before I could execute my PFP and ushered me to the medical tent where I plonked myself in a chair. I was given a couple of sports drinks which I demolished in nothing flat. I would've preferred a bed and an intravenous drip. The helpful and extremely caring fellow runner even trudged off and returned with some sliced orange pieces. The kindness of the long-distance runner.

I squatted in the medical tent for about 20 minutes hoping to revive. It didn't work. Nevertheless, when I figured I'd outstayed my welcome, I rose to my feet and attempted to move. That didn't work either and I felt dangerously close to passing out.

I gathered enough strength to shuffle to the bag drop after collecting my race T-shirt and 'finisher' medal, the weight of which, though relatively light, almost caused me to topple over when it was hung around my neck. I couldn't sit down on the grass or bend over and ease into my tracksuit bottom. I was too numb and spaced out to stick around and savour the post-race euphoria. I slung my bag over my shoulder, missed and belted myself in the head. That helped not one bit. I then hobbled towards the Southport light rail stop. The 500 metres to the station seemed like running the last 10 kilometres of the race all over again, and took me about the same time.

Being so woefully slow in rising to my feet, I came close to missing the Cavill Avenue light rail stop. Some kind young person (probably, in fact, in his or her mid-eighties — I couldn't determine the sex or the age at that point) had taken pity on me and had given me their seat. The same, kind young/old sexless person helped me back to my feet and gently eased me out the door just before it could slam me from both sides.

I limped my way down Cavill Avenue. Walking in a straight line was non-negotiable. Incapable of deviating a centimetre left or right, when people approached, I'd wildly gesticulate to get the fuck out of my way, and clearly articulated the same instruction. (The same kind of helpful advice I gave to soccer refs back in the day.) After what seemed to be light years, I arrived at my hotel, which, to me, was an oasis in the desert. And nothing like Camp 25 in the Pilbara desert.

I don't like spas much. There's a limit to how much even *I'm* prepared to stew in my own juices. But on this day, I thought a soak in a hot tub would help relax my aching body, which was fast approaching meltdown. I lay in the spa (about the size and depth of an

Olympic swimming pool) and passed out after a few minutes, only waking when I felt water running down my nostrils and gurgling in my throat.

After witnessing the bathwater disappear down the plughole and feeling comforted that no body part had vanished with it, I failed miserably in my several attempts to get to my feet. Each time I contorted one part of my body into a position where standing fully upright seemed possible, I'd cramp in another. In the end, I heaved myself up with the aid of the shower taps only to encounter another problem: how to get *out* of the spa.

My brain had turned to mush. Like soggy blancmange. Each time I hoisted one leg over the edge of the spa, I'd cramp in the other. At one point, I cramped in both legs at the same time. In desperation, I did the only half-sensible thing my mushy brain could rationalise which wasn't rational at all. I held my breath, crossed my fingers and dived out of the spa headfirst, executing a perfect 'somersault with pike'. I 'stuck' the landing on the bathroom floor and lay there prostrate for a few moments suffering, inevitably, a *full* body cramp, including my fingers, which by then couldn't be uncrossed.

I assumed things couldn't get worse. False assumption. I was back in the horizontal position which was, as I proved in the spa, a wonderful achievement. But, now, I had to get back on my feet again. Being too buggered to start the whole ridiculous and agonising process all over again, I simply breaststroked / Australian crawled / dog paddled my way along the floor and into the bedroom. I slothed myself up onto the bed like an amoeba oozing from a primeval pond. I was barely able to don a T-shirt which, luckily, rested on the bed from the night before. I crawled under the covers and slept for three hours, wet hair and all.

I woke in the late afternoon with the hair trend we didn't see coming. I could hardly move. Despite that, I was overcome by an urgent need for food and drink. A slightly dickie tummy meant nothing. All I could visualise was a burger, fries and a chocolate thickshake. I struggled for about 30 minutes to squeeze into a trackie bottom, a different T-shirt to the one I'd woken up in and some loose-fitting shoes. If I'd had thongs or my favourite comfy slippers, I would've gladly worn them. If I'd had a walking frame, I would've gladly used that, too. Must've left it behind at Camp 145.

I flicked into survival shuffle mode and made my way back up Cavill Avenue to find a burger joint. If I'd been walking any slower, I would've been arrested for vagrancy — if that's still a crime these days. About halfway into my trek, it dawned on me that, in my 'haste' to get dressed, I'd forgotten to wear undies. If I'd been arrested, a second charge would've surely been slapped on me, particularly if the rest of the jaunt had involved even a modest amount of friction down south. But the embarrassment of the moment didn't last. Stuff it. I was ravenous for a burger, fries and a thickshake.

I found a suitable burger joint, no problems, and ordered double everything. The young guy who served me looked puzzled as he took my order. He must've twigged that I wasn't wearing undies — or maybe I was being overly self-conscious. Regardless, the service was lightning fast, as far as my still mushy brain could compute, and I was soon outta there and back in slowmo (frictionless) walk mode down Cavill Avenue carrying my brown paper bag of goodies.

I munched some of the fries on the way and slurped/dribbled some of the thickshake, like when the dentist unfairly demands that you rinse and spit. Maybe it was paranoia or maybe I was halluci-nating through lack of food but I had the feeling that I'd be arrested at any moment. I made it back to my hideout without drawing any more attention to myself, especially from the cops, and scoffed what remained of the burger, fries and thickshake. I almost polished off the brown paper bag, too.

Having suitably grossed myself out, I plucked up enough courage to survey the body parts that had suffered the most damage from the morning's light exercise and which, until then, I'd completely ignored. For good reason, as it happened.

The scene was ugly: three blackened toenails, including those on both big toes, which required urgent amputation and cremation; an assortment of blisters on the remaining toes that needed popping and draining, despite my having liberally smeared each of the buggers with a generous dollop of Vaseline before the race. Both feet resembled lumps of hamburger mince and my right foot was so swollen I thought I'd grown a sixth toe - bleeding nipples also, which I'd earlier discovered post-race and pre-spa.

I could easily have scored a gig as an orc in the next *Lord of the Rings* movie — and without the need for the slightest hint of make-up.

Putting aside the post-race bleeding nipples, at least I wasn't peeing blood, which had been the scary result of a bad marathon many years before. My right hamstring was throbbing, tight and tender to the touch. Worst of all, though, my quadriceps were in dreadful shape. They were almost locked solid. I could only manage the shuffle of a 90-year-old, but straight-legged like a teenage girl wearing spray-on jeans.

It may sound crazy but I slept only on and off that night. I woke at about 5.30am the next day, again ravenously hungry and thirsty. My legs were in worse condition than the day before. No spa for me this time, but I still had to negotiate getting into and out of the wretched thing to shower.

I was aching, bone weary, sleep deprived and generally grumpy with the world, though being grumpy isn't an unusual state for a card-carrying curmudgeon like me. I'd waited for the post-marathon euphoria to kick in but was sadly let down. Quite the reverse in fact. Still, once dressed (wearing undies this time), I crept back up my old friend Cavill Avenue looking like I'd staggered out of a B-grade Hollywood zombie movie. I plonked myself down at the nearest breakfast joint I could find and ordered the biggest Big Brekkie on offer.

Again, I craved a chocolate thickshake which, when presented to me, was demolished in the new world record time of 5.2 seconds, despite the clogged straw. I barked at the poor young waitress (sorry, female food attendant) that I needed another before she'd even had a chance to draw a second breath.

In hindsight, I embarrassed myself hugely that morning, but I really couldn't have given a hoot. I was too hungry, too thirsty and too sleep deprived to care. Food and drink were consumed with no regard for modesty, reasonable dining etiquette or the feelings of other patrons. One young family vacated the adjoining table, such was their disgust at my very ordinary table manners. I'd let everything hang out in a most disturbing way.

Après la grande bouffe, I stumbled back to the hotel and slept for four hours. It was still only mid-morning.

During the afternoon, I took some time to reflect on the race. For some reason, I hadn't dwelt on it up to this point. I was probably too preoccupied with the physical aftermath.

How did I feel about it? Was I happy with the outcome? If pushed, I'd confess to having mixed feelings. On the plus side, I'd finished, and run a time that I was hopeful would secure me a Boston start. That had been the main aim of the exercise. I was also quite sure that my preparation had been pretty much spot on. Apart from some minor tweaks here and there, I got that part right.

After five years of miscellaneous mishaps, at least I could now get that bloody gorilla off my back. On paper, I was well under Boston qualifying time. All that was left now was to wait for 14 September to register and hope my time was good enough.

I was stuffed but chuffed.

Why I didn't feel more euphoric is a mystery. It was as if I'd merely ticked it off as an item on a to-do list – but, not a bucket list. It was more like: job done, move on. Of course, it was more than that, however, I wasn't hearing the 'Hallelujah Chorus' playing in my head or experiencing a grand sense of achievement, either. I guess it was more a feeling of having the job only half done. The real deal, Boston, was yet to come.

On the minus side, I was a trifle, but only a trifle, annoyed that I'd blown up so badly. I really coulda/shoulda/woulda run under the 3:50 mark. I was ticked off with myself that I hadn't run a 'smart' race. I'd started too quickly, especially over the first 20 kilometres, and had paid the price later, being totally spent at the end. That was *not* how it was supposed to play out. In effect, I'd broken the cardinal marathon rule and disrespected the intolerant marathon monster once more. The result: a firm clout over the ear.

There was one crucial thing that I hadn't factored in from the outset, though — just how bloody hard it was going to be to train for, and run, a marathon at my age. Especially after a 34-year gap. I'd massively underestimated this. I had no realistic concept of how difficult and draining it would prove to be. And to think I'd be doing it all again if my Boston application was successful.

There was a lesson to be learned. (There always is.) Next time, be disciplined enough to hold back and finish without blowing up.

That was the plan. I wouldn't make the same mistake again, would I? If, indeed, I even got the chance.

18

BONNIE AND CLYDE RIDE AGAIN!

So put me on a highway
And show me a sign
And take it to the limit
One more time

The Eagles, 'Take it to the Limit'

Running-wise, the two months after the Gold Coast race were, predictably, very forgettable. In terms of total kilometres covered, successive weeks went like this: 8, 5, 15, 28, 40, 42, 42, 5, 12. And I wasn't even close to neutralising the night-time TV couch munchies: chips, Cadbury's Hazelnut, Snickers and dark chocolate bullets (Darrell Lea, preferably). And truckloads of Twisties.

Since the marathon, I'd been struggling with a lack of motivation. That wasn't surprising, either. It was as if the body was pleading with the brain (they've never been soulmates, as you know): 'No, you're *NOT* going to put me through this again — no way, get fucked, fuck off.'

It wasn't until towards the end of September that I started to string some reasonable running weeks together. By then, I'd lost fitness, but I wasn't in panic mode at that point. That would come later.

At the end of August, we hit the road again for a short trip to Merimbula to attend the 90th birthday of my uncle Bruce, who married us back in 1977 and who I've been fond of all my life.

After a brief stop in Melbourne on the way back, we headed north-west, calling in at Ballarat, Castlemaine and Bendigo. In Ballarat, I ran a few times on the cycle path bordering Lake Wendouree which, these days, goes under the official name of the Steve Moneghetti Track, another marathon legend.

8 September: A momentous day. My left big toenail finally fell off after two months of literally hanging around at the end of my foot. It was uncrematable, so simply got binned. The toenail on the right big toe proved to be more stubborn and difficult to dislodge, despite forlorn and painful attempts to detach it with the aid of a pair of rusty pliers.

14 September: Applied online for entry into the 2017 Boston Marathon.

17 September: Woke early. Overnight, I'd received an email from the Boston Athletic Association: 'This is to notify you that your entry into the 121st Boston Marathon on Monday, 17 April, 2017 has been accepted.'

Text message from Hamish later that day: 'Congratulations Dad, lifetime's ambition fulfilled, proud to be your son'. Then, later, a message from Jess: 'Brilliant!! Such great news!! Go Dad. Congratulations!!! x'

These messages meant more to me than making it to Boston.

After almost 40 years of dreaming and five years of mishaps, false starts and disappointments, that bloody gorilla was finally off my back. For the second time. Gorillas are, infuriatingly, like that. They hang around for as long as gorillas choose to.

Unless cleaned up by the same or a different 5-tonne truck, I'd be running the 2017 Boston Marathon, four days after my 65th birthday. I'd get to experience the pleasure and pain of marathon madness all over again: more bouts of extreme physical fatigue in all kinds of shitty weather. More stress piled onto already tender-to-the-touch Achilles tendons. More knife-like jabs from a dickie lower back. More gut-busting time trials. More rogue potholes. More blistered toes and bleeding nipples. More self-doubt. More pain, less pleasure.

I couldn't wait.

* * *

We spent some unscheduled time in Venus Bay from about mid-September. With welcome, settled weather for a change, I was able to venture out for some relaxed beach running, my favourite kind.

The track from our back gate to Beach 1 begins with a short but steep climb through the entrance to Cape Liptrap Coastal Park. From the top of the hill, the track twists and turns and undulates through the dunes to a point where it hits the beach — about 200 metres to the east of the Beach 1 car park. The track is just short of 500 metres from 'gate to beach'.

On reaching the beach, my habit had always been to turn left and run in an easterly direction, past the wreck of the *Magnat*, a steel barque that ran aground during a storm in the early 1900s. Rusted parts of the ship can still be seen from the shoreline on a very low tide.

This section of the beach is more isolated and tends to have fewer people — none, in most cases — apart from the very occasional park ranger patrol, bike rider or salmon fisherman.

It wouldn't be possible to enjoy a more peaceful and soul-restoring beach run anywhere. Beach running forces me to run slower and leaves me more relaxed. I barely concern myself with my Casio runner's watch. I just run for a particular time then turn around and, somewhat anally, retrace my steps — almost footprint by footprint. For some inexplicable reason, bitumen stirs me up and pumps the juices. Beach running is calming and soothing, as beaches always are for me.

That stretch of the South Gippsland coast is always spookily quiet, as if existing in its own timeframe, or time warp, more accurately. Sometimes I have the distinct but unearthly feeling that I'll bump into Margaret Clement, out for a pleasant beach stroll. I even look for her. I wish we'd meet. I think we'd get on well. She sounds like my kind of person, rare though they may be: practical, down to earth, a straight shooter. The real deal. A true stoic. Unpretentious, self-reliant, resilient, a dog lover and, crucially for me, humble.

Very few people brave it along that expanse of beach. That's its main attraction. I can run out and back for an hour or more and not see another soul. It's never unsettling, more like feeling you're the only person on the planet. The best place to be. Sometimes, the only place to be.

* * *

For the first three months after the Gold Coast race, I'd been suffering from a depressing lack of motivation.

But by the end of September, I'd at least mapped out a rough training plan for the six months leading up to Boston Marathon day on 17 April. It wasn't vital at that stage to put much science into it. In October, I'd increase the mileage to 60-kilometre weeks, November 70 kilometres and December 80 kilometres, allowing one rest week, involving fewer kilometres, in each month. By running at least two 80-kilometre weeks in December, I'd have a solid platform to launch into the more serious months of January, February and March, leaving the two to three weeks before race day on 17 April as the usual taper period.

All running throughout October, November and December was intended to be relaxed and easy. In reality, though, it was a slow, tough slog. Having done so little in the months after the Gold Coast race, my overall fitness had dropped off rapidly and alarmingly.

Like many things of significant value, fitness is diabolically hard to attain and depressingly easy to lose, especially when age is factored in. It was also likely that I was still overcoming the effects of the Gold Coast race, which had taken a much greater toll than expected. The problem then, was twofold: gradually increasing the volume of running, while at the same time, recovering from the effects of the July marathon.

It proved to be a grind to reach the monthly targets I'd set myself, and to be honest, those targets weren't always met.

* * *

Having previously had both hips 'done' and her left shoulder reconstructed, the good Mrs Burns decided to square the ledger, anatomically speaking, by having surgery on her right shoulder, just before Christmas. A combination of wear and tear and overuse had caused a tendon to tear from the shoulder muscle and she was in heaps of pain. At this point, neither knee worked terribly well, and she had no properly functioning shoulder. In other words, she was starting to resemble the multi-hacked version of the Black Knight from *Monty Python and the Holy Grail*, flesh wounds and all. And just as feisty and cantankerous.

Again, we found ourselves grounded, this time in Melbourne, before our planned return trip to Tasmania in the new year.

By the time Christmas rolled around, I was pretty much ready, at least mentally, to launch into serious marathon preparation in January. But there was now an additional physical problem to overcome. In the month or so before Christmas, I'd experienced an unusually high level of fatigue during my daily runs. After having run for the best part of 40 years, I knew my body well enough to recognise when it was under stress, and if it was, I'd ease back enough to allow adequate recovery. Throughout that period, though, every run was a mirror image. By about 5 kilometres into a 10-kilometre run, extreme fatigue would set in and I'd feel totally drained, even if the pace of the run was light. By mid-January the situation hadn't changed, and despite urging myself not to, I was beginning to slide into panic mode.

At one point, it seemed that the only practical way to break out of the malaise was to book myself into the nearest sports doping clinic — I think there's one called The Last Resort — and order the full Lance Armstrong Package. All intravenous meals are included with complimentary spa and pedicure. (Spa and foot treatment - happy days!) In the end, I decided against it, though. I figured it might be stretching things a bit too far and would do little to enhance my much-cultivated cleanskin image.

Towards the end of January, we again headed for Tasmania to avoid what was left of the summer heat on the mainland. This time we headed for the west coast, which we hadn't visited in the previous summer because of bushfires that raged there at the time.

We spent most of late January and early February cruising along the north-west coast, including Burnie (runs along Somerset beach as in the year before) and Stanley (runs along Tatlows beach). Later, we travelled to the west coast where we stopped at Arthur River (where I ran to the aptly named 'Edge of the World'), Rosebery and Zeehan, before basing ourselves in Strahan for five days.

As I've mentioned, when you arrive in a town in the late afternoon, often you have little opportunity to check out the likely places to run the next day. You're forced to compromise and improvise, such as doing a lap of the town in Rosebery and, to make up extra distance, running multiple laps of a bitumen cycling velodrome which I'd stumbled across in semi-darkness.

On the first Monday in February, during our stopover at Strahan, I decided to have another crack at a long run to determine whether I was still suffering from the general fatigue I'd experienced for the previous several months. I'd handled the shorter runs reasonably well in the weeks since arriving in Tassie, but a stiffer test was essential.

It was a fateful day. Without overstating it, I judged that if the run didn't prove to be stress-free, I'd be in deep trouble and would have to reconsider whether I'd be running Boston at all.

The result (a 25-kilometre run at 5:28 pace) was solid enough to convince me to keep ploughing ahead. Though tired at the end (no surprise there), I wasn't out on my feet and the last 5 kilometres had been the quickest. It gave me at least some degree of confidence that the preparation was back on track.

I followed up the long run a few days later with another decent hit-out of 13 kilometres at sub-5:20 pace, and then a further 11-kilometre run on the road between Derwent Bridge and Lake St Clair in pouring rain, both of which were additional reassurance that the training was on target.

We camped ourselves at Huonville for the next week. There, I ran 11 kilometres at a pleasing 5:08 pace — the best 'result' I'd had since the pre-Gold Coast preparation in Venus Bay during May and June 2016.

A few days later we made our way back to Seven Mile Beach, which we'd used as our Hobart base the year before. A 27-kilometre Sunday morning run at 5:32 pace, though not out of the box, consolidated the training to that point. Another hard 10-kilometre hit-out at 5:08 pace during the following week was further reinforcement.

* * *

While staying at Seven Mile Beach, Diana suffered yet another medical setback. She'd been experiencing light-headedness and general dizziness when she stood to walk. A trip to a very helpful GP in nearby Sorell, and subsequent blood tests, revealed a dangerously low level of iron in her system. She was rushed into the Royal Hobart Hospital, where she received a much-needed blood transfusion and an intravenously administered iron supplement.

The internal investigations in Hobart proved inconclusive and we were advised to have them performed again upon our return to Melbourne. We didn't hesitate. We booked Di on the first available flight to Melbourne where she immediately contacted her local GP who arranged the necessary procedures.

Because we'd previously booked our return ferry crossing for 8 March, I spent four days at Turner's Beach with Taffy. I was especially pleased with a 30-kilometre Sunday run which I managed at 5:26 pace.

I returned to Melbourne in the first week of March and immediately felt absolutely crap again. I attempted a long run at the end of the week but could barely manage 20 kilometres. I was forced to cut it short because of general exhaustion. Superstitiously thinking that the cause of the problem was some kind of 'big city' syndrome, I headed back to Venus Bay until my Boston departure on 11 April.

On 19 March, I completed a long run around my old dirt road course from the beach house — 31 kilometres at 5:29 pace. On 25 March, again in Venus Bay, I ran a 10-kilometre time trial at 4:56 pace, faster than any similar run during my pre-Gold Coast preparation.

I reckon Melbourne's a great place and well deserves its multi-year status as the 'world's most liveable city'. All I know for sure is that I felt incredibly fatigued in Melbourne but fine elsewhere. If anybody out there can offer a logical, scientific or medical explanation for that, I'm dying to find out. It's a mystery to me which I'm not qualified to answer. Even if you have a half-plausible theory, that doesn't involve alien abduction, you know where to find me.

* * *

I'd never experienced the damaging psychological effects of being unemployed until I'd been unemployed myself for well over two years.

After Diana had been diagnosed with breast cancer and I'd left work in May 2013, I wanted to believe that the end of my working life was within reach. By then, I was too bone weary to contemplate returning to full-time employment.

But, by the start of the following year, I knew this hope was just that — an unrealistic expectation. It simply wasn't feasible to believe that we could survive on the finances we had. The cost of daily living, recurring medical bills (despite medical insurance) and expensive mortgages effectively ruled that out. That's basically what forced me back to work in February 2014.

By the end of my time with Ansaldo in November that year, I was confident that the contracts management consultancy I'd set up would bring in enough work to earn at least reasonable income and mean I wouldn't have to return to full-time employment, either up north or in Perth. That was a plan that didn't come to pass. I hadn't anticipated the depth and strength of the mining construction downturn. I wasn't, of course, the only one.

In the 18 months between early 2015 and the middle of 2016, I literally applied for hundreds of jobs right across Australia, South-East Asia, Africa, the UK and the Middle East. The result of that effort was a handful of interviews, but no job offers. I received lots of positive comments, the occasional half-promise and sometimes a backhanded swipe at my age. Job recruiters, who'd ritually contacted me during the boom to coax me into taking on the latest high-paying role they were promoting, had taken me off speed dial. Let's face it, most of them would've been looking for jobs themselves.

I can well understand why people in a similar position simply gave up. By mid to late 2016, so had I.

It's infinitely less painful to stop applying and know you won't get a job than it is to apply countless times over and routinely suffer the humiliation and despair of actual rejection. In 2011, I'd successfully applied for a position as a senior commercial lawyer in a moderate-sized legal practice in Perth. By the early part of 2016, my sights had been lowered substantially to the point where I was reduced to applying for jobs well below my qualifications and experience level. But still there were no offers.

The lowest point, however, came in about November of that year. I decided to bite the bullet and apply for FIFO positions, not in my field of contracts management, but as a 'FIFO utility', that is, a housekeeper/cleaner, laundry attendant, kitchen hand or catering and dining attendant.

On 17 November, almost two weeks before applications even closed, I received an email which stated, apart from the other standard job-rejection BS: 'Your application has been reviewed and assessed in line with the specific requirements of the position. After careful consideration we regret to advise that your application has been unsuccessful in this instance.'

On the basis that the 'specific requirements' of most of these FIFO utility positions involved (with all due respect) not much more than the ability to recite my full name, and perhaps having a reliable pulse, this really was one of the lowest points in my life. It was way past being merely soul destroying to realise that I couldn't even score a job cleaning dunnies in dongas.

However, there is a lighter side, even to mind-numbing hopelessness of being unemployed. You may be intrigued to learn that, at one stage, I became an official Newstart applicant. Thereafter, I became known simply as 'Jobseeker 0365494019'.

I had my 'participation interview' by phone with a wonderfully dedicated young fellow from Centrelink who, in the end, was highly embarrassed that the pro forma questionnaire he ran through was in no way relevant to me or my qualifications and experience. We pressed on and, by the end of our cosy chat, we'd become great pals.

The next day, I ventured to a Centrelink office, this time for a face-to-face interview with an equally kind soul. I sought advice from my kids on how I should present myself. Hamish was particularly forthcoming:

Dad, correct me if I'm wrong. One aim here is to get as many benefits as you can for as long as you can, until such time as you actually find work (a 'job' in itself). You must realise that you're now walking a tightrope, and a thin one at that.

Don't try hard enough, consequence = no benefits. Try too hard, consequence = you may, indeed, be found a job, though I appreciate this is your ultimate, and preferred, aim.

I suggest a middle ground, somewhere between mild confidence and early onset dementia. Shouldn't be too hard for you.

Shaving only half your face, shirt buttons in non-opposing holes, loose-fitting belt, frayed cuffs, badly polished shoes and a little dab of either mustard or tomato sauce strategically placed on your tie. (Both would be going a bit too far.)

Consider seeking out the older, heavy-set lady in the Centrelink office. The one with the reading glasses attached to a chain around her neck and wearing a green cardigan with a distinct fragrance of eau de mothballs. And usually occupying a workstation towards the rear of the room adjacent to the toilet.

Stopping at the local bakery, I suggest purchasing one eclair and one custard-filled, not jam (too sweet), donut. Present it to her upon arrival, just to let her know how much you appreciate and value her help during this difficult transition.

Such empathy. Aren't kids wonderful?

19

17 APRIL 2017

To capture the essence of the Boston Marathon experience, one must live it, watch it, drink it and run it. Each perspective provides a unique and special look at why a simple road race has taken on the mantle of a legendary event. The Boston Marathon is life itself.

Michael Connelly, 26 Miles to Boston

Largely due to Diana's ever-growing list of medical issues, we decided that only I would travel to Boston for the race.

Though that decision was practical, it was incredibly disappointing. Diana had played a substantial role in me getting to Boston in the first place, and she of all people deserved to be there. However, pragmatism ruled the day, as it often does with us. Financially, and because of Di's less than robust health, there was simply no choice.

Prior to leaving for Boston, I spent two nights in Melbourne. As it happened, both nights were spent in The Van parked on the street near Jess's house. It's not what I'd planned. On our first night in the house (indeed, the first hour) the noise-making machine next to me in bed forced an early exit out to The Van. When Mrs Burns lets rip, the bone-jarring grunt is a cross between the noise made by a chainsaw about to run out of juice and an Antarctic fur seal on heat. Her only serious contender for heavyweight snoring champion of the world is the not-so-heavyweight Rupert — Jess's 13-year-old Cavalier King Charles Spaniel. Unbelievably, poor old Rupe can snore while still being wide awake and the noise is what you'd imagine to be the seismic result of sexual intercourse between a trombone and a tuba.

Mind you, Mrs Burns (but not Rupert) has some legitimate complaints of her own in this area so I can't be too critical.

I left for Boston on 11 April, two days short of my 65th birthday.

I don't like plane travel. It's right up there with crowds, snakes, spas and all the other things (like meetings of *any* description and *any* duration) which are too numerous to mention, so I won't. (Maybe there's another book to be written — *100 Things That Piss Me Off*. Shouldn't be too difficult to write, for me at least.)

The 14-hour flight from Melbourne to Los Angeles was jogging along brilliantly until it was time to take off. I'd gone through the usual scoping ritual that we all undertake as we assess who of our fellow passengers, as they march single file down the aisle, would be mildly tolerable to sit next to:

'*Oh please God, not him.*'
'*Oh please God, not her.*'
'*Yes, you pass, just.*'
'*Bugger off, stinky.*'
'*No way, get fucked, fuck off.*'

At almost the last possible opportunity, a red-faced couple raced down the aisle and plonked their butts next to me. This was an annoyance, though unavoidable. The wife/partner sat next to me in the middle seat. Almost immediately, it became obvious that she was unwell. I didn't need to be sitting next to someone with a cold for the remaining 13 hours and 59 minutes. The first time she sniffed (there were to be gazillions more), I winced. When she sneezed, I barely stopped myself from leaping out of my seat. When she reached for the Codral Cold & Flu tablets, I almost wet my pants.

It probably won't come as a surprise to learn that I'm not hugely fond of children either. And, this has nothing to do with the fact that I'm grandchild-less. Their much-touted cuteness (kids, not grandads) is lost on me, I'm afraid. Am I mistaken in thinking that we're all supposed to be overjoyed to be living in a dummy-less world? Or am I just behind the times? When it comes to plane travel, I reckon dummies should be handed out with headsets, as standard issue — with an adult-size supply as well for serial dummy-spitters like me.

On QF 0093 we were blessed with a smorgasbord of squawking toddlers. I hesitate to use the word 'brats' as I accept that, most times, they know not what they do. Except for one little treasure who knew exactly what she was doing when she swiped my muffin during one of her laps around the cabin — as if she were training for the mini-marathon at the next Grots Olympics. Her name was likely something trendy and incredibly obnoxious, like Rocket, Skylar, Zot or Racer.

Of course, the mother laughingly dismissed this brat-like terrorist attack as just another example of baby gorgeousness. I didn't see the funny side. Even less so after we'd finally prised the helpless bakery treat from her tiny mitt by which time it (the muffin, that is, or what was left of it) was reduced to a mangled mess, and then promptly deposited it into *my* mitt to eat if I dared. I *did* dare and shoved it down my gob right in front of the horror just to piss *her* off. It must've done the trick as she let out a high-pitched wail (as only small children can) and high-tailed it back to Mum. Dopey Mum starred incredulously at me as if I'd mentally scarred the kid (and Dopey Mum) for life. I wouldn't have been at all concerned if I had.

Anyway, I managed to safely navigate my way through the rest of the journey. Except that my TV screen suddenly froze, and couldn't be fixed, about 20 minutes from the end of *Manchester by the Sea* (I wanted to get into the Massachusetts spirit as early as possible). Can someone please let me know how it ended?

* * *

I'd left it late to organise accommodation in Boston. (Over forty years in the making and a planning failure at one minute to midnight!) For many months prior to Patriots' Day each year, bookings in and around the city fill rapidly. After some frantic online searching and a dose of luck, I scored a room in a guesthouse in Cambridge near the Massachusetts Institute of Technology, and only one subway station away from Harvard.

My main concern prior to the race was the notoriously unpredictable springtime New England weather. The history of the race over the previous 120 years provided ample evidence that weather conditions could fluctuate wildly between snow and oppressive heat. Conditions in the early part of pre-race week had been quite settled, around the mid-teens during the day with a light to moderate breeze. It looked hopeful for decent race conditions on Patriots' Day — Monday.

That changed dramatically on the Sunday. The temperature rocketed to 27 degrees — insane conditions for running a marathon. Most people headed for the beach. I stewed in my room at the guesthouse.

The forecast for the Monday was for the temperature to drop to the low twenties. And so it did. The maximum temperature for Boston that day was 23 degrees, cooler than the day before, but still very ordinary marathon-running conditions. Even temperatures in the high teens are acknowledged to be unpleasantly warm.

* * *

As you may imagine, the logistics of conducting an event like the Boston Marathon are nothing short of staggering, especially given the expected 32,000 registered runners.

Runners were grouped into starting 'waves' according to their qualifying times. Wave 1 was scheduled to start the race at 9.50am. Wave 2 was scheduled for 10.20, Wave 3 at 10.50 and Wave 4 at 11.20. Each wave was divided into several 'corrals'. I was assigned to Corral 7 in Wave 3.

On the morning of 17 April, I made my way to the race precinct and finish line at Copley Square in downtown Boston. I'd packed my drop-off bag (to be left at the finish line) with the gear that I'd be wearing after the race. Any gear that was taken to Hopkinton and not worn during the race was gathered into bags and donated to the homeless. I had no problems with that. Great idea.

By the time I'd lined up to catch one of the dozens of yellow school buses to Hopkinton, at about 8.30am, the sun was already making its presence felt. It wasn't hot yet, by any means, but it was still uncomfortably warm and sticky. Enough to raise a more than decent sweat, even on a slow walk.

I planned to grab the first available seat on my allocated bus. Two kind young women noticed my soggy brow and let me on first. One held out her hand to help me onboard. I was about to run a marathon as a 65-year-old and she was already taking pity on me. Pride took over and I declined. That error of judgment proved costly as I clumsily (predictably?) cracked my shin on the first step.

The chatter on the bus was decidedly nervous. No one spoke of the weather directly but you could tell from the 'I really only want to finish' comments (me included), and the universal cry for the windows to be opened, that race time expectations were being adjusted on the spot at a furious rate (me included).

I didn't engage in much of the bus chat. But I did break my

silence long enough to learn that the guy sitting next to me was a Seventh Day Adventist pastor from Tennessee who would be running his 57th marathon. I felt like a marathon virgin all over again. He had the further advantage that, when the going got tough, as it most assuredly would a few hours later, he could draw on some divine intervention for help. Though sorely tempted, it would've been shockingly hypocritical of me to attempt the same.

By the time the bus had pulled into the massive Athlete's Village at Hopkinton, the sun was high and the air more than just cosily warm. Most runners were diving for the shade offered by the biggest marquee I'd ever seen — about half the size of a soccer field — or guzzling down the free water and sports drinks on offer. Or cramming in last-minute carbs: apples, bananas, oranges and energy bars. The only venues more in use were the sunscreen stands and the 50 or so portable toilets where runners lined up in queues of a hundred deep. In one such queue, I waited 20 minutes for the chance to have my own final nervous pee.

At 10.20am, 30 minutes before start time, Wave 3 was called. In contrast to the excitement of the village, the atmosphere suddenly turned deathly quiet as if the significance and difficulty of what we were about to undertake had finally sunk in. In almost dead-man-walking fashion, we shuffled about 800 metres to within 200 metres of the starting line, where we waited for the starter's gun. There was no dry retching this time, but close enough.

As I would already be running 42.195 kilometres, I had no intention of running a step further. Circumstances didn't oblige, unfortunately. Immediately the gun was fired, each runner broke into a slow trot and jogged the extra 200 metres to the actual starting line. By then, and after having spent over 20 minutes in the rapidly warming sun, I'd already worked up quite a lather.

As with the Gold Coast race the year before, I'd determined my 10-kilometre 'splits' well before Boston. I'd planned to run about 55 minutes for the first 10 kilometres, a little quicker for the next ten, and hopefully to run strongly to the finish from there.

That's how it went, but only to a point — that point being the halfway mark. I passed the 10 km mark in 55:22, just as planned. I ran the next 10 kilometres in, would you believe, the *exact* same time. By then, however, the real effects of the sun had kicked in.

My recollections of the race after the halfway point are blurred and very sketchy. I remember events only as a series of unconnected images. At times, all I could hear was the almost deafening roar of the thousands of people who lined the road. A PA system belted out 'Born to Run' and 'We are the Champions'. Thankfully, it wasn't the other Queen hit, 'Another One Bites the Dust'. The irony of 'Stayin' Alive' didn't escape me either.

I remember that some runners had begun to walk after only a few kilometres. I remember garden sprinklers being turned on in front yards to cool runners down. I remember the hundreds of discarded, sodden paper cups strewn in thick, slippery clumps all over the road. I remember the frantic crush as runners approached each drinks station. I remember runners stopping to stretch to ease the effects of dehydration and cramp. I remember some runners declaring to anyone who'd listen: 'I'm done'.

One of the few things I recall with any degree of clarity was running through the town of Wellesley, the home of Wellesley College — an exclusive, private all-women college attended by a young Hillary Clinton at one time and located just after the halfway mark of the race. The time-honoured tradition has been for students to form what's known as the 'scream tunnel' in which, as the name suggests, young college women scream out encouragement to runners as they pass by, or pass out. They also hold up signs with encouraging messages such as 'Gimme a kiss for extra energy'. On this day, one such sign was a tad more risqué: 'Kiss Me, Fuck Trump'. Even I was sufficiently compos mentis to appreciate that one. Given my crusty old fart status, even well before race day, I didn't take up the smooch offer with any of the young ladies along the course.

There was a sign further along the route that read: 'You run much better than how Trump runs the country'. Mind you, we were in Massachusetts, where there was very little love lost for the 45th president.

I remember running past people handing out oranges, ice-creams, lollies on sticks, ice and beer, and I remember the strong smell of meat cooking on barbecues in front yards. I remember the picnic rugs and blankets laid out on the front lawns of homes along the course. I remember a marine band thumping out 'The Halls of Montezuma'. It was a stirring rendition. By that stage, I was shaken, but not stirred.

I remember the constant crowd encouragement:

'Good job!'
'Way to go!'
'Awesome!'
'You got this!' — my personal favourite, especially when it was yelled out rather optimistically at the 3 km mark. Even I wanted to stop and give each of these well-wishers a serious hug.

Above all else, I vividly remember admitting to myself at about the 25 km mark: 'Holy crap, I'm in big trouble'. After that, and for the remainder of the race, it was purely a matter of survival and making it to the finish line. Not everyone did. Some parked themselves on the side of the road and refused to budge. Some chose to walk the rest of the way, or to jog/walk to the finish.

At about the 26 km mark, we hit the first of the four major hills on the course - very ordinary timing, to say the least. The four hills spread out over the next 7 kilometres, with some flattish stretches in between, culminating in the infamous Heartbreak Hill at about 33.5 kilometres. Once I'd made it over Heartbreak, I was confident that the worst was over. There would be another 8–9 kilometres of flat running with some gentle downhills too.

Then my legs cramped. First, in my right hamstring. Next, in both calves. I knew that if I kept running — even if by now it was no more than a hesitant hobble — I'd make it. I also knew with greater conviction that, if I stopped, I wouldn't be able to start again.

I remember shuffling past Fenway Park, the legendary home of the Boston Red Sox. I remember running past the famous Citgo sign. I remember the small but extremely nasty hill just before the 40 km mark where I witnessed the bizarre spectacle of a couple (both of whom were competing in the race) engaging in a full-on argument. The female of the couple was having a major hissy fit. The male was calmer but still visibly annoyed. How they could summon the energy to do battle at that juncture was incomprehensible to me. My memory flashed back to the same kind of male/female relationship angst I'd witnessed with Mr and Mrs at the Manly Metro movie theatre milk bar 50 years before, minus the projectiles.

I continued to do my very best impersonation of the Cliff Young survival shuffle down Commonwealth Avenue, but not remotely doing it justice. Just before the right-hand turn into Hereford Street, I knew I was into the final kilometre. Right onto Hereford. Left onto Boylston Street and the final 800 metres. As I rounded the corner onto Boylston, I was greeted with the most deafening crowd noise I'd ever experienced. I realised that they weren't, though my gut tried to convince me that they were, cheering just for me.

I felt as if I'd taken a hat trick in an Ashes Test at the 'G. It was overwhelming and very moving. Very humbling. And very emotional, especially for a big sook like me.

As I ran that last 800 metres, it hit me that this was the end point of what I'd set myself to do decades before. It was over. It was done. So was I. I no longer had to lay awake at night wondering whether Boston would ever come to pass. It wasn't accomplished in the glorious fashion I'd hoped. I hadn't stormed down Boylston Street and smashed across the finish line with energy to burn. Not even close. I'd done it tough — very tough. It'd taken *every* ounce of willpower I could muster just to finish. It hurt. It hurt a lot. I was drained in *every* way imaginable. I'd rarely experienced such a level of extreme physical exhaustion.

I was even too stuffed to shed a tear. That would come later. I did feel disappointed that I hadn't paid the kind of tribute I would have liked, to Boston and its people. I finished in 4:26:30, a very ordinary time by any measure, particularly mine. For me, it was borderline embarrassing. But right then and there, it mattered little. I was 65 years old and I'd run the Boston Marathon. And I'd run all the way. I hadn't stopped once. Not even on Heartbreak Hill.

I was proud.

* * *

After I'd run across the finish line (I'm using the word 'run' rather loosely here) I stopped, as you do. I'd already run 200 metres further than planned and my body/brain refused to run another step and shut down completely. I tried to walk but couldn't. My shoes seemed concreted to the road. I just stood on the spot and swayed in the breeze like an inflatable air dancer outside a car dealership. I then managed to plonk one leg after the other, like a baby taking its first, tentative steps. I didn't loudly proclaim, 'Rejoice, I conquer.' It was even too much to mumble: 'Holy crap, I'm stuffed!'

I was offered a bottle of water. The heat seemed to have sucked every drop of fluid from my body. I was bone dry. The last remaining drop of sweat had long since disappeared, leaving a dry and salty crust on my skin. My cap, which is usually sopping wet after any type of run, felt like coarse sandpaper. I had a strange feeling it was about to snap, crackle and pop, and I had an even stranger feeling that I was about to snot, crumple and poop.

I sculled the bottle of water in seconds. I was offered another bottle and that suffered the same fate. I poured yet another onto my head, hoping to absorb the fluid by osmosis into my body. I then moved on to have the finisher's medal hung around my neck. I negotiated that exercise successfully, but only just. The only task remaining was to stagger through the gauntlet of caring volunteers who lined the finish area and provided food, drinks and energy gels.

A foil cape was wrapped around my shoulders, making me feel remarkably like Superman — the post-Kryptonite version. There was even a separate group of volunteers whose sole job was to provide tape to stick the ends of the cape together so that runners could proceed hands free. I was struck by so many acts of genuine kindness and concern.

When quadriceps muscles are stiff and painful after a long run or race, one of the most agonising things to do is walk downstairs. As a runner, a trick you learn is that the task is a whole lot easier if you proceed backwards. Believe me, it works. I decided to put theory into practice to cope with the long downstairs haul to the bowels of the Boston subway after I'd collected my bag of gear.

It's human nature that once a pattern is set by the first, others follow — even if the first act makes no apparent sense, like faithfully following footprints on a beach. So it was that several runners followed my lead in true Pied Piper fashion. Goodness knows what must've been going through the minds of non-running commuters who were confronted by a technicoloured assortment of bums proceeding down the stairs as they walked up.

The heat inside the train was suffocating, mirroring the stifling conditions outside. No spare seats were on offer, which was most likely a good thing as I wasn't convinced I'd make it back onto my feet in any case. Still, during the subway trip and the kilometre-long crawl back to the guesthouse, I was stopped and congratulated by three complete strangers, two of whom proudly introduced me to their kids as someone who'd just run the Boston Marathon. The wonderful people of Boston are proud of their city and proud of their marathon. It's deeply meaningful to them, especially after the tragedy of 2013. And they show it.

The guesthouse, luckily, had no spa. But it did have stairs, lots of them, and they were exceedingly steep. There's no point at all in attempting to proceed upstairs backwards, though.

After a quick email to Diana, Hamish and Jess, I lay on the bed and passed out for over an hour, wearing nothing more than my race shorts and singlet (I'd discarded the cape by then) and my running shoes, which I couldn't bend down to remove. I woke up with the usual post-marathon cravings. Not for a burger, fries and thickshake, this time, but for fluids — as long as they were cold, sweet and fizzy.

I shuffled to the pizza shop on the corner in tracksuit bottoms, plus undies this time, T-shirt and slippers — the only footwear I could manage after the 20-minute ordeal of extricating my burning feet from my running shoes. I grabbed two Powerades, two cans of sickly-sweet orange soft drink and two cans of Pepsi, all drinks that I'd never touch in normal circumstances. Both cans of orange soft drink and both Pepsis disappeared one after the other in dou-ble-quick time. The two Powerades were saved for later that night when I'd demolish (as my own DIY post-race dinner) the large meatball pizza I'd order from the same pizza shop. In the same pair of slippers. And in the same pair of undies.

I mistakenly left the slippers behind — but not the undies — when I left Boston. They're comfy slippers. Hopefully, a homeless person inherited them as well, after emptying out a blackened toenail or two. After a shower, I fell into bed at about 9pm and slept for 12 hours straight. The brain easily beat the bladder that night.

* * *

Did I, as the quote at the start of this chapter contends, feel that the Boston Marathon was 'life itself'? In all honesty, no. In the spirit of keeping all things real, I have doubts whether any event, particularly a sporting event, could ever rightly claim that title. Nevertheless, that doesn't in any way detract from what I know at the deepest level to have been one of the most memorable experiences of my life.

I'd achieved what I'd set out to accomplish several decades before — not with any bravado, flourish or fanfare, but accomplished all the same. I'm thankful that I gave myself the chance. I was truly grateful that I'd fulfilled a promise I'd made to myself.

Just like my very first marathon back in 1979, it could never be taken from me. I'd have my finisher's medal framed. I'd hang it, fittingly, in the Venus Bay beach house, the place where I'd done the bulk of my serious marathon training. Maybe this was a touch self-indulgent, but so be it. I'd have the memory, and would cherish it, forever.

There remained only one unresolved issue – more unfinished business.

How would I 'celebrate' my 70th?

20

ONCE MORE UNTO THE BREACH

Wish I could find a good book to live in
Wish I could find a good book
Well if I could find a real good book
I'd never have to come out and look at
What they done to my song

Melanie Safka, 'Look What They've Done to My Song, Ma'

In early 2017, I made a solemn pact with myself that once Boston was run and done, I'd throw every scrap of energy into one last ditch attempt at finding a job.

I'd made literally hundreds of unsuccessful attempts over the previous couple of years. I'd reached the point in late 2016 where I'd virtually given up on job hunting as a forlorn and fruitless lost cause. Without being conscious of it, I'd taken the concept of casualisation to a new and depressing level. I'd become, inadvertently, a full-time 'permalancer'. CEO at Unemployed Inc.

I also promised myself that this would be my final shot. There's a limit (even for a stoic like me) to how often and how much you can let yourself be brutalised by rejection.

I brainstormed several employment possibilities. Maybe I could become a business mentor. After all, I'd co-run a fish 'n' chip shop in the past and occasionally read the *Australian Financial Review*. (Surely, that's all it takes?) Personal trainer was out, as I'd long since stopped looking 18 years of age and my quads, pecs, glutes, abs etc. had all gone missing in action many years before. Shovelling shit in Siberia? That'd do, provided the money stacked up, along with the other stuff. I was a more than capable shit handler, as you're by now well aware.

I set myself an absolute deadline of the end of August. In other words, about four months after returning from Boston. If it hadn't worked out by then, the fallback was reading gas meters on a casual basis. Not kidding here folks. Read on.

As with my previous efforts, I applied for contracts management positions right across Australia. I adopted a flexible (read: desperate), scatter-gun approach. Being selective or the tiniest bit finicky was not an option. Anything in that field, or moderately associated with it, like reading gas meters, would've been good enough. *Had* to be good enough.

As before, I scored a handful of screening interviews with recruitment agents but nothing more substantive. It was blindingly obvious from the earliest stage that the greatest stumbling block (apart from the unspoken age barrier) was the sheer length of time I'd been out of the workforce. It doesn't take a genius to understand that the longer you're out, the more difficult it is to get back in. When you're asked the question, 'Where have you been working recently?', no amount of fluffing, fudging or faking sounds remotely believable. Saying straightforwardly, and honestly, that you've been swanning around Tassie in a van for several months, or training to run the Boston Marathon, is hardly likely to form part of a relevant or impressive resumé. Recruiters immediately switch off the interest button and you never get the chance to proceed to the 'oh yes, but' phase.

Irrespective, it'd also become very apparent that, if I *was* to find a job, my best prospects would be in WA. That's where my most recent experience had been, albeit several years before.

So, in early July 2017, I packed up The Van with as much stuff from the Venus Bay beach house as I could load into it and set off to trek across the Nullarbor, back to Margaret River. Diana had travelled back several weeks before to undergo knee replacement surgery - a bit like loyally journeying across town to visit your favourite motor mechanic. This bung knee meant five extremities down (two shoulders, two hips and one knee) and only one to go. Not counting the feet, of course, which even the limb-challenged Mrs B would have to admit are more Hobbit-like than human.

Apart from Taffy, my other travelling companion for the trip was a medium-sized photocopier/printer, which I slept next to each night. Don't ask me to explain. At least it didn't make weird bedtime noises. It was unplugged, just like me.

Day 6 of The Odyssey. Some people 'do' lunch. I'd just 'done' the Nullarbor, including the straightest stretch of highway in Australia — 146.6 kilometres. Good thing I do boring very well. I can stare at a blank wall for several hours and still be mildly entertained. I must confess, though, that the combination of a tedious drive and many hours of ABC afternoon regional radio was almost too much, even for me. Sorry, Auntie. I love you dearly, but …

The Van held up remarkably well. At the merest suggestion of an oncoming heart attack, I did the usual: shoved on a CD and cranked up the volume – often, fittingly, it was Joe Cocker's version of 'With a Little Help from My Friends'.

You'd think that, after six days on the road, I would've mastered the art of the 'one finger wave'. Not so. My problem was that I drive, contrarily it seems, with my right hand on the side of the steering wheel, not at the top. This made the wave near impossible. By the time I'd successfully managed the awkward adjustment, the passing vehicle was long gone, no doubt with its occupants aghast at how rude I'd been in not reciprocating the time-honoured tradition with my fellow Nullarborians. Mind you, it might've also had something to do with the fact that, in my haste, I sometimes got confused and deployed the middle finger by mistake.

* * *

The depressingly painful job search blues continued into July and August. The dreaded, self-imposed end of August deadline was just visible over the horizon. Several weeks earlier, I'd been knocked back for a gas meter reading job in Busselton, north of Margaret River, the only practical requirement for which was a modest level of fitness. Having recently run the Boston Marathon, which I mentioned in my CV, you'd imagine that I'd stand a fair chance of landing the gig. Yeah, nuh. Obviously underqualified.

The universe wasn't unfolding as it should. It wasn't unfolding at all. It was superglued shut. The gods weren't smiling down upon me. Shit was happening. Good karma wasn't.

I spied a job cleaning the toilets at a local Margaret River caravan park. It had my name written all over it, so I thought. I was a shoe-in, wasn't I? I was a good cleaner and knew my shit, as you know. It was on my daily job-hunting list to make the call.

Then the phone rang. It was a recruitment adviser from a mining services company, MAS Australasia, following up a job application I'd submitted some days earlier. Somehow, I managed to fudge my way past the embarrassing 'where have you been working recently' question. Showing my level of desperation, I cowardly threw in Mrs B's dodgy medical history to garner sympathy. It must've worked. A phone interview hook-up was scheduled for a few days later. During the interview, the shattering comment was made that I was too senior for the position I'd applied for.

Underqualified, overqualified, I couldn't get it right. My heart sank and my bum fell out of my pants. Another knockback was about to be dumped on me. More shit was about to happen.

Then the universe tilted ever so slightly on its axis, if a universe can do such things. The gods took pity on me, even if they weren't in an overly cheery mood. It was the end of the week. They were tired and grumpy, but somehow still mildly accommodating.

Did I want to be considered for a more senior role as a contracts manager on a FIFO basis to work on the Ichthys LNG Onshore Facilities Project about 40 kilometres outside of Darwin? I'd be paid a decent salary as well as the usual FIFO site uplift. I wouldn't be housed in a camp, but in my own self-contained apartment close to the Darwin CBD. I'd also be paid a food allowance and would be working a 4-weeks-on, 1-week-off roster, but would have every Sunday off. Was I interested?

It was as if I'd been asked casually whether I was mildly interested in winning the 2020 Olympic Marathon. I promptly shoved my heart and bum back where they belonged. Two weeks later, I was seated on a plane heading for Darwin and counting my blessings. I'd effectively dodged another financial bullet in much the same circumstances as when I'd moved west in 2011 to work in the Perth law firm.

Naturally, I'd pay a price. There's always a price to pay. Every action has a consequence: 60-hour work weeks and 4am starts to the day; long, boring hour-long bus commutes to and from work during which *I'd* be the one who'd sleep or doze fitfully; trekking to work in the dark, which I still find disturbing; working the 'suicide swing'; impossible to perform morning stretches at pre-start meetings minus the gorgeous Bec/Bac. Steelcapped boots, hard hats and high-vis shirts. Becoming a 'bro' again. A tough commercial environment in testing physical conditions. More stomach-churning feelings of insecurity.

And I was way past 'ripe old age'. I was starting to rot – and the low-hanging fruit was beginning to drop off.

Still, it was a chance to breathe again, a chance to restore a measure of control, for the gazillionth time. To steel myself to do battle once more. I'd have to flick the imaginary switch and jump quickly into work mode, after an almost three-year enforced lay-off. I'd have to grab the chance by the throat, squeeze hard and run with it for as long as my flagging energy levels held out.

That's the only kind of 'running' I'd be able to handle for the foreseeable future. Running, as such, would have to be content with a distant second place, as it had many times in the past. Full-on, or even part-time, commitment was out of the question. My mate was used to it, though. It knew me well enough by then to understand and accept that I'd be back, some day, when the timing was right.

And, make no mistake, I would be back.

But, just now, life's giant hairy bum would obstruct again, and other 'life things' were vastly more important. It was time to re-prioritise. To regroup. To hunker down. To be selective about what I could cope with and what I simply couldn't. To settle for something less than the flow of the good life but be thankful nevertheless. I'd done it before and could do it again.

And I *was* thankful. Unreservedly so. Someone had faith in me and had seen something in me worthwhile. The self-esteem balloon had been reinflated again, without the need — temporarily at least — for that daggy lump of Blu-tack.

At 65 years of age, that reassurance and emotional boost were irreplaceable.

* * *

In March 2017, we learned that the lawyer to whom we'd sold our Canberra legal practice in 2008 had, in connection with an unrelated matter, been sentenced to three years in prison for defrauding the Australian Legal Aid Office.

On 27 July, the ACT Supreme Court handed down its judgment in the action for negligence and damages against me and our former legal practice. The court found in favour of the firm and, in addition, awarded costs against the plaintiff, my former client.

21

WHAT'S NEXT?

I've looked at life from both sides now
From win and lose and still somehow
It's life's illusions I recall
I really don't know life at all

Judy Collins, 'Both Sides Now'

You would expect that, as a silver-haired senior citizen who'd accumulated his fair share of life experiences (particularly over the previous ten years or so), I'd have something profound to say at this point, or at least be able to share with you a few pearls of wisdom. You'd be forgiven for imagining that, just by virtue of the number of years I've been on the planet, I'd have things worked out. That I'd have life sussed.

Sorry to disappoint, but I've come up a bit short.

Even tentative answers to 'what's the meaning of life?' had eluded me at the start of this book and I've made minimal headway since. I've come to terms with one or two painful life experiences that have troubled me for some time, but overall, life still confounds me. I'm sure I'm not alone.

Looking at the 'Both Sides Now' quote at the start of this chapter, I wonder if maybe we're not *meant* to 'know life'. After all, it's not something we study with the aid of a textbook, or online for that matter. Although there are surely lessons to be learned, we're rarely schooled or tutored on the subject, at least in a formal sense. There's no course we can undertake. We're not awarded with a university degree at the end, or even a 'certificate of attainment'.

But, we may not have to *know* life. We may just have to *live* it to the best of our personal capacities, avoiding as many painful cock-ups as we can in the process. (Please don't ask me for guidance on that one. If you've read this far, you'll know why.)

Maybe the question 'What's Next?', posed as the title of this chapter, can only be answered in a meaningful way when you've examined and come to grips with what's gone before. That's a difficult one for me as I'd be quite content to obliterate large chunks of my past if I could. A strategically targeted dose of amnesia would do wonders if I could ever swing it.

Of course, that's never going to happen, however much it might appeal. Life doesn't work that simplistically or naïvely. Arguably, it shouldn't. Coping as best you can with the good, the bad and the grossly ugly in equal measure is simply part of the deal, isn't it? Part of what we sign on for as human beings.

Throughout the writing of this book, I regularly stopped to ponder why I'd decided to write it in the first place. It wasn't dissimilar to training to run a marathon. As with some not-so-successful past marathon attempts, I came perilously close to abandoning the book idea completely. Coincidentally, long, drawn-out non-writing periods mirrored equally long, drawn-out non-running funks.

I had regular misgivings because the book was always going to be mostly about the one subject I'm reluctant to focus on, or talk about. It's not as if I have an incredibly earth-shattering story to trumpet to the world. I'm nothing special. I've never fought in a war. I've never lost a child. I haven't suffered an unimaginable tragedy. At least as far as the sporting world is concerned, I'm certainly no Kurt Fearnley, Dylan Alcott or Turia Pitt who are, quite surely, brave, inspiring and truly heroic individuals.

In a wider context, it's not as though I'd won the Nobel Peace Prize or discovered the cure for a mysterious life-threatening disease or overcome some crushing, life-changing adversity ... and become a celebrity TV chef.

I've never regarded myself as anything more than an everyday person. But, maybe that's the point. Maybe it's the commonplace, and the common person's story, that may resonate with most people. Can't the modest can rise, fall and rise again in equal measure and significance to the mighty?

Arguably, none of us is 'average' or 'ordinary' in the first place though, are we? We're all unique, even in the humblest of ways. We all have stories to tell. And, each story is equally genuine, worthy and valid.

In any case, just about everyone, celebrity guru or otherwise, writes a book these days, don't they? Compelling life stories are commonplace. Even stuffing up big time in some form or another, in the manner of a 'disgraced former businessman' or failed politician, at least warrants a gong on the Australasian speaking circuit and several guest appearances on *Q&A*.

So why did *I* decide to write one?

Partly, as a form of therapy. You've probably heard that one before. Like many people, there were a few demons lurking in my past that needed to be exorcised and I figured that writing a book, and exposing them, might achieve that. I've only been partially successful there, I have to say, but some progress has been made.

Apart from that, I simply wanted to know whether I could write a book as an intellectual exercise. Check.

As you might appreciate, I didn't wombat myself away in some cosy burrow to write it. Most of the book was written 'on the run' in all types of unlikely places, and on-and-off over several years.

I've written sitting in a donga at a rail camp in the middle of the Pilbara desert, at various airports, on plains, on the train or bus between Perth and Margaret River, in hotel rooms, on the bus to or from mining construction camps or doubled up in The Van with my knees, and laptop, wedged under my chin. In Boston. In Darwin. Even making copious but scratchy notes on the backs of the waxy, brown paper chip bags we used at The Fishy, when trade was slow. The book certainly wasn't leisurely written on a sabbatical or in my gap year.

In some ways, the writing of the book has forced me to undergo some honest self-analysis and self-appraisal. Unsurprisingly, I didn't come up with too many answers at the end of that process either. I haven't always been comfortable with what I revealed to myself. Sometimes, I squirmed uneasily in my chair. Often, I became incredibly emotional. For better or worse, though, in searching my past, I've learned more about myself and I'm grateful.

It's been amazing to discover how the simple act of writing can somehow unlock so much emotional 'stuff' that's been buried by the passing of time.

And, through that simple act, I've discovered something even more revealing and magical. Writing, I've found, takes me to an entirely different level of wellbeing. I disconnect from the here and now and plug into a world of comfort, solace and creativity. I become immersed in the words, phrases and sentences – and in the feelings and emotions they stir within me. Time and place are meaningless. I switch off, and I switch on.

Melanie would be pleased for me. I've found 'a real good book' to live in. It's home to me, be it ever so humble, and I never want to come out.

* * *

What's emerged after Boston and the fulfilling of a longstanding athletic ambition? Did Boston fundamentally change me?

I can't honestly claim that it did. But, as I've mentioned, I was immensely proud of the fact that I'd run Boston, and even more so that I'd committed to the idea over so many years and had seen it through, despite various speed bumps encountered along the way. *That* was the most satisfying result and had the greatest personal impact.

It strengthened my deeply felt belief that resilience in the face of adversity — great or small, real or perceived — is the essence of the human condition. Resilience. Courage. Hope. They're intertwined. They reinforce each other.

Despite appearances (can I run the Boston Marathon as a 65-year-old? Can I write a book? Can I leap back into the professional workforce in my mid-sixties after a near three-year lay-off?), I don't consciously thrive on challenge. I don't readily, or enthusiastically, aspire to take it on or rise to it. The mind, body and spirit simply aren't robust enough for too much of that these days. Challenge just seems to have fallen in my lap, or followed me around like a lost dog — particularly over recent years.

Like most of us, I'm occasionally asked the question: 'Are you happy?' That's a difficult one for me, and right up there with 'what's the meaning of life?' Happiness, for me, can simply mean that un-deniably soul-restoring first sip of coffee in the morning, a gentle run on a deserted beach or beating the Poms at cricket. I guess it comes down to what your personal concept of happiness is. If it means being in a constant state of 'today is the first day of the rest of my life', or otherwise being perpetually perky, then I'm afraid I'll be coming in a distant last in the happiness race. I'm simply not that kind of person. That brand of happiness isn't for me, or part of my DNA. Being sad, or harmlessly melancholy, from time to time isn't always dangerous. To me, it's as natural to be sad at times as it is to be joyous. It's only when my melancholy moments slide into more sinister and threatening feelings that I tend to sit up and take notice.

For me, it's less a state of happiness and more a state of wellbeing: a positive feeling of contentment, achievement, equilibrium, security, good health, a lack of stress and, above all, inner peace. I'm not there yet, but I'm working on it as best I can. It's a work in progress and I can't place a date on when, or even whether, I'll achieve it. Maybe I should throw in a dose of 'forest bathing' to kick things along, or at least spend more holiday time in Bhutan.

With each successive year, am I anxious about the future as many are in these difficult times? What I'm most fearful of, aside from those malevolent melancholy moments, is losing my independence. I won't live a life of reliance on other people. I simply won't. I dread experiencing that demoralising feeling of a total loss of control, a loss of self-sufficiency – when a steadfast reliance upon my own 'human resources' simply isn't good enough. It remains a matter of real and present concern.

What does the future hold? In truth, the future for me is a complete mystery. I hazard a guess that most people of my vintage have arrived at a stage where the rest of their lives is reasonably well settled and predictable. You'd expect that, or at least hope it to be the case. Not so for me. I have no clear picture of *where* I'll end up or *how* I'll end up. I even have no idea *when* I'll end up. The possibilities are wide-ranging and at times unsettling. A continuing (possibly forlorn) pursuit of the so-called good life in Margaret River? Maybe. Touring around endlessly in The Van? Maybe. A return to FIFO life? Increasingly likely. I honestly don't know with any degree of certainty. I regularly preface my internal deliberations about my future with the words, 'All things being equal'. Problem is, they rarely are.

In the meantime, the only certainty for me is life's unpredictability and I find myself continuing to make up life as I go along. My own unusual DIY version of it, a day-by-day, limited-choices existence with no clear plan in mind.

The crystal ball remains far from crystal clear. I continue to go with my own peculiar kind of flow. To where, who knows? Not me.

* * *

But, despite the uncertainties, at least I've discovered in more recent times a much greater sense of self-acceptance. Not acceptance of the world around me, though, which I still find threatening and alien. I'm snug, not smug, in being a misanthrope, but a harmless, respectful and accommodating one, if that makes any sense. I'm content to live my life at marginally below passion level. I have no burning desire to shake things up or to grow old disgracefully. I don't crave to make a statement, or even make an impact - just to tread lightly and leave the smallest possible footprint, perhaps.

Importantly for me, I've now arrived at a point in my life where I don't feel the need to prove myself to anyone — on any level. That feeling is both precious and priceless.

Although I'm still a firm advocate of the shit happens principle, I've mellowed somewhat in recent times and consider that the Ned Kelly 'such is life' approach sounds slightly less hostile. Mind you, Ned made that comment (even if mythologically) just before being hanged, so there's probably not much in it. And he was likely only stating the nineteenth-century equivalent of the shit happens principle in any case.

These days, I remind myself that I am, fundamentally, a decent human being. I remind myself to be satisfied that I've done my best. That I've made a contribution and to be content with the results. That, as a minimum, I've maintained a sense of integrity and a clearish conscience. I'll settle for an epitaph that reads, 'At least he wasn't an obnoxious dickhead.' Or even just to be remembered as a 'Good Bloke', like my dad.

It's important for me to know at a gut level that I'm a good citizen, and to generally conduct myself with a thought for the greater good.

I continue to open doors — for both sexes, despite the strange looks I sometimes get — and always will. I give way and I give in. I always thank the bus driver. I even wait in line until it's my turn. How crazy is that? 'Please' and 'thank you' are natural parts of my vocabulary. Even these unexceptional personal habits, along with other acts of basic politeness and courtesy, are to me integral parts of what makes a decent and successful human being, even if a somewhat reclusive one. I'm content to live a life based on simplicity, commitment and discipline.

But I still don't, and never will, talk to people in lifts.

I've long since accepted that I'll never reach the heights of someone like Abebe Bikila in athletic terms, or Deny King, in terms of how an ideal life might be lived. I know I could never have been the best marathon runner or could ever be the best human being.

But, I'm okay with that. Though I've fallen short at times, I think I've come near enough and often enough to being the best *I* could ever have been. I'll cling to that, proudly. Isn't that all we can, and should, rightly ask of ourselves?

* * *

How's Mrs Burns travelling these days?

Despite recurrent medical setbacks, she's still as mad as it's possible for her to be. Loving, and consumed by, every square centimetre of Orchid Ramble. Strangling the last drop out of life. Continuing to remind the world that it can go take a flying leap at itself. Continuing to live life gloriously in Diana World. Wreaking total havoc wherever she ventures. Smashing her way through life like a juiced-up, out-of-control, cyclonic Tassie Devil.

Undeniably brilliant. In her own crazy, F-bomb kind of way.

Here's a true story which, for me, says it all and sums up Mrs Burns to a tee. A couple of weeks before Christmas 2017, I received the following text message:

Mrs Burns (seriously): *'I'm in the Margaret River bookstore. Is there a book I can buy you to read over Christmas?'*

Me (facetiously): *'The only book I'll be reading is* Long Road to Boston: An Autobiography of No One You'd Know.'

(30 minutes later)

Mrs Burns (seriously): *'The lady in the bookstore has searched her system and can't find the book listed anywhere. Do you know the name of the author?'*

* * *

Do I dare offer my own philosophy on life? Sounds a bit pretentious, but I'll have a crack.

It is what it is?
Shit happens?
Such is life?

Change what's within your capacity, inclination and energy level to change. Accept what you can't. Live with it and deal with it as best you can. Take care. Stay safe. Keep it real. 'Go placidly amid the noise and the haste'. Above all, never lose your sense of humour. It's a wonderful and life-saving vaccine for many of life's problems that plague us.

* * *

Is there an underlying message that I wanted to convey in writing this book, aside from the obvious that even people of my vintage can perform at a reasonable level and that we do have something meaningful and worthwhile to offer? — and even if some of us are unconventional square pegs.

If anything, it's simply this: everyday people *can* achieve special things. What that special thing is depends on the individual and, most times, it's highly personal. If it's realistic and important enough to you, achieving that special thing is entirely possible. It needs to be kept real. It needs a road map, a plan that's flexible and adaptable to change. Surely I'm a testament to that.

Above all, never let go of that special thing — whatever it is — for any reason. You'll regret it if you do. I'm a testament to that, too. Grand or modest, it just takes a heartfelt desire to accomplish it. Keep that special thing within reach, even if you have to tuck it away in a drawer, stick it in your back pocket or park it in some safe place for another day. Even if it's barely held together by a lump of worn-out Blu-tack or invisibly attached to you by the most fragile or flimsy thread, never let it go.

Don't worry that you'll lose it. You won't if it's special enough to you.

* * *

What's next for me? Any long term plans?

None really. In a sense, I'm still drifting.

But there *is* this famous ultramarathon in South Africa, the Comrades Marathon, that's run between Durban and Pietermaritz-burg in June each year. It was first run in 1921, so the race has a rich and colourful history which, as you may appreciate, is a great attraction to me. The race is about 89 kilometres, so it's more than *twice* the standard marathon distance and, therefore, a staggering but glorious physical challenge.

* * *

And, I must get to know more about my Uncle Dick. Not knowing is unfinished business.

I owe it to him to find out.

www.ingramcontent.com/pod-product-compliance
Lightning Source LLC
Chambersburg PA
CBHW030917090426
42737CB00007B/224